THE DIAGNOSTIC TEACHER

Constructing New Approaches to Professional Development

THE DIAGNOSTIC TEACHER

Constructing New Approaches to Professional Development

Edited by Mildred Z. Solomon
Foreword by Arthur L. Costa

TEACHERS COLLEGE PRESS
Teachers College
Columbia University
New York and London

**To the classroom teachers, principals,
and other professional staff
with whom we have worked so closely
from whom we have learned so much**

Published by Teachers College Press, 1234 Amsterdam Avenue, New York, NY 10027

Library of Congress Cataloging-in-Publication Data

The diagnostic teacher: constructing new approaches to professional development / edited by Mildred Z. Solomon ; foreword by Arthur L. Costa.
p. cm.
Includes bibliographical references and index.
ISBN 0-8077-3863-8 (cloth). — ISBN 0-8077-3862-X (paper)
1. Teachers—United States. 2. Teachers—In-service training—United States. 3. Action research in education—United States. 4. Constructivism (Education)—United States. I. Solomon, Mildred Z.
LB1775.2.D53 1999
371.1—dc21 99-12986

ISBN 0-8077-3862-X (paper)
ISBN 0-8077-3863-8 (cloth)

Printed on acid-free paper
Manufactured in the United States of America

06 05 04 03 02 01 00 99 8 7 6 5 4 3 2 1

Contents

Foreword

In an effort to improve my golf game, I occasionally take a lesson from the golf-pro at a nearby municipal golf course. Recently, I had to wait for Tasho to finish his lesson with another student, an eager young woman who was obviously a polished player. As I waited, I thought I might observe them and even eavesdrop so as to pick up some extra, unsolicited pointers that might improve my sorry game.

Soon they finished and Tasho turned to me. Let me see you hit a few, he commanded. Trying to demonstrate my new skills, I attempted to remember and employ those purloined instructions given to his previous student. To my surprise, he instructed me to do just the opposite from what he had told her. "No," he said, "address the ball more off your left foot." "No, step back more." "No, hunker down on the club handle more." Finally, in exasperation I stammered, "But that's not what you told that lady you taught before me!" "I know," he said. "But she's not a 66-year-old out-of-shape man who doesn't practice often enough!"

Tasho displayed some of the attributes of a diagnostic teacher. He held a vision of a proficient golfer and could compare his pupil's performance with the model of excellence he held in his mind. He was keenly observant of the unique and sometimes subtle characteristics of his pupils' skills, dispositions, and levels of commitment. He was able to locate them at a correct level of developmental readiness; he was able to break down the learning into teachable, incremental steps; he was able to articulate to his pupils in clear and precise terms how to employ the body and mind to perform certain moves at increasing levels of complexity. And he was able to provide clear and corrective feedback to his pupils about their performance.

How does one learn to become a diagnostic teacher? This volume contains a collection of action research studies, experiments, and learning strategies intended to serve staff developers in their efforts to transform practices from a traditional towards a more constructivist approach. Unlike my coach, Tasho, in the opening vignette, the intent of this book goes well beyond the learning of kinesthetic golfing skills. It focuses on the complexities of how humans construct meaning and how those new insights promulgate refined practice. It discloses how changing one's mind is a prerequisite to changing one's instructional behaviors.

Constructivism: Paradox and Promise

The essence of this volume is that meaning-making is not a spectator sport. Knowledge is a constructive process rather than a finding; it is not the content stored in memory but the processes of constructing it that gets stored. Humans don't *get* ideas; they *make* ideas. And those ideas, once constructed, are robust, enduring, and not easily extinguished. This view of learning provides a paradox for staff developers who devote their energies to the transformation of teaching practices.

We tend to teach as we were taught. Our perspectives, beliefs, and actions regarding curriculum and instruction are the constructed products, visions, and meanings born out of our own experiences over time, and thus we tend to perpetuate those same practices. The constructivist dilemma, therefore, is how to facilitate a change from a highly entrenched and deep-seated traditional, didactic, rote, competitive perspective about learning to one of mediating learners to become producers of their own knowledge rather than consumers of someone else's knowledge. And the trick is to do it in such a way as to model the characteristics and components which are consistent with constructivist learning.

Drawing on years of research and experience, the authors have contributed a treasure of staff development strategies and techniques based on a constructivist framework intended to engage, activate, and transform the mind. When these powerful strategies are applied, a set of beliefs about how human beings learn in most effective ways are exemplified and manifested and thus, through analogous learnings, the same values and beliefs are constructed and transferred to more refined instructional practices with students. The theme here is congruity: The mediator employs constructivist practices in the interventions with teachers who, in turn, transform their meanings to apply those analogous constructivist interventions with their students.

In this volume, the authors offer interventions which challenge learners with perplexing situations, intriguing discrepancies, and metaphorical tasks—the resolution to which are not readily apparent and therefore must be designed and constructed. During and after the activities, participants are invited to reflect on their thinking and to make meaning from their experiences—to compare intended with actual outcomes, to analyze and draw causal relationships, to synthesize meanings, and to apply their learnings to their own situations.

In this role, the diagnostic teacher, whether working with children or adults, assumes the identity of a facilitator of meaning-making. The diagnostic teacher interposes him or herself between the learner and the learning, causing them to approach events, tasks, and problems strategically, monitoring their own progress, constructing meaning from their experience, and applying their learnings to other contexts and settings. Learning is viewed as a continual process of engaging the mind, which then transforms the mind. Instruction is organized so that learners are typically the producers of knowledge rather than consumers of knowledge. Anyone who serves others—children or adults—with the intent of producing learning will find this book to be a valuable resource.

Managing an Atmosphere for Meaning-Making

Many out-of-conscious factors influence teachers' thinking as they make daily decisions about curriculum and instruction. Their culture, knowledge of content, cognitive style, knowledge about their students, and professional values and beliefs influence their judgments about when and how to teach what to whom. Less obvious, but vastly more persuasive influences on teacher thought, are the norms, culture, and climate of the school setting in which teachers work. Hidden, but powerful cues emanate from the school environment. These subtle cues signal the institutional value system which governs the operation of the organization. Knowing this, the constructivist leader constantly monitors and manages the environment to enhance conditions which will be conducive to intellectual growth. The following are some of the recurring patterns and themes which pervade the interventions described in this volume. All are basic to creating conditions for constructivist learning.

- *Building and Maintaining Trust.* Trust is a vital element in enhancing cognition. Experimentation implies that an atmosphere of choice, risk-taking, and inquiry exists. It is well established that higher-level, complex, and creative thinking closes down when trust is lacking in the environment or in the relationship. Creativity will more likely grow in a low-risk atmosphere. Teachers will be encouraged to inquire, speculate, construct meanings, experiment, self-evaluate, and self-prescribe when the leader manages a trusting environment.

  The essence of building trust and collegiality happens when people work together to better understand how to work together. People are more likely to engage and grow in higher-level, creative, and experimental thought when they are in a trusting, risk-taking, cooperative climate. Risk-taking requires a non-judgmental atmosphere where information can be shared without fear that it will be used for evaluative or coercive purposes.
- *Communities of Learners.* Humans, as social beings, mature intellectually in reciprocal relationships: The individual influences the group and the group

influences the individual. While meaning-making may be a personal experience, it is also a socio-cultural phenomenon. There are social processes of interaction and participation which enhance and refine meaning. Constructivist learning is rich with group work and interactions. Collaboratively, individuals generate and discuss ideas eliciting thinking that surpasses individual effort. Together and privately, they express different perspectives and beliefs, agree and disagree, display style diversity, point out and resolve discrepancies, and weigh alternatives. Because people grow their intellect through this process, deliberately structuring collegial interaction is a powerful intervention.

- *Constructivist Coaching.* The act of teaching is, itself, an intellectual process. The behaviors observed in the classroom are artifacts of decisions that teachers make before, during, and after instruction. The purpose of coaching, therefore, is to enhance the teacher's capacity to plan, monitor, reflect upon, and thus build meaning about their own instructional decision-making. The intent of coaching is to modify teachers' capacities to modify themselves.

  The constructivist leader, in an atmosphere of trust, challenges existing practices, assumptions, policies, and traditional ways of delivering curriculum. Intellectual growth is found in disequilibrium, not balance. It is out of chaos that order is built, that learning takes place, that new understandings are forged, that new connections are bridged and that instruction becomes more consistent with principles of constructivist learning.
- *Process Curriculum.* Curriculum is the pulse of the school; the currency through which teachers exchange thoughts and ideas with students and the community. It is the passion which binds the organization together. When we address curriculum, we address the very heart of the educational enterprise.

Changing our curriculum means changing our mind. Constructivist curriculum challenges the basic educational views of knowledge and of learning with which most schools are comfortable. It causes us to expand our focus from educational outcomes that are primarily collections of sub-skills to include successful processes of participation in socially organized activities and the development of students' identities as conscious, flexible, efficacious, interdependent, and continual learners. Teachers of constructivist curriculum let go of having learners acquire *their* meaning and have faith in the processes of individuals' construction of personal and shared meanings through social interaction.

Constructivist leaders make curriculum interventions when teachers behave as mathematicians, historians, writers, or composers. What makes a discipline a discipline is a disciplined mode of inquiry—the kinds of problems it defines and solves. Each content has a logic which is defined by the thinking that produced it: its purposes, problems, information, inferences, concepts, assumptions, implications, points of view, forms of communication, technology, and its interrelationships with other disciplines. Bio-logy, for example, is the logic of the study of lifeforms. Anthropo-logy is the logic of the study of mankind and culture. Psycho-logy is the logic of the study of the mind, etc. All areas of study are topics of interest in which something has to be reasoned out. Mathematics means being able to figure out a solution to a problem using mathematical reasoning. History means learning how to figure out a reasonable answer to a historical question or problem. Any subject or content must therefore be understood as a mode of figuring out reasonable answers to a certain body of questions. Thus, teachers construct new meaning about the structure of the disciplines through experiencing the modes of inquiry basic to that discipline.

Since these process-oriented goals cannot be assessed using product-oriented assessment techniques, the existing evaluation paradigm must shift as well. Thus assessment of students' and teachers' thinking will focus on their becoming more conscious, more reflective, more efficient, more flexible, and more transferable.

- *Action Research.* Construction of meaning is nurtured when people engage in active experimentation and wrestle with crucial, strategic, and real issues. Action research marshals the motivations and unleashes the talents of those who work directly with children day after day. Constructivist leaders assist the teaching staff in surfacing real problems, designing multiple strategies for collecting data, establishing criteria for judgment, developing common understandings and reliability of observations, and reporting of results. In action research, assessment data is the energy source that fuels informed and reflective practice. This is because:

  - the information is linked (scaffolded) to previous learnings;
  - learners feel a need for it, are interested in it, or request it;
  - it is delivered in a manner which matches the learner's learning style;
  - it is relevant to the learner's developmental levels;
  - it is drawn from multiple sources: visual, auditory, kinesthetic, tactile;
  - it is acted upon and processed—synthesized, evaluated, and applied to contexts beyond the one in which it was learned.

  There is no such thing as failure or mistakes—only learning from experience. As a result, learners feel empowered—they feel a responsibility for their own learning and knowledge building.
- *Metacognition.* Leaders invite learners to make meaning from experiences. Time is taken to invite reflections on learning, to compare intended with

actual outcomes, to analyze and draw causal relationships, to synthesize meanings, and to apply their learnings to new and novel situations. They are invited to share their metacognition—to reveal their intentions, strategies, and plans for solving a problem, to describe their mental maps for monitoring their strategy during the problem solving, and to reflect on the strategy to determine its adequacy.

- *Monitoring Growth in Self and Others.* Constructivist leaders are alert to indicators that constructivist practices are being incorporated into decision-making. Self-monitoring implies asking oneself: What are my intentions and motives at this moment? It means keeping in mind the criteria and characteristics of individual meaning-making. While self-monitoring implies being aware of one's own words, values, and actions, monitoring others means listening to their words and implicit thoughts about lesson design, curriculum decisions, assessment strategies, or staff development plans as indicators that principles of constructivist learning are being internalized.
- *Modeling.* Imitation and emulation are the most basic forms of constructivist learning. Teachers, parents, and administrators realize the importance of their own display of desirable learning behaviors in the presence of students. Thus, in day-to-day events and when problems arise in schools, classrooms, and homes, students must see adults and teachers must see leaders employing the same types of constructivist learning listed above. Without this consistency, there is likely to be a credibility gap. As Ralph Waldo Emerson is often quoted as saying, "What you do speaks so loudly, they can't hear what you say."

Constructivism: The Humility of Continuous Learning

A great paradox about humans is that we confront learning opportunities with fear rather than mystery and wonder. We seem to feel better when we know rather than when we learn. We defend our biases, beliefs, storehouses of knowledge rather than inviting the unknown, the creative, the inspirational. Being certain and closed gives us comfort, while being doubtful and open gives us fear.

From an early age, experiencing a curriculum of fragmentation, competition, and reactiveness, we are trained to believe that deep learning means figuring out the truth rather than developing capabilities for effective and thoughtful action. We are taught to value certainty rather than doubt, to give answers rather than to inquire, to know which choice is correct rather than to explore alternatives.

Our wish is to develop creative human beings who are eager to learn. That includes the humility of knowing that we don't know, which is the highest form of thinking we will ever learn. Paradoxically, unless we start off with humility we will never get anywhere, so the first step in becoming diagnostic teachers is to have already what will eventually be considered the crowning glory of all constructivist learning: to know—and admit—that we don't know.

The Payoff

What are the benefits of implementing a constructivist approach? The payoff will be found in the excitement of learners' self-discovery, the exuberance of their participation, the enhancement of their self-esteem, their intrigue with the mysterious, and their joyous expressions of insight. Furthermore, when you assume the identity of a mediator and devote your energies to serving other's construction of meaning, a profound transformation in your own thoughts and values occurs. You find enormous power within yourself to positively influence others and you gain personal satisfaction in using your talents to enhance their achievement. You expand your repertoire of instructional strategies and you will soon find yourself applying this view of learning in a variety of life-situations beyond the school. You embark, along with those you teach, on a magical journey of continuous and lifelong learning. After all, isn't that what education is all about?

Arthur L. Costa, Ed.D.
Kalaheo, Hawaii

Introduction

MILDRED Z. SOLOMON

Metaphors are helpful because they allow us to view the all-too-familiar from a new vantage point, one that brings hidden assumptions and overlooked detail into sharper focus. Yet metaphors can also be misleading, or even dangerous. After all, teachers are not doctors, and students are not patients. What, then, could we possibly mean by the term "diagnostic teacher"?

The concept of the diagnostic teacher emerged through a process of institutional inquiry and individual self-reflection by a group of colleagues who have worked together at Education Development Center for many years. Each of us has struggled in our own way to develop collaborations with teachers, staff developers, and principals that would enrich school life and the learning experiences students encounter there. Some of us worked with young children, others with adolescents, still others with adults only. With some exceptions, most of us focused specifically on one content domain—math, science, social studies, or language arts—and each of us developed, with our respective teams of colleagues and partners, a fairly distinct, perhaps even idiosyncratic, way of working.

And yet many of us had felt for some time that our work was more than the sum of individualistic parts—that there were core commonalities infusing, impelling our work. At a minimum, we knew that we could locate ourselves within a certain intellectual history. We could say with clarity and a common voice that our work grew out of the insights first of John Dewey; later out of the mathematics and science communities of the 1950s and 1960s and the ideas of Jerome Bruner, who worked with EDC in the late 1960s. EDC President Janet Whitla discusses this in her Afterword to this volume. Based on this history and a shared set of values, our work was clearly grounded in an "inquiry" approach to learning—one that assumes that schools must strive to develop active learners rather than passive recipients of isolated facts or disembodied skills.

There were other common characteristics, too: We all had discovered the vitality and power for change inherent in cultivating schools and teachers as communities of learners. Learning for all of us was a *social* endeavor, grounded in the idea that learners, whether they be teachers or students, should be encouraged to develop ideas in exchange with other ideas and in the context of participating in a field of inquiry with a history and direction.

Most, but not all, of us located our work within a set of perspectives known as constructivism, an orientation that sees knowledge as the dynamic and conditional by-product of individuals working in intellectual communities, constructing their understandings through interaction with their own and other's ideas, problems, and questions. Strikingly though, even those of us who did not consider ourselves constructivist seemed to be operating in ways that shared fundamentally similar assumptions and characteristics with those who did consider themselves constructivist.

Although we could see common principles and strategies reflected in our very different-looking projects, these broad generalizations about our work were unsatisfying. The principles we relied upon to characterize our work, while important, seemed too general or abstract, clichés even. Several of us began to feel that there was something deeper, an important common core, at the center of all our activities, yet at that point we still couldn't name it. We wondered: Is there an elusive, but fundamental, concept that our work embodies? If there is, what is it? Can we name it? Can we illustrate it? Can we talk about it in ways that might be helpful to others? In ways that might make a difference in how teachers teach and are themselves taught?

It was only after the writing of our stories and reflection upon them that the concept of the diagnostic teacher became clear. What we now see running through all our staff development efforts, and what we can finally articulate, is an effort to cultivate a certain stance in teachers. We call that stance "diagnostic," a gem of a term for which we are grateful to Dan and Molly Watt, who used it in the chapter they contributed to this volume to describe one of the teachers in their action research project. The Watts' phrase resonated with me, and, as I read more and more of these chapters and talked with the authors, I began to see it as a very powerful conceptual framework for understanding all our work.

By using the term "diagnostic teacher," we want to signal the importance of looking closely, looking for and in the details. A diagnostic teacher is one who casts oneself as an observer, scrutinizer, and assessor, as well as an engaged leader. More specifically, throughout these chapters we see staff developers encouraging teachers to develop assessment capacities in three domains. Diagnostic teachers (1) seek to know students' current understandings and misconceptions; (2) deepen their own subject-area knowledge and make judgments about what concepts are worth teaching, that is, what ideas and curriculum content they will encourage students to develop; and, finally, (3) assess their own beliefs and practices, selecting, designing, and redesigning appropriate pedagogical strategies and curriculum materials that make sense given students' understandings and the concepts and skills they want to promote.

It is gratifying, and validating of the inductive process we undertook, that these three domains precisely parallel the three domains the National Commission on Teaching and America's Future identified as central for reinvigorating teachers' professional skills. As the commission states: "American students are entitled to teachers who know their subjects, understand their students and what they need, and have mastered the professional skills required to make learning come alive" (National Commission on Teaching and America's Future, 1996, p. 7).

The concept of the diagnostic teacher is a helpful one because it highlights the importance of focusing intently on students and subject matter as well as pedagogy and striving to keep all three lenses actively in use and in constant relation to one another. This insight stands in sharp contrast to the predominant forms of staff development and teachers' curriculum planning that have, historically, focused on the *teacher's* behavior, as though it could be determined and evaluated independent of student needs. Too often the focus has been on what the teacher will or will not, did or did not, do; rarely have teachers been invited to begin by looking closely outside themselves—at what individual students understand, can do, find confusing or stimulating.

Diagnostic teachers, on the other hand, actively assess students' understandings, misunderstandings, interests, and skills in the light of teaching goals. Such teachers realize that any particular task or pedagogical strategy is not inherently appropriate or inappropriate, but something that should be chosen, or crafted, on the basis of one's specific teaching goals and students' interests and capacities.

Yet traditionally principals, staff developers, and teachers themselves have focused on teachers' practices—what they say or do in the classroom. Professional development has primarily been operationalized as the transmission of "teaching tips" or curriculum strategies in brief workshops or pull-out "training" conferences. The concept of the diagnostic teacher helps to clarify what is inadequate about this model of professional development.

If we are serious about meeting the challenge outlined in the commission's report, we will have to reexamine many of our most basic assumptions about professional development and school reform, and the concept of the diagnostic teacher can help us do that. Until recently, the emphasis of a great deal of school reform efforts has been on district restructuring and on school management and curriculum, not on student and teacher learning. These broader issues are often presumed to have a strong connection to student achievement, yet the connection is, in fact, tenuous. By and large, general reorganization of management and curriculum structures has not had an impact on what goes on in classrooms.

In an article aimed at discovering what we can learn from the school restructuring movement, Peterson, McCarthey, and Elmore (1996) analyzed cases of restructuring experiments in several elementary schools, with ethnically diverse populations, located in large urban school districts in different parts of the United States. They argued that far too much planning only posits or assumes a connection between the planned change and its impact on classroom practice. Instead, they suggest that reformers should "map backward" from desired teaching practices to organizational structures:

> If researchers, reformers, and teachers understood and agreed on what kind of teaching practices they wanted, and if they understood what would need to be learned to create these practices, then they might create structures that would support this learning and these practices. While some might continue to map forward from structural changes in schools to changes in teaching practice, we prefer to map backward. Why not begin by attempting to understand teaching practice? Then researchers might try to understand what [teacher] learning would need to occur to create such practices and what school structures might support this learning and these practices. (p. 151)

The staff development practices collected in this volume can be understood as a first step in "planning backward." Each chapter provides a portrait of the kind of teaching and learning worth aiming for and the sorts of supports we need to put in place to help teachers teach in those ways.

In Chapter 10, Catherine Cobb Morocco and I reflect on these portraits and present what we see as common across them. In that chapter, we provide a more detailed account of the concept of the diagnostic teacher and underscore how essential professional *communities* of adult learners are for teachers developing a diagnostic orientation to their craft. In Chapter 11, we propose a revitalized model of professional development, arguing that the current conception of one-shot workshops and didactic presentations of disembodied teaching techniques is inadequate for cultivating diagnostic teaching and, worse, actually undermines the professional identity of teachers. We recommend five actions that staff developers, teachers, and principals can undertake together to promote and sustain the professional growth of teachers, and we begin to sketch out the implications this model of professional development would have for how we organize our schools, school schedules, teaching roles, and norms.

First, though, we turn to Barbara Scott Nelson's introductory chapter, in which she articulates the reasons why we must strive for a new kind of teaching. Her chapter launches our reading of a remarkable set of in-depth accounts of teachers, teacher educators, principals, and researchers working collaboratively to strengthen what goes on in our country's classrooms. We hope readers will find that their experiences contribute, in some small measure, to the

Carnegie-Rockefeller commission's call for a national drive to revitalize teaching and teacher development.

REFERENCES

National Commission on Teaching and America's Future (1996). *What matters most: Teaching for America's future.* New York: Author.

Peterson, P. L., McCarthey, S. J., & Elmore, R. E. (1996). Learning from school restructuring. *American Educational Research Journal, 33*(1), 119–153.

Acknowledgments

This book would not exist without the contributing authors who have shared their time and their experiences so generously, nor without Janet Whitla, the president of Education Development Center, Inc., who has been our mentor and guide for nearly two decades. The concept for the book occurred to me somewhere mid-course in a series of interviews I was conducting with senior EDC staff. Janet and I had become interested in probing more deeply to see if we could articulate both common themes and possible discontinuities across EDC's many professional development projects. Through those interviews, the idea for a collected volume of essays emerged. It has been a privilege to have been allowed in for such a close-up look at the work of my colleagues. Thank you for the opportunity to reflect with you on the meaning and implications of your work.

The editing of this volume has also been gratifying because it has provided the opportunity to work closely with other senior EDC staff—Catherine Cobb Morocco, Barbara Scott Nelson, Myles Gordon, and Dan Tobin. These colleagues, in addition to Janet Whitla, have served as the editorial committee for this project. The editorial committee reviewed and selected abstracts for inclusion in the volume and then reviewed drafts of each chapter as they were submitted. Working closely with Cathy Morocco as co-authors of the two final chapters was a special treat that fulfilled my longtime desire to find an opportunity to work with her and her keen mind.

There is no way to adequately thank Dan Tobin, who joined this project in mid-course yet literally ensured its success. When we were well along in the production of chapters still far from finished, I found myself starting up a new center at EDC and five new projects all at once. Dan cheerfully stepped up to the plate and thereafter gracefully hit many home runs. Agreeing to serve as developmental editor to the volume, he met with individual authors to help focus and refine their chapters and to ensure that the collection would cohere. He also supervised many production aspects, including the securing of permissions, completing the references, and doing a thorough edit of the whole manuscript. Dan's conceptual abilities, his outstanding writing and editing skills, his ease with people, and his reassuringly calm presence were an enormous help to me and of great benefit to the book.

Karen Skipper and Bill Kuhlman provided cheerful and invaluable help with manuscript production and coordination with all the authors. Thank you all for your time and helpful contributions.

I am grateful to Brian Ellerbeck and Faye Zucker, our editors at Teachers College Press. Thank you for your early and sustained enthusiasm for this book idea and for your guidance throughout the project. Thanks, too, to Sarah Biondello for a topnotch job editing the penultimate version of the manuscript.

I would like to underscore that there were other EDC staff whose thinking and good work have enriched us all but who do not have chapters included in this book (most often because the particular projects they were working on at the time were at a stage where there was not yet enough data to allow them to flesh out a full narrative). Nevertheless, they participated in the early interviews, often contributed thoughtfully to our deliberations, and sometimes joined the lunchtime meetings we held to discuss our work. In particular, I would like to thank Linda Davenport, Sue Gordon, Vivian Guilfoy, Deborah Haber, Katherine Hanson, Carol Howard, Brian Lord, Eva Marx, Shira Persky, Arlene Remz, Annette Sassi, Joyce Malyn Smith, and Cheryl Vince Whitman.

A special thanks to Cheryl Vince Whitman, Senior Vice President and Director of Health and Human Development Programs at EDC, and Vivian Guilfoy, Director of the Center for Education, Employment, and Community, for their longstanding friendship and collegiality, which has created so productive and gratifying a work environment for many years. Also, a special thanks to the staff of the Center for Applied Ethics and Professional Practice at EDC for their patience with me as I completed this task—Karen Heller, Denise Matulis, Tim McIntyre, Stacy Piszcz, Anna Romer, Deborah Sellers, Karen Skipper, Judith Spross, and Molly Lynn Watt.

Finally, a word of appreciation to Manson Solomon and our children, Sara and Joshua, for putting up with all those nights and weekends when they just could not unhitch me from the computer. Thanks for being there.

EDC would like to thank the following organizations and institutions for providing funding for the projects described in this book: the National Science Foundation (Chapters 2, 3, 6, 7, and 8); the U.S. Department of Education (Chapters 4 and 5, through the Office of Special Education and Rehabilitative Services; and Chapter 9, through the Office of Special Education Projects); and the Lilly Endowment (Ch. 9). Any opinions, findings, and conclusions or recommendations expressed in this book are those of the authors and do not necessarily reflect the views of the funders.

THE DIAGNOSTIC TEACHER

Constructing New Approaches to Professional Development

"On the whole, the school reform movement has ignored the obvious: What teachers know and can do makes the crucial difference in what children learn."

—*What Matters Most: Teaching for America's Future: Report of the National Commission on Teaching & America's Future*, Summary Report, September 1996, p. 5

CHAPTER 1

Reconstructing Teaching

Interactions Among Changing Beliefs, Subject-Matter Knowledge, Instructional Repertoire, and Professional Culture in the Process of Transforming One's Teaching

Barbara Scott Nelson

Center for the Development of Teaching at EDC

Many studies of student achievement in relation to the cognitive demands of contemporary employment and informed citizenship indicate that *all* students in this country need an education that provides them with more conceptual and critical habits of mind than is currently the norm (Carnegie Corporation of New York, 1986; Educational Testing Service, 1989; Population Reference Bureau, 1989). Increasingly, well-paying jobs will require people who can read and understand technical material, write clearly, speak articulately, and solve complicated problems. Democratic government will require citizens who can understand and weigh difficult social and technical issues. Though American schools have always successfully taught a small number of students to handle such demands, very large numbers of students must now receive this kind of education (Resnick, 1987). As both wage earners and citizens, Americans need habits of mind that function as powerful, flexible tools to meet the challenges that lie ahead.

A significant body of research conducted over the past 20 years provides substantial guidance about how students can learn school subjects in ways that promote habits of mind such as creativity and problem solving. Students should *do* mathematics, science, writing, or history. They should work on meaningful tasks, explore multiple ways of approaching problems, express their thinking in speech and in writing, engage in discussion of complex ideas, and carry out long-term projects and investigations. That is, students should be part of serious intellectual communities.

To promote and sustain this new kind of learning, all parts of the education system need to change in concert. Curricula need to be redesigned to encourage student inquiry, new assessment instruments need to be developed to permit students to demonstrate their thinking, and, above all, teaching needs to be transformed. Because teachers stand at the intersection between the subject and the student, education change ultimately depends on them. Their knowledge of the subjects they teach, their ideas about the nature of learning and teaching, and the intellectual climate that they create in their classrooms are essential ingredients for student learning. But important ideas in all these domains have been changing.

Contemporary ideas about what constitutes a sound education in mathematics, science, and language and literature are undergirded by a new conception of the nature of knowledge itself (National Council of Teachers of English & International Reading Association, 1996; National Council of Teachers of Mathematics, 1989, 1991; National Research Council, 1996). By and large, the view of knowledge that current reforms are based on is a socio-constructivist one. Knowledge is considered to be the dynamic and conditional product of individuals working in intellectual communities, not a fixed body of immutable facts and procedures. In this view, learning proceeds through the individual's construction of understanding, not only by accepting facts and rules from teacher or textbook; teaching is the facilitation of knowledge construction, not only the delivery of information or opportunities to practice new skills. Further, in the fields of literature, history, and the social studies, the texts through which learners build their knowledge include not only the traditional classics, but also contemporary literature reflecting many cultures, oral histories, media-based materials, and students' own life experiences.

Teaching that provides opportunities for students to develop rigorous thinking is different in kind from what tends to occur in American schools today. Providing students with the opportunity to learn how to think flexibly and rigorously means more than *telling* students about previously accepted facts and procedures. Such teaching also involves understanding how knowledge is crafted by the students themselves and making a commitment to teaching as the facilitation of that process. In some subject areas it also requires seeing that meaning is constructed in a social context and that classroom conversation about texts of all kinds necessarily entails a complex ecology of interpretive processes. In all subjects, teaching involves creating a culture of inquiry in the classroom, in which both students and teacher are engaged in the serious exploration of the ideas at hand, and teachers are open to discovering what it is that their students understand.

An example from elementary mathematics makes the nature of such an exploratory classroom clear. In a recent teacher enhancement project, a kindergarten teacher described the following event from her classroom. She had been exploring her students' ideas about subtraction through the vehicle of stories about children who had a number of fruit roll-ups and gave some away to friends. She decided to investigate her students' thinking by asking what would happen if a child had promised fruit roll-ups to five friends but only had a single one to share. While some students said it couldn't be done, others said that the child would owe fruit roll-ups to four friends, and one student said she should "cut it in half into 5 pieces," to share it fairly. The teacher was surprised by the range of answers that her students saw as valid. Some kindergartners could imagine negative numbers (owing fruit roll-ups to four friends), and some could imagine division and fractions ("cut it in half into 5 pieces"). This event formed the basis of several days of excited classroom exploration into the several ways that fruit roll-ups could be shared among different numbers of children, with the teacher busily engaged in understanding the children's mathematical thinking (Nelson & Hammerman, 1996).

In another example, from science, an elementary school teacher portrays not only how the students in her classroom inquire into the nature of electrical systems, and what she learns about both electricity and their thinking, but also how this is different from the way she had previously taught.

> In the years past, I would give students a battery, a wire, and a bulb and show them how to make the light work. I would then have a discussion about why this is a system and that this is a light system.
>
> This year, I gave them the light bulb, a wire, and a battery and asked, "What are these things?" "What can we do with them?" I heard comments like, "We're going to make a system." Then they broke into groups of two and discovered how to make the bulb light. In one room, they discovered two different ways. I was so excited! They were teaching me some new ideas! We came back together and shared what they discovered. Then I let them go back to their groups and try these discoveries. Two girls discovered a third way to make the bulb light! . . . The excitement level was very high and they were ALL on task looking for new ways to make the light work. And they did! I was so excited about how smart they were and how much growth can take place in the right atmosphere! (Cohen, McLaughlin, & Talbert, 1993, pp. 94–95)

Some teachers have always centered their teaching on their students' thinking, and many more are in the process of transforming their teaching in this way. But for many teachers, because of the way they were educated, developing this kind of practice is not accomplished simply by adding new techniques to their current ideas about teaching and learning. It requires an epistemological shift—changing their beliefs about the nature of knowledge and learning, deepening and expanding their knowledge of the subject they teach, and reinventing their classroom practice from within a new conceptual frame. If education reform is to succeed, we need to carefully examine what it will take to support teachers as they make these necessary changes. However, our knowledge in this domain is recent and emergent (Fennema & Nelson, 1997).

RECENT INTELLECTUAL HISTORY

Only since the mid-1970s has the mental life of the teacher become a central topic in studies of teaching. Early work was based on research on human information processing, seeking to describe the psychological processes by which teachers perceived and defined their professional responsibilities and situations. Substantial research programs were developed to investigate teachers' planning, teachers' interactive thoughts and decisions while teaching, and teachers' theories and beliefs about teaching. This body of research provided a good start at describing teachers' cognitive behavior; but it did not provide rich descriptions of the tasks of teaching, nor did it pay much attention to the role of teachers' subject-matter knowledge itself (Clark & Peterson, 1986).

In the mid-1980s researchers began to elucidate teachers' understanding of subject matter and the nature of learning, and to trace out the relationship between such understandings and the instruction that teachers provide (Shulman, 1986; Zimpher & Howey, 1990). Such studies have included explorations of the nature of teachers' knowledge of the subject that they teach—mathematics, physics, English literature, and so on—with an eye to seeing if that knowledge is sufficiently flexible and deep to enable teachers to analyze the strengths and the weaknesses in their students' thinking. There has also been research on teachers' beliefs about what learning is and on how those beliefs affect teachers' ideas about what *teaching* is.

More recently, as the education reform movement has picked up speed, the dynamics of *change* in teachers' knowledge, beliefs, and practice have come under scrutiny. These changes typically are studied in the context of an actual professional development program, in which teachers are provided support for reconsidering their views of the nature of knowledge in the subject they teach, observing and analyzing children's thought and work, and exploring new modes of teaching. A number of studies of teachers in such programs suggest that, as teachers move toward basing their teaching on the development of children's thought, they experience an interrelated set of changes—in their beliefs about both the nature of learning and the nature of mathematical, scientific, literary, or historical knowledge; in the depth and flexibility of their own subject-matter knowledge; in their sense of the kind of intellectual environment a classroom could be; and in their repertoire of instructional practices (Fennema & Nelson, 1997; Goldsmith & Schifter, 1997). Such changes in knowledge and belief are considerably enhanced when the professional development program in which they are enrolled itself provides a professional culture for teachers that supports inquiry into how students' thinking develops and how to facilitate that thinking.

The following four sections discuss emerging evidence about changes in teachers' beliefs, knowledge, and classroom practice, as well as the nature of an emerging new professional culture of teaching. The chapters that follow describe particular aspects of such changes among teachers of a variety of subjects and cite research literature appropriate to those subjects.

Beliefs

For most teachers, changing their teaching to better facilitate students' mathematical thinking appears to require several interconnected changes in belief about the nature of learning (Carpenter, Fennema, Peterson, & Carey, 1988; Fennema, Carpenter, Franke, & Carey, 1993; Lampert, 1987; Schifter & Fosnot, 1993; Schifter & Simon, 1992; Thompson, 1991; Wasley, 1990; Wiske & Houde, 1988). Among the beliefs that evolve are the following:

- The belief that students are "empty vessels" waiting to be filled evolves toward the belief that students are intellectually generative, with great capacity to pose their own questions and develop their own solutions to problems.
- The belief that students learn by being told what to do and how to do it evolves toward confidence that students will learn through their own effort and can take greater responsibility for their own learning.
- The belief that the subject (for example, mathematics, science, or history) consists of a series of isolated facts and topics that should be taught in a certain order, or hierarchy, evolves toward a view of the subject as a flexible network of ideas, with many interconnections, which can be approached in a variety of ways.
- The belief that instruction should follow the textbook and that the teacher's responsibility is to cover the material evolves toward the belief that instruction should build on what students know and can do and should focus on important questions and ideas in the field.

Often teachers begin to question prior beliefs when they encounter unexpected evidence about children's ideas and knowledge. For example, teachers may come to question the belief that demonstrating how a mathematical algorithm works is a sufficient teaching strategy when they see that students who know how to work the algorithm cannot explain how and why it works. Such an experience leads many teachers to question whether their previous beliefs have led to instructional practices that do not actually meet their educational goals.

Often such changes in belief begin in summer programs or workshops where teachers are provided the opportunity to examine data about student thinking, but changes in teachers' beliefs about teaching and learning also take place in their classrooms and in interaction with changes in their classroom teaching practice (Franke, Fennema, & Carpenter, 1997; Guskey, 1986; Richardson, Anders, Tidwell, & Lloyd, 1991; Wood, Cobb, & Yackel, 1991). Indeed, classrooms are important contexts in which teachers can explore the power of new explanations for children's mathematical behavior. In their classrooms, the evidence teachers see of children's thinking has the power of being undeniably *there*—not the artifact of a research program or videotape editing, not something that children elsewhere might do. Further, changes in conceptual lenses and in behavior are iterative—through new lenses teachers can see children's intellectual work differently and act differently. When one acts differently, others respond to the new situation, and then there is a new set of actions to be interpreted through the new lenses.

This suggests that a summer institute or pull-out program alone, disconnected from teachers' own classrooms, may not be sufficient to provide teachers with the stimulation and support they need to change prior beliefs. There is some discussion in the literature about which comes first—change in belief or change in teaching practice. However, it is not clear that the relationship between beliefs and practice is a simple, linear, causal one. The research suggests that the relationship between beliefs and practice is dialectic, moving back and forth between change in belief and change in classroom practice (Cobb, Wood, & Yackel, 1990; Franke et al., 1997; Thompson, 1992).

Several chapters in this volume address the role of changing beliefs in the process of teacher change. Driscoll (Chapter 4) cites teachers' surprise at the role of students' family and cultural backgrounds in their interpretation of mathematics problems; Riley and Morocco (Chapter 5) report on the dissonance between what teachers expected and what happened in classrooms; and Cutler and Ruopp (Chapter 6) focus squarely on the belief/practice interplay.

Subject-Matter Knowledge

Teachers' ideas about the nature of knowledge in the subject they teach, and the depth and flexibility of their own subject-matter knowledge, are important ingredients in their teaching (Schifter & Fosnot, 1993; Shulman, 1986). To take mathematics as an example, when mathematics is considered to be a set of memorized rules and procedures for correctly solving particular quantitative problems, mathematics learning can reasonably be thought of as becoming proficient at applying the rules and procedures for arriving at the correct answer. In such a view of mathematics, it may be adequate for teachers to know how the algorithms work. However, when mathematics is considered to be a body of knowledge that has been created, refined, challenged, and modified by generations of men and women, learning mathematics comes to be viewed as a process of conjecturing, discussing, testing, playing with, revising, and extending ideas about mathematical objects. For this form of instruction, teachers need much deeper and more flexible mathematical knowledge.

However, because of the way they were educated, many teachers do not have such conceptually based and flexible subject-matter knowledge. In mathematics, for example, because their own mathematics education often has been primarily algorithmic, teachers themselves may not have thought through the mathematical meaning that underlies formal mathematical expressions (Borko et al., 1992; Schifter, 1993). If teachers do not have a strong enough grasp of the mathematics they are to teach, they may not be able to engage their students in an exploration of mathematical ideas beyond calling attention to a variety of solution strategies. They themselves may not be able to distinguish valid from invalid reasoning. This can leave them with no way to assess the various solutions offered.

There is evidence that deeper knowledge of the subject results in more emphasis on conceptual explanations; that seeing the relationships between topics may lead to more effective teaching; and that teachers' subject-matter knowledge itself may become transformed in the process of teaching, as it becomes enriched by teachers' knowledge of students, curriculum, and teaching context (Grossman, Wilson, & Shulman, 1989). But the process of deepening one's own subject-matter knowledge for the purpose of teaching may not be straightforward, and taking a typical university course in the subject may not be sufficient. For example, Barnett's studies of teacher change through the analysis of teachers' use of case studies on the teaching and learning of rational numbers indicate that changes in teachers' mathematics knowledge is multidimensional and context-embedded. Barnett reports that teachers typically discuss several different but intertwined dimensions of the instructional incident represented in a case—mathematical concepts, mathematical relationships, assessment, language, strategies for promoting mathematical thinking, strategies for promoting understanding and meaning, and strategies for fostering motivation and positive disposition (Barnett, 1991).[1] There also are indications that teachers can learn their subject while teaching it. Russell and colleagues (1995) describe several ways in which teachers engaged in a professional development program in elementary mathematics learned mathematics while teaching it—through exploring the mathematics content of a lesson before teaching it; by thinking through the mathematical significance of students' mathematical representations and problem-solving strategies; and by looking at the mathematical structures that underlay student reasoning.

Change in teachers' subject-matter knowledge is a theme in several of the chapters in this volume. Driscoll (Chapter 4) shows changes in teachers' ideas of what mathematics is; Schifter, Russell, and Bastable (Chapter 2) focus on teachers' increasing awareness of the "big ideas" that underlie the elementary mathematics curriculum; Cutler and Ruopp (Chapter 6) show teachers regularly exploring mathematics for themselves; and Riley and Morocco (Chapter 5) depict teachers changing their views of the nature of writing.

Instructional Repertoire

As noted earlier in an example of inquiry-based science teaching, conventional instruction tends to emphasize whole-class instruction, with students listening to the teacher's explanation and watching the teacher work sample problems or following the teacher's instructions about how to do the experiment, and then working on their own on the assigned task. The goal of student activity is to produce the single, right answer, which is already known by and will be validated by the teacher (Cohen & Ball, 1990; Porter, 1989; Stodolsky, 1988). Teaching that facilitates students' construction of knowledge, on the other hand, is largely based on inquiry (Duckworth, 1991a; Richards, 1991; Schifter & Fosnot, 1993). Teachers attend carefully to students' oral and written expressions of ideas; use these to develop conjectures about students' understanding; and offer questions, counterexamples, or activities meant to check the depth, breadth, or robustness of students' ideas.

The knowledge and skills needed to conduct instruction based on inquiry include the ability to *do* mathematics, science, or history oneself; the ability to listen to students' thinking and identify the seeds of an important idea or a conceptual stumbling block; the ability to devise activities that provide the opportunity for students to extend their knowledge; and the ability to help students learn to explain their own thinking and listen to their peers' ideas (see Simon, 1997). Teachers also need to be able to recognize unexpected but promising ideas that arise in the classroom and weave these into the ongoing discourse. In short, teachers need to be able to create and maintain classroom environments that function as cultures of inquiry in a particular subject.

The following episode from a science classroom illustrates how a classroom can become a context in which each student's pursuit of answers to her emerging questions builds knowledge and expands the concepts that all students are understanding.

> A group of girls studying whales became interested in fertility rates and the fate of low birth-weight babies. They discovered that one reason that certain species of whales are endangered is that their reproduction rate has slowed dramatically. The same was found to be true of sea otters. These students introduced the concept of declining fertility rates into the discussion, and it was taken up in the common discourse in two forms: simply as the notion of the number of babies a species had, and more complexly as the notion of reproductive strategies in

> general. The skilled teacher appropriates students' spontaneous interest in the common problems of endangered animals—amount of food eaten, amount of land required, number of young, etc.,—and encourages them to consider the deeper general principles of metabolic rate, and survival and reproductive strategies. (Brown & Campione, 1994, p. 13)

The degree to which such techniques are similar in all academic subjects is an open question at the moment. Surely, making space in the classroom for students to exhibit their thinking is requisite, as is intelligent and informed engagement with students. But the particulars of how subject-matter knowledge is represented, and the nature of the questions and activities that will enable students to extend their knowledge and their thinking, will vary from subject to subject and require very particular knowledge of the subject on the part of the teacher. Knowing the "facts" of a discipline, and *its* particular ways of validating knowledge, will be essential for teachers if classrooms are to be places where students can build knowledge well.

Research on teachers' change of instructional practice and the development of a new instructional repertoire is under way, but it is in the very early stages. There are indications that teachers need to work through the new instructional methods over time in the context of their teaching practice; that they see different aspects of the problem at different points in the process of change; and that they become proficient and flexible in their use of new methods only over an extended period of time, often 2 or 3 years. Teachers' initial attempts at changing their teaching may be disjointed and they may face classroom management problems because the kind of classroom they are trying to envision and develop is significantly different from the kind of classroom they currently know how to create and manage.

A number of studies in mathematics education shed light on the early stages of the process and on what is involved for teachers as they move to a mature and self-sustaining instructional practice based on inquiry. Schifter and Simon (1992) have observed four different stages that occur as teachers change their instructional practice. Teachers may begin by holding a view of learning that is not learner-centered at all, then develop a rudimentary understanding of what learner-centered learning is but have difficulty basing their instruction on that understanding. At a third stage, teachers may progress to being comfortable with learner-centered instructional techniques, but their instructional decisions are based on teaching behaviors that they know, rather than on their students' thought. At the final stage, the teacher is focused on students' learning from a constructivist perspective and designs instruction based on *students'* mathematical thinking (Schifter & Simon, 1992). Thompson (1991) has a compatible three-level model that describes changes in teachers' epistemology and mathematics knowledge as well as their classroom practice. At level 0, the role of teacher is perceived as that of demonstrator of well-established procedures. At level 1, teaching is viewed as involving conceptual understanding, but this is understood as requiring the teacher to possess a collection of pedagogical techniques for explaining isolated concepts, procedures, algorithms, and formulas. At level 2, the teacher's role is to steer students' thinking in mathematically productive ways. The hallmark of this level is the presence of cognitively based principles that are explicitly used to guide instructional decisions. Finally, Franke and colleagues (1997) suggest that it is as teachers develop the practice of practical inquiry focused on understanding children's mathematical thinking that they move to a self-sustaining level of change in their beliefs about learning and teaching—and in their practice.

Several chapters in this volume address the issue of changing instructional repertoire. Driscoll (Chapter 4) sees teachers posing different kinds of mathematical questions; Cutler and Ruopp (Chapter 6) trace the difficult path between beginning to change one's beliefs and trying to change one's practice; Zorfass (Chapter 9) describes the process of coaching teachers through incorporating new instructional practices into an interdisciplinary unit; and Hammerman (Chapter 8) discusses the role of a supportive professional culture in supporting teachers' efforts to change their instructional practice.

Professional Culture

Research on professional development for teachers, in general, repeatedly emphasizes the necessity of collegial interaction for teachers (Fullan & Hargreaves, 1992; Little, 1993; Little & McLaughlin, 1991; Lord, 1994). In particular, researchers have observed that groups of teachers who are in the process of examining their own thinking, and are learning to facilitate students' thinking, sometimes develop what amounts to a new culture of teaching that legitimates and supports reflection, experimentation, ongoing learning, and collegiality (Duckworth, 1991b; Hammerman, 1995; Wasley, 1990). Studies of teachers who are in the process of changing their practice show that such teachers want the freedom to express their doubts and uncertainties but find it difficult to admit they do not have all the answers, that they are themselves continuing to learn. Finally, teachers truly enjoy working together with colleagues, although many find it difficult to emerge from their traditional isolation (Wasley, 1990). Part of the work of teaching, redefined, is to continually question, critique, and explore ways to interpret the meaning of what happens in the classroom and to develop the next instructional step. This is best done with colleagues who share the enterprise.

Conversely, the process of learning together can provide teachers with a rich picture of the world they might make for their students. In the passage below, a group of teacher researchers describe what they learned about the circumstances in which ideas develop, by reflecting on the nature of their own learning community.

> We began to realize how much our own collaboration was a context for us to learn about learning. As we examined ourselves in light of these changes, we wondered at the factors that made it possible for us to experiment, to watch one another and find ways to adapt our own teaching given these new experiences. Watching one another over time, and seeing how children's skills and knowledge developed over a sequence of classes—rather than from a single experience—was exciting and a rich contribution to our own learning. It made us want to find ways to give students the same kind of time to stew in ideas, to consider alternative explanations, to generate and then challenge hypotheses, to explore territories that mattered to them in ways that were genuine. (Cohen et al., 1993, p. 95)

A change in the professional culture for teachers is a salient feature of change in several of the projects described in this volume. Watt and Watt (Chapter 3) report increased collegiality among teachers doing action research; Matsumoto (Chapter 7) describes how teachers and principals began to transform their relationships and their school culture through joint engagement in hands-on learning activities and long-range planning; Driscoll (Chapter 4), Cutler and Ruopp (Chapter 6), Zorfass (Chapter 9), Riley and Morocco (Chapter 5), and Hammerman (Chapter 8), all describe similar changes in culture and professional relationships. In each case, the growth of a collegial learning community among teachers appears to provide an important context for taking the risks inherent in change.

CHAPTERS IN THIS BOOK

Most recent research on teacher change has consisted of conceptual work elucidated by case studies of teachers in the process of change, studies of teachers engaged in innovative professional development programs (Fennema & Nelson, 1997), and writing by teachers themselves about their own changes in belief and practice (Schifter, 1996a, 1996b). The chapters in this book add the view of experienced teacher educators to that body of work. It should be kept in mind that, while the findings from many studies appear to be congruent, they do not yet represent either the experience of large numbers of teachers or, for the most part, the experience of teachers who were not voluntary participants in experimental programs.

The chapters in this volume emerge from the practice of teacher education, as it has been conducted in a variety of funded projects at EDC. As a collection, the chapters describe a variety of contexts for teacher change and examine the process in a variety of academic subjects and at different grade levels. Each paper illuminates one or more aspects of the process of teacher change described above, showing how it occurred in the particular project in which the teachers and teacher educators were working. The view of teacher change that emerges from the set of papers is not uniform, but rather kaleidoscopic, and in each paper the pieces of colored glass fall in a slightly different configuration.

By and large, these are stories of action—the actions of both teachers and their mentors and guides in the change process. The action may be guided by intuition or theory. As the stories unfold we see many of the themes discussed earlier combine and recombine from chapter to chapter. We see worked out in concrete detail the relation between changes in belief and changes in practice, the effects of the opportunity to think deeply and critically about the subject matter itself, what it is like to begin to explore an inquiry-based mode of instruction, and the powerful effects of the development of a new form of collegiality and community among teachers. We also see here the kind of knowledge that emerges from the process of grappling with the world rather than researching it: It may not fall into neat categories and tends to be anecdotal rather than systematic; it is often context-dependent; but it also contains gripping stories of the struggles of real teachers whose dedication to their students propels them through months of struggle and self-doubt to the hard-won emergence of a new view of learning.

Schifter, Russell, and Bastable (Chapter 2) describe the structure of a project designed to help teachers transform their practice to one organized around teaching to the big ideas—the central organizing principals of mathematics with which students must wrestle as they confront the limitations of their existing mathematical conceptions. In the authors' view, big ideas are never fully and finally comprehended. Rather, their construction is always provisional—they will be successively reorganized, acquiring additional content, as new areas of mathematics are explored.

The authors identify five principles crucial to the process of transforming mathematics pedagogy:

1. In-service instruction should be organized to facilitate teachers' construction of new pedagogical theory and practice.
2. Teachers' mathematical understanding is central.
3. Regular school-year follow-up support is an indispensable catalyst.
4. Teacher development and curriculum reform must support one another.
5. Schoolwide collaboration is essential to the process of reform.

Within such a context, they report that grappling with the big ideas of the elementary mathematics curriculum provides teachers with an intellectual structure for identifying what may be most important in the ebb and flow of ideas in the elementary classroom, for choosing or adapting curriculum materials, and for planning the course of a year's work so that it involves opportunities for children to have deep engagement with these ideas rather than providing a relatively arbitrary series of mathematical activities.

Watt and Watt (Chapter 3) focus on teachers' classroom-based, action research as the engine for change. Action research is conducted by teachers for the purpose of improving the teaching and learning in their own classrooms. It focuses on the particular circumstances of an individual teacher's classroom and is designed to resolve real teaching and learning issues that are occurring in that classroom. The Watts lay out for us the process by which teachers can be supported in learning to do action research. Focusing on a few individual students at the outset, among other things, allows teachers to base their observations on specific data rather than generalizations and to ground their discussions in that data. Teachers learn to focus on what knowledge students are using and what potentially useful or relevant knowledge they are *not* using. Group discussions of collected data make possible the surfacing of alternate interpretations of student thinking and a variety of possible instructional interventions.

The action research perspective helps teachers learn how to take a descriptive, research frame of mind into their classrooms—a frame of mind that is analytically distinct from the subsequent instructional decisions that might be based on what was observed. To focus on student thought, freeze the moment of observation, and to make a space in which "disinterested" discussion about the phenomenon can take place is an important moment for teachers. It also is an important component of the inquiry-based mode of teaching that many teachers are moving toward.

Finally, as is evident in other chapters in this volume, the opportunity to talk with one another about what they observe, how they interpret it, and what they might do next instructionally provides teachers doing action research with an openness to others' ideas and a set of collegial relationships that may have previously been lacking in their professional lives.

Driscoll (Chapter 4) presents the story of what happens when teachers focus their attention on their students' mathematical thinking. Classroom-based assessment activities provide the context for this new focus. When the teachers set out specifically to ascertain how well what they were teaching was being learned so that they could make appropriate adjustments to instruction, they found themselves looking directly at their students' mathematical thought. And what they saw often "drove" professional growth on the part of the teachers themselves. It prompted the development of new ideas about what is important in mathematics—concepts or algorithms; increased teachers' awareness of the number of different, and mathematically legitimate, ways in which problems could be approached by students; and supported the emergence of a link for the teachers between undertaking activities to learn what a student knows and undertaking activities in order to instruct. But teachers also sometimes discovered that they had not been fully aware of the impact of students' home and community backgrounds on their engagement with mathematics assignments and had not created truly equitable opportunities for all students to learn. And sometimes it was clear from the results of classroom assessments that teachers needed to examine the clarity of their own explanations or directions to students. Professional inquiry into the nature of classroom events revealed by assessment became an important feature of the Classroom Assessment in Mathematics (CAM) community.

Riley and Morocco (Chapter 5) extend the range of discussion still further in their chapter about teachers who come to create constructive conversation formats with their students as contexts for developing thought and writing. Riley and Morocco describe a view of writing instruction that was new for the teachers with whom they worked—that writing is a process of social construction of meaning; that certain kinds of conversation can facilitate that process; and that teachers have critical, highly intentional roles to play in facilitating students' talking and thinking for writing. As in Chapter 9, the experience for teachers was designed according to the same principles that would undergird teachers' design of student instruction. Teachers had the opportunity to see their own thinking and writing develop through useful conversations with others; and, by reflecting on their own processes of learning, they generated new hypotheses about what might facilitate their students' learning. As in Chapter 4, in-class assessment of children's work was an important vehicle for refocusing teachers' attention on individual student thinking. The teachers were often surprised at how much students knew and knew how to do. Riley and Morocco postulate that it was the surprising dissonance between what they expected (of themselves and of their students) and the experience of being scaffolded in their own growth, as well as figuring out how to scaffold growth for their students, that spurred the teachers on.

Cutler and Ruopp (Chapter 6) return us to the field of mathematics with their chapter on the process by which middle school teachers examined their mathematics teaching. Cutler and Ruopp focus on the belief/practice interplay. In half-day workshops, teachers explored the mathematics of the middle grades—grappling with problems, reflecting on their own learning, and exploring classroom applications of what they were learning. Moving back and forth between using new curricula and materials *themselves* and discussing how one would teach with them, as well as moving back and forth between teacher workshops and trying things out in their own classrooms, teachers were encouraged to examine their beliefs about mathematics and teaching. As in the other chapters in this volume, project leaders engaged in a practice with teachers that instantiated the same principles that teachers might use to inform their teaching. Also present is the important theme of a growing sense of collegiality and community among teachers.

Moreover, through their portraits of the struggles of individual teachers, Cutler and Ruopp remind us of the complexity and interrelatedness of ideas about mathematics, learning, and teaching in teachers' lives. The pathways to change are quite individual and appear significantly related to teachers' hopes for themselves and their students and to their dispositions to take risks and to experiment. Also present here is a glimpse of the distance between teachers' changing vision for their classrooms and what they are, as yet, actually able to make happen.

Matsumoto (Chapter 7) continues the theme of supportive professional cultures, discussing the nature of the school culture that will be necessary to support new forms of science teaching. In particular, she explores what school principals need to know and know how to do if they are to provide necessary support for teachers who are working to change their science teaching. Not only will principals need to understand what it means to do science and what science classrooms might look like, but they also will have to reconceptualize the nature of the teachers' role and, suggests Matsumoto, rework the hierarchical relationship between principal and teacher, so that it is more collegial. The work reported in this chapter suggests that just as most teachers need the support of a principal to make real changes in their classrooms, principals need the support of teachers to make real changes in the school.

Hammerman (Chapter 8), in his discussion of collaborative explorations among teachers of a changing practice, brings into focus a theme that has wound its way through other chapters as well—the nature of a new professional culture for teaching. Hammerman suggests that there is a dynamic relationship between teachers' learning and growth and the development of the teacher communities that support those processes. That is, it is *as* teachers do mathematics together and explore the pedagogy of their teaching that they create a new, less isolated, and more collaborative culture for teaching itself.

Zorfass (Chapter 9) broadens the focus beyond mathematics in her discussion of the process by which middle school teachers learn to operate as interdisciplinary teams, coaching students to conduct long-term multidisciplinary investigations on socially relevant themes. She focuses on curriculum design, rather than classroom assessment, as the precipitating context for teacher change. In order to develop interdisciplinary inquiry-based units, teachers found that they needed to explore the nature of inquiry-based learning itself, think deeply about the important ideas they wanted students to be thinking about, share their knowledge of the several relevant disciplines and together forge goals for students, and reflect on both their own learning and the likely effectiveness of the unit they were developing. In this chapter, it is clear that the experience was designed according to the same principles that project leaders hope teachers will use in their own teaching. Teachers thereby had the opportunity to reconstruct their own knowledge of both discipline and teaching in a socially meaningful context and to experience both the joys and struggles of the process. Teachers worked hard to identify the overarching concepts of the unit, coming to see that it was these big ideas that were fundamental and should drive the choice of student activities. They also learned to take risks with one another and became bonded into a new community.

Teachers talk about feeling part of a community or family that has made them feel less isolated as professionals. They talk about how their team has gradually developed a shared language that works its way into conversations about students, teaching, and assessment. The actual curriculum unit, a document that contains their plans, becomes a shared history that reflects their knowledge about students, concepts, learning objectives, and instructional activities. These plans not only anchor their thoughts, discussions, and present work, but also provide a solid foundation for future work.

WORKING WITH TEACHERS

The chapters in the book are not meant as a "how-to" of constructivist teacher education. Rather, they are reflections from the field, from experienced teacher educators, about elements of the process of teacher change as it has occurred in particular projects of which they have been part. The question remains: What might those who work with teachers expect to draw from the chapters in this book?

The same revolution in ideas about learning and teaching that undergirds the new vision of what classrooms should be like if robust and flexible learning is to happen underlies new ideas about working with teachers. The Association for Supervision and Curriculum Development (ASCD) devoted its entire 1992 Yearbook to the issue of *Supervision in Transition*. In that volume Nolan and Francis offer some implications for supervision of our changing perspectives on learning and teaching:

1. Teachers should be viewed as active constructors of their own knowledge about learning and teaching. That is, just as it is impossible for teachers to pour knowledge into the minds of students, so it is impossible for teacher educators and supervisors to pour knowledge into the heads of teachers.

2. Teacher educators and supervisors should be collaborators in the creation of knowledge about learning and teaching. That is, rather than being a critic of teachers' practice, the supervisor or teacher educator would be a collaborator in thinking through puzzling dilemmas of teaching.
3. The classroom data that is relevant for understanding teaching becomes more varied. That is, single pencil-and-paper observation instruments that focus on teacher behavior need to be replaced by a variety of items that bring the nature of student thinking into the discussion—student products, videotapes, student interview, and so on.

Just as teachers need to reinvent their craft from within a new conceptual frame, so do teacher educators and supervisors. Those who work with teachers will have to construct their way into this new world, using the same general principles that teachers are using in their classrooms. There are few proven guides.

In her Preface to this book, Mildred Solomon introduces the concept of the diagnostic teacher as a helpful metaphor for elucidating not only new approaches to teaching but also new models of professional communities and professional development. In Chapter 10, Solomon and Morocco expand on the concept of the diagnostic teacher and use it to synthesize and pull into focus the orientations and practices described in the preceding chapters. The chapter ends with an examination of the critical importance of professional communities in fostering and nurturing a diagnostic stance. In Chapter 11, Morocco and Solomon extend that discussion by looking at what kinds of staff development efforts help to cultivate diagnostic teachers and what kinds work against it. The chapter describes the conditions that support re-formed teaching, traces implications for the practice and policy of teacher education and supervision, and suggests implications for the nature of school culture.

NOTES

An early draft of this chapter formed the basis for another essay, written with Jim Hammerman, which appears in *Teacher Learning: New Policies, New Practices.* In that chapter, some of the same ideas are treated from a slightly different perspective.

1. The effectiveness of using cases in teacher development is viewed by Shulman (1992) as related to the situated nature of cognition—"the specificity and localism of cases . . . may [make them] far more appropriate media for learning than the more abstract and decontextualized lists of propositions or expositions of facts, concepts and principles" (p. 24). Further, the criterion for validity in case-based learning is verisimilitude—does the case ring true? Well-written cases can feel to teachers like the real thing and thus provide rich contexts for their teaching. Finally, sets of cases

provide the opportunity for multiple representations of teaching incidents, so that the limitations of any single case, or misunderstandings that might arise from it, are counterbalanced.

REFERENCES

Barrett, C. (1991). Building a case-based curriculum to enhance the pedagogical content knowledge of mathematics teachers. *Journal of Teacher Education*, *42*(4), 263–272.

Borko, H., Eisenhart, M., Brown, C. A., Underhill, R. G., Jones, D., & Agard, P. C. (1992). Learning to teach hard mathematics: Do novice teachers and their instructors give up too easily? *Journal for Research in Mathematics Education*, *23*(3), 2194–2224.

Brown, A. L., & Campione, J. C. (1994). Guided discovery in a community of learners. In K. McGilly (Ed.), *Classroom lessons: Integrating cognitive theory and classroom practice*. Cambridge, MA: MIT Press/Bradford Books.

Carnegie Corporation of New York. (1986). *A nation prepared: Teachers for the 21st century* [Report of the task force on teaching as a profession]. New York: Author.

Carpenter, T., Fennema, E., Peterson, P., & Carey, D. (1988). Teachers' pedagogical content knowledge of students' problem-solving in elementary arithmetic. *Journal for Research in Mathematics Education*, *19*, 385–401.

Clark, C. M., & Peterson, P. L. (1986). Teachers' thought process. In M. C. Whittrock (Ed.). *Handbook of research on teaching* (3rd ed.). New York: Macmillan.

Cobb, P., Wood, T., & Yackel, E. (1990). Classrooms as learning environments for teachers and researchers. In R. Davis, C. Maher, & N. Noddings (Eds.), *Constructivist views on the teaching and learning of mathematics* [Journal for Research in Mathematics Education Monograph No.4] (pp. 125–146). Reston, VA: National Council of Teachers of Mathematics.

Cohen, D. K., & Ball, D. L. (1990). Policy and practice: An overview. *Educational Evaluation and Policy Analysis*, *12*(3), 233–240.

Cohen, D. K., McLaughlin, M. W., & Talbert, J. (Eds.). (1993). *Teaching for understanding: Challenges for policy and practice*. San Francisco: Jossey-Bass.

Duckworth, E. R. (1991a, April). *Teaching and research in one: Extended clinical interviewing*. Paper presented at the annual meeting of the American Educational Research Association, Chicago.

Duckworth, E. R. (1991b). Twenty-four, forty-two, and I love you: Keeping it complex. *Harvard Educational Review*, *61*(1), 1–24.

Educational Testing Service. (1989). *A world of differences: An international assessment of mathematics and science*. Princeton, NJ: Author.

Fennema, E., Carpenter, T. P., Franke, M., & Carey, D. (1993). Learning to use children's mathematical thinking: A case study. In R. B. Davis & C. A. Maher (Eds.), *Schools, mathematics, and the world of reality* (pp. 93–117). Boston: Allyn & Bacon.

Fennema, E., & Nelson, B. S. (1997). *Mathematics teachers in transition*. Mahwah, NJ: Erlbaum.

Franke, M. L., Fennema, E., & Carpenter, T. (1997). Teachers creating change:

Examining evolving beliefs and classroom practice. In E. Fennema & B. S. Nelson (Eds.), *Mathematics teachers in transition.* Mahwah, NJ: Erlbaum.

Fullan, M., & Hargreaves, A. (1992). *Teacher development and educational change.* London: Falmer.

Goldsmith, L. T., & Schifter, D. (1997). Understanding teachers in transition: Characteristics of a model for developing teachers. In E. Fennema & B. S. Nelson (Eds.), *Mathematics teachers in transition.* Mahwah, NJ: Erlbaum.

Grossman, P. L., Wilson, S. M., & Shulman, L. S. (1989). Teachers of substance: Subject matter knowledge for teaching. In M. C. Reynolds (Ed.), *Knowledge base for the beginning teacher* (pp. 23–36). New York: Pergamon.

Guskey, T. R. (1986). Staff development and the process of teacher change. *Educational Researcher, 15*(5), 5–12.

Hammerman, J. K. (1995). Teacher inquiry groups: Collaborative explorations of changing practice. In B. S. Nelson (Ed.), *Inquiry and the development of teaching: Issues in the transformation of mathematics teaching.* Newton, MA: Center for the Development of Teaching, Education Development Center.

Lampert, M. (1987). *Teachers' thinking about students' thinking about geometry: The effects of new teaching goals.* Cambridge, MA: Education Technology Center, Harvard Graduate School of Education.

Little, J. W. (1993). Teachers' professional development in a climate of educational reform. *Educational Evaluation and Policy Analysis, 15*(3), 129–151.

Little, J. W., & McLaughlin, M. W. (1991). *Urban mathematics collaboratives: As the teachers tell it.* Palo Alto, CA: Stanford University, Center for Research on the Context of Secondary School Teaching.

Lord, B. (1994). Teachers' professional development: Critical colleagueship and the role of professional communities. In N. Cobb (Ed.), *The future of education: Perspectives on national standards in America* (pp. 175–204). New York: College Entrance Examination Board.

National Council of Teachers of English & International Reading Association. (1996). *Standards for the English language arts.* Urbana, IL: Authors.

National Council of Teachers of Mathematics. (1989). *Curriculum and evaluation standards for school mathematics.* Reston, VA: Author.

National Council of Teachers of Mathematics. (1991). *Professional standards for teaching mathematics.* Reston, VA: Author.

National Research Council. (1996). *National science education standards.* Washington, DC: National Academy Press.

Nelson, B. S., & Hammerman, J. K. (1996). Reconceptualizing teaching: Moving toward the creation of intellectual communities for students, teachers and teacher educators. In M. W. McLaughlin & I. Oberman (Eds.), *Teacher learning: New policies, new practices* (pp. 3–21). New York: Teachers College Press.

Nolan, J., & Francis, P. (1992). Changing perspectives in curriculum and instruction. In *Supervision in transition, The 1992 ASCD Yearbook* (pp. 44–60). Alexandria, VA: Association for Supervision and Curriculum Development.

Population Reference Bureau. (1989). *America in the 21st century: A demographic overview.* Washington, DC: Author.

Porter, A. C. (1989). A curriculum out of balance: The case of elementary school mathematics. *Educational Researcher, 18*(5), 9–15.

Resnick, L. B. (1987). *Education and learning to think.* Washington, DC: National Academy Press.

Richards, J. (1991). Mathematical discussions. In E. von Glasersfeld (Ed.), *Radical constructivism in mathematics education* (pp. 13–51). Norwell, MA: Kluwer Academic Publishers.

Richardson, V., Anders, P., Tidwell, D., & Lloyd, C. (1991). The relationship between teachers' beliefs and practices in reading comprehension instruction. *American Educational Research Journal, 28*(3), 559–586.

Russell, S. J., Schifter, D., Bastable, V., Yaffee, L., Lester, J. B., & Cohen, S. (1995). Learning mathematics while teaching. In B. S. Nelson (Ed.), *Inquiry and the development of teaching: Issues in the transformation of mathematics teaching.* Newton, MA: Center for the Development of Teaching, Education Development Center.

Schifter, D. (1993, September). Mathematics process as mathematics content: A course for teachers. *Journal of Mathematical Behavior, 12*(3), 271–283.

Schifter, D. (Ed.). (1996a). *What's happening in math class: Envisioning new practices through teacher narratives* (Vol. 1). New York: Teachers College Press.

Schifter, D. (Ed.). (1996b). *What's happening in math class: Reconstructing professional identities* (Vol. 2). New York: Teachers College Press.

Schifter, D., & Fosnot, C. T. (1993). *Reinventing mathematics education: Stories of teachers meeting the challenge of reform.* New York: Teachers College Press.

Schifter, D., & Simon, M. A. (1992). Assessing teachers' development of a constructivist view of mathematics learning. *Teaching and Teacher Education, 8*(2), 187–197.

Shulman, L. S. (1986). Paradigms and research programs in the study of teaching: A contemporary perspective. In M. C. Whittrock (Ed.), *Handbook of research on teaching* (pp. 3–36). New York: Macmillan.

Shulman, L. S. (1992). Toward a pedagogy of cases. In J. H. Shulman (Ed.), *Case methods in teacher education* (pp. 1–30). New York: Teachers College Press.

Simon, M. A. (1997). Developing new models of mathematics teaching: An imperative for research on mathematics teacher development. In E. Fennema & B. S. Nelson (Eds.), *Mathematics teachers in transition.* Mahwah, NJ: Erlbaum.

Stodolsky, S. (1988). *The subject matters: Classroom activity in mathematics and social studies.* Chicago: University of Chicago Press.

Thompson, A. G. (1991, November). *The development of teachers' conceptions of mathematics teaching.* Paper presented at the annual meeting of the International Group for the Psychology of Mathematics Education, Blacksburg, VA.

Thompson, A. G. (1992). Teachers' beliefs and conceptions: A synthesis of the research. In D. A. Grouws (Ed.), *Handbook of research on mathematics learning and teaching.* New York: Macmillan.

Wasley, P. (1990). Stirring the chalkdust: Changing practices in essential schools. *Teachers College Record, 93,* 28–58.

Wiske, M. S., & Houde, R. (1988). *From recitation to construction: Teachers change with new technologies* [Technical Report]. Cambridge, MA: Educational Technology Center.

Wood, T., Cobb, P., & Yackel, E. (1991). Change in teaching mathematics: A case study. *American Education Research Journal, 28*(3), 587–616.

Zimpher, N. L., & Howey, K. R. (1990). Scholarly inquiry into teacher education in the United States. In R. P. Tisher & M. F. Wideen (Eds.), *Research in teacher education: International perspectives.* New York: Falmer Press.

CHAPTER 2

Teaching to the Big Ideas

Deborah Schifter, Susan Jo Russell, and Virginia Bastable

Ever since Jill Lester transformed her mathematics instruction to engage her second graders in meaningful mathematical explorations, she finds certain themes emerging year after year. One of these involves the inverse relationship of addition and subtraction. The issue first arose the year she gave her class the following problem: *I have 24 pencils. I give 1 to each of the 18 children in the class. How many am I left with?* Although all her students came up with the answer, half arrived at it by taking away 18 from 24, while the other half added 6 onto 18 to get 24. But what struck Lester was the children's conviction that those who had "done it the other way" had solved the problem incorrectly. It seemed that because they understood the two operations as distinct and contrary actions, they were unable to concede that this problem could be solved using either one.

When the issue again arose the following year, her new crop of second-graders already had experience with problems that could be solved in different ways. Still, they were intrigued that the same problem might be solved by either adding or subtracting. Taking advantage of their curiosity, Lester assigned the children to work in pairs—one partner having solved the problem by addition, the other by subtraction—making up and then testing similar problems with missing addends. After 1 week most children were satisfied that if adding on worked, so would taking away, and vice versa. (See Lester, 1996, for her account of yet a third group of children exploring the relationship between addition and subtraction.)

THE NEW MATHEMATICS PEDAGOGY

Because a near-universal consensus has lately developed that mathematics education in the United States is seriously inadequate to contemporary needs, an alternative pedagogy has begun to find the support necessary to contest the one in place. Recent reports and documents (California State

Department of Education, 1985; Mathematical Association of America, 1991; National Council of Teachers of Mathematics, 1989, 1991; National Research Council, 1989, 1990) have charted a course for reform that brings mathematicians and mathematics educators together in an effort to make school mathematics reflect more accurately the nature of mathematical inquiry and the modes of generating knowledge that are characteristic of the discipline. They call for a redefinition of the content of school mathematics, of how it is learned, and of what it means to be successful in mathematics.

Among the forces that have shaped the vision of the current mathematics education reform movement is constructivism. According to this perspective, learning is primarily a process of concept construction rather than a matter of absorbing and accumulating received items of information—the usually unstated assumption underlying most traditional mathematics instruction. The construction and subsequent elaboration of new understandings is stimulated when a person's established structures of interpretation do not allow for satisfactory negotiation of an encountered situation. The disequilibrium attendant upon failure to understand or to anticipate leads to mental activity and the modification of previously held ideas to account for the new experience (Kamii, 1985; Labinowicz, 1980; Piaget, 1972, 1977; Simon & Schifter, 1991; von Glasersfeld, 1983, 1990).

Simultaneously, an alternative view of the nature of "doing mathematics"—one that differs from that associated with reigning instructional practice—has contributed to the new vision of mathematics instruction. In contrast to the static conception of the discipline—"all the math there is, is already out there"—conveyed by the math-fact, drill-and-practice approach, this view recognizes the reality that mathematics is a human pursuit—as much invention as discovery—with a long history: Schools of thought compete, fashions change, and some questions may never be settled. Thus doing mathematics is not simply a matter of applying rules for arriving at answers to particular problem types. Rather, it involves describing and predicting mathematical patterns, conjecturing, testing, and revising hypotheses (P. J. Davis & Hersh, 1980; Ernest, 1991; Lakatos, 1976; Lampert, 1988; Tymoczko, 1986).

A constructivist understanding of the learning process and a different conception of the nature of school mathematics converge to form a drastically revised picture of what should be taking place in the classroom. If the creation of the "conceptual networks" that constitute each individual's map of reality—including that individual's mathematical understanding—is the product of constructive and interpretive activity, then it follows that no matter how lucidly and patiently teachers explain *to* their students, they cannot understand *for* their students. The mathematics classroom becomes a problem-solving environment in which developing an approach to thinking about mathematical issues is valued more highly than memorizing algorithms and using them to get the right answers. And it is in this spirit that the new pedagogy aspires to convey at all levels of instruction an experience of mathematics approaching that of the mathematician's. Posing questions, making and proving conjectures, exploring puzzles, solving problems, debating ideas, describing and predicting patterns—these constitute the mathematics of the classroom. As students learn what it means to establish mathematical validity, they are doing so in the context of explorations of number, operations, data, and space. In the process, they are building a rich network of connections among mathematical objects, various representations, intuitive notions, and conventional notation (Ball, 1993a, 1993b; Cobb, 1988; R. B. Davis, Maher, & Noddings, 1990; Schifter & Fosnot, 1993).

Thus Jill Lester introduces her mathematics lesson each day by posing a single problem to which the entire period will be devoted. Work begins with whole-group discussion of the feasibility of possible solutions before students break into pairs to explore the problem using manipulatives. Toward the end of the period, the class comes together again to discuss their findings and questions. Lester's approach to instruction, which is based on the thoughts and questions students raise as they work on the mathematics, allows them to engage with the big ideas inherent in the second-grade curriculum.

By "big ideas" we, the authors of this chapter, mean central organizing principles of mathematics with which students must wrestle as they confront the limitations of their existing conceptions. Through our work as mathematics teachers and teacher educators, we have found that there are particular themes—themes that embody critical mathematical concepts—that arise time after time with different groups of learners. We hypothesize that the big ideas that underlie these themes are tied to developmental issues inherent in the process of learning mathematics.

For example, when children are introduced to addition and subtraction, they construct the operations as distinct and unrelated actions. Thus, like Lester's students, they are surprised or intrigued to discover that some problems can be solved either way. As they work through the big idea—that addition and subtraction are systematically related—they come to see these operations in a new light. *Any* problem context that can be solved using subtraction can also be solved by finding a missing addend, and vice versa. At this point, the operations become objects of study in themselves, separate from any *particular* problem context. They have begun to work with whole numbers and their operations *as a system.*

Big ideas are never fully and finally comprehended. Rather their construction is always provisional—they will be successively reorganized, acquiring additional content, as new areas of mathematics are explored. The same principle that Lester's second-graders are working on arises in the analogous relationship of multiplication and division, and understanding it is an important prerequisite for dealing with equivalent equations.

For example, Joanne Moynahan (1996) has asked her sixth-grade class to solve a set of problems like the following: *There are 15 people at a picnic and $\frac{1}{3}$ of them are Davises. How many are Davises?* After working in pairs, the class comes together and discusses their strategies and solutions. Then, pointing to the board that summarizes their results—for example, "$\frac{1}{3}$ of 15 = 5" —Moynahan challenges her students to identify which operation could replace the word "of." They have solved the picnic problem by dividing 15 into groups of 3, but they see that "$\frac{1}{3} \div 15$" does not describe the problem. They also find that, although $\frac{1}{3}$ added to itself 15 times leads to the answer, 5, it isn't clear why repeatedly adding $\frac{1}{3}$ to itself is an appropriate way to solve the problem. After two days of discussion, one student makes a connection with the relationship between multiplication and division: "$12 \times 2 = 24$ and $24 \div 2 = 12$," she points out to the class. She also discovers that she can make sense of the equation "$5 \div 15 = \frac{1}{3}$" in terms of the problem situation. Therefore, she convinces the class, "$\frac{1}{3} \times 15 = 5$" must be the number sentence for their problem. (They have yet to reconsider the very meaning of multiplication—which they understand as repeated addition—to account for the picnic problem.)

In another sixth-grade class, the addition–subtraction relationship arises among Geri Smith's students, who are writing equations with variables (Smith, 1993). Students who understand the operations as inversely related can readily see that the two equations, $A + 2 = S$ and $S - 2 = A$, are equivalent. Both describe the situation: "Ms. Smith's scale shows everything 2 pounds heavier than its actual weight." However, those students who have never thought through the issues that Lester's second-graders explore are unable to follow their classmates' reasoning. They believe that if "$A + 2 = S$" is correct, then "$S - 2 = A$" must be wrong.

From the standpoint of mathematics considered as a body of formal results, the inverse relationship of addition and subtraction is a fact. However, reflection by a mature mathematician cannot, in itself, reveal the particular significance of its recognition by primary-aged children. Identifying big ideas and gaining insight into how and why they play the role they do in the development of mathematical thinking can only come from listening to students, recognizing common areas of confusion, and analyzing the issues that underlie that confusion.

For example, one frequently hears questions and comments like the following among students engaged in mathematical explorations: "Is ¼ the smallest number after 0?" "We're multiplying, but the answers come out smaller. That doesn't make any sense!" "How can that piece of cake be ½ and ¼ at the same time?"

When statements such as these are repeatedly heard, indicating persistent difficulties and confusions, points at which students need to step back and take time to ponder, they likely flag crucial conceptual-developmental issues. The big ideas that may be implicated in the quandaries of these students involve the fact that much of what they learned about numbers in the context of whole numbers must be reconsidered for the domain of fractions. For example, children originally encounter numbers through counting, learning the sequence of number names—What comes next? However, the density of fractions implies that there is no "next" number or point. If they first learned multiplication as repeated addition, they must extend their understanding of the meaning of the operation to account for multiplication of numbers between 0 and 1. And in the realm of fractions, the role of unit takes on greater complexity: The same quantity can be represented by different fractions, depending on their reference to the whole.

Misconceptions commonly found among large numbers of students do not necessarily flag big ideas. For example, those derived by generalizing from symbol patterns (the sum of two fractions is found by adding the numerators and adding the denominators; ½ = 1.2) might not directly relate to central, organizing principles of mathematics.

In general, students do not attain an understanding of the big ideas by listening to teachers explaining what they are or by being shown how to solve sets of problems. Rather, they must have opportunities to confront the limitations of their extant conceptions; they must be given time to work through their confusion in order to construct new, more inclusive conceptions that take account of initially unassimilable information. Teachers with an understanding of the big ideas embedded in the topics of their grade-level curriculum can look for opportunities to present situations that will allow students to confront them. In fact, we would argue that teaching for mathematical understanding is teaching for the construction of the big ideas.

In this chapter, we describe the structure of a project designed to help teachers transform their practice to one organized around teaching to the big ideas.[1] Specifically, we (1) lay out the principles we believe underlie successful efforts to support teachers' changing practice, (2) identify research questions that will move our own practices forward and will contribute to the larger mathematics education community, and (3) describe project activities that we believe will support both professional development and national research efforts.

Staff from SummerMath for Teachers at Mount Holyoke College, Talking Mathematics and *Investigations in Number, Data, and Space* at TERC, and the Center for the Development of Teaching at Education Development Center (EDC) have drawn upon their collective experiences and resources to design and run a mathematics project for practicing teachers of grades K–6.

Readers are invited to consider which aspects of the project apply to their particular circumstances, including professional development in other subject areas and for different grade levels.

PRINCIPLES OF PROFESSIONAL DEVELOPMENT

Since 1983, the SummerMath for Teachers Program at Mount Holyoke College has worked to introduce teachers of grades K–12 to a constructivist view of mathematics learning and to help them enact a classroom practice based on that view (Schifter, 1993; Schifter & Fosnot, 1993; Simon & Schifter, 1991, 1993). Since 1990, the Talking Mathematics Project at TERC has worked with a small group of K–6 master teachers to explore techniques, principles, and models of mathematical talk in the elementary grades (Russell & Corwin, 1993). Staff at TERC have also worked with teachers who piloted either of two curriculum projects: *Used Numbers: Real Data in the Classroom* (Russell, Corwin, Friel, Mokros, & Stone, 1990) and *Investigations in Number, Data, and Space* (TERC, 1994). Through our experiences working intensively with 200 teachers (and less intensively with several hundred more), we have come to identify five principles crucial to the process of transforming mathematics pedagogy.

1. *Just as mathematics instruction must be organized to facilitate construction of mathematical concepts, so should in-service instruction facilitate construction of a new pedagogical theory and practice.* Thus in-service programs must provide participants with experiences that challenge dominant instructional paradigms, inviting them to confront and work through such experiences if they wish to develop a more coherent and personally compelling practice for themselves. For example, based on their own pre-service instruction as well as assumptions generally held in our society, many teachers tend both to under- and overestimate children's mathematical understanding. On the one hand, they do not believe that their students can figure something out on their own, can know something before it is "covered" in class. On the other, they often do not recognize that severe misunderstandings can lie behind correct answers. Observing videotapes of children working on mathematics problems—analyzing their solution processes, assessing the extent of their understanding, and exploring the significance of the gaps that are exposed—can cause teachers to rethink their estimates of their students' capabilities as well as their assumptions about what "understanding mathematics" really means.

In-service activities should be designed to facilitate teachers' constructions of a practice based on their evolving understandings of mathematics and the learning process. Once an activity is set in motion, generally the role of the staff developer is to listen to teachers as they articulate their beliefs and understandings and to pose questions to promote further reflection.

Teachers' responses to the contrast between their developing understandings and well-established, often unarticulated, assumptions about classroom process might lead to confusion, frustration, anger, and self-doubt as often as to excitement and enthusiasm. In-service programs must offer opportunities to work through such emotions with the support of staff developers. For example, on the third day of an intensive introductory institute, SummerMath for Teachers schedules an activity explicitly designed to address affective response. This provides participants an occasion to discuss their feelings with one another and with project staff. In addition, reading articles that tell individual teachers' stories of change can help place participants' own immediate experience in the context of a long-term process. (See, e.g., chapter 6 in Schifter & Fosnot, 1993; Schweitzer, 1996; Yaffee, 1996.)

2. *Teachers' mathematical understanding is central.* To achieve a successful practice grounded in constructivist principles, teachers require a qualitatively different and significantly richer understanding of mathematics than most now possess. After all, most teachers were themselves students in traditionally taught mathematics classes. They must now be given opportunities to learn a new version of mathematics if they are to be expected to teach it. This does not simply mean that they work through activities they might later use with their own students, but that they engage in mathematics lessons designed for adults. When challenged at their own levels of mathematics competence and confronted with mathematical concepts and problems they have not encountered before, they both increase their mathematical knowledge and experience a depth of learning that is for many of them unprecedented. Such activities allow teachers, often for the first time, to encounter mathematics as an activity of construction rather than as a finished body of results to be accepted, accumulated, and reproduced.

For example, we have posed the following problem to elementary teachers: Given a set of base-5 blocks, devise a number system using the symbols "0," "A," "B," "C," and "D," in which you can add, subtract, multiply, and divide. Most teachers begin by developing idiosyncratic systems or systems that resemble those of ancient Greece or Rome (such as those shown in the middle three columns of Figure 2.1), but eventually they come to base-5 place value (as shown in the last column of Figure 2.1). This activity offers teachers the opportunity to endow the symbols and procedures of our number system with meaning. Since the activity involves base 5, they cannot rely on remembered procedures that may have no conceptual depth for them. However, once the logic of that system has been explored, many teachers can translate their insights back into the system they teach. (For a more detailed description of this activity, see chapter 3 of Schifter & Fosnot, 1993.)

Figure 2.1.

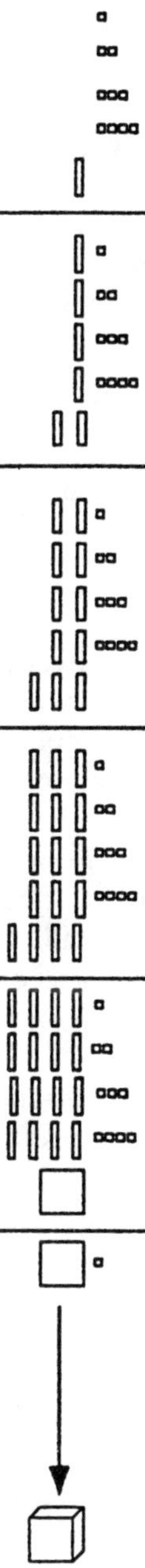

A	A	Aa	A
AA	B	Ab	B
AAA	C	Ac	C
AAAA	D	Ad	D
B	| (stick)	Ba0	A0
BA	| A	BaAa	AA
BAA	| B	BaAb	AB
BAAA	| C	BaAc	AC
BAAAA	| D	BaAd	AD
BB	||	Bb0	B0
BBA	|| A	BbAa	BA
BBAA	|| B	BbAb	BB
BBAAA	|| C	BbAc	BC
BBAAAA	|| D	BbAd	BD
BBB	|||	Bc0	C0
BBBA	||| A	BcAa	CA
BBBAA	||| B	BcAb	CB
BBBAAA	||| C	BcAc	CC
BBBAAAA	||| D	BcAd	CD
BBBB	||||	Bd0	D0
BBBBA	|||| A	BdAa	DA
BBBBAA	|||| B	BdAb	DB
BBBBAAA	|||| C	BdAc	DC
BBBBAAAA	|||| D	BdAd	DD
C	[d] (doozie)	Ca00	A00
CA	[d] A	Ca0Aa	A0A
↓	↓	↓	↓
D	[db] (doozie box)	Da000	A000

While a series of lessons in a summer institute can provide a starting point—an opportunity for teachers to begin to think about mathematics in a new way—the new mathematics pedagogy calls for a much deeper and broader understanding of mathematics content. It must be recognized that such understanding, which develops over years rather than weeks or even months, involves connections among mathematical concepts, various representations, and real-world contexts; knowledge of how mathematical truth is pursued and how validity is established; and construction of an integrated picture of the mathematics curriculum. Furthermore, the notion that mathematics is about ideas is a novel one for many teachers, and we have found that most are prepared to seriously consider the big ideas of the mathematics curriculum only after at least a full year's participation in a teacher development program that focuses on such issues.

3. *Regular school-year follow-up support is an indispensable catalyst of the change process.* Translating the insights grasped in an in-service course into new classroom methods is always a difficult, and often a frustrating, process. Pressure from administrators and parents to cover traditional curriculum, lack of institutional support, resistance from students, and competing demands on teachers' time—all may reduce the actual effect that in-service programs have on instruction. A more profound and longer-lasting impact can usually only be realized when programs provide regular activities during the school year that allow teachers to find ways to overcome these daily obstacles.

Furthermore, the classroom is an incomparably rich environment for continued learning about learning. Each day, students' thoughts, questions, and behaviors offer new information to be incorporated into an evolving instructional practice. Teachers must be given opportunities to reflect on classroom events in the light of their new conceptions of the nature of mathematics and how it is learned.

One possible strategy for providing this kind of support is to integrate clinical supervision of classroom practice with courses and institutes (Joyce & Showers, 1988; Simon, 1989). A classroom consultant can provide support and perspective to teachers who are struggling to implement new classroom goals. An outside observer can also alert teachers to particular events and behaviors whose significance they might not appreciate and to stimulate reflection on these. In this way, teachers can become more self-conscious about their own decision-making processes. Once teachers learn how to learn from their own classroom experiences, they can continue their own development beyond the follow-up period.

4. *Teacher development and curriculum reform must support one another.* A fifth-grade teacher who was piloting units written by curriculum developers at TERC confided, "I really got fired up about using pattern blocks to teach

fractions, and we worked on this for several weeks, but then I didn't know where to go. So I went back to the textbook." Another teacher, who was involved in Talking Mathematics, described how she had come up with individual mathematical investigations that she knew provided opportunities for genuine mathematical thinking among her students, but she felt that her year as a whole was fragmented and incoherent. These are two examples of a dilemma commonly voiced: While teacher-enhancement experiences leave participants convinced that they must bring about change in their practice and new curricular materials provide a taste of what better mathematics teaching and learning might be, most teachers have neither the time nor expertise to create a whole new curriculum.

In the past, curriculum has been primarily a set of activities for students. TERC's experience with the *Used Numbers* and *Investigations in Number, Data, and Space* curriculum development projects has shown that innovative materials can aid teachers in rethinking their mathematics programs; indeed, we are convinced that curriculum must be thought of as a vehicle supporting ongoing teacher development, especially with regard to teachers' mathematical understanding. A curriculum traditionally includes a sequence of activities, examples for the teacher to present to students, and lots and lots of problems to provide practice on each topic. At one extreme, directions for the teacher may approach a script, but even in less extreme cases they are largely prescriptive. Much of the information for the teacher focuses on what to do next, even if the curriculum incorporates hands-on activities and manipulative materials.

As teachers focus their teaching on students' mathematical thinking, they develop needs that traditional curriculum materials do not address. Promoting mathematical reasoning requires that teachers listen hard and observe carefully, try to make sense of their students' mathematical thinking, consider how students' understandings relate to central mathematical ideas, and carefully choose new questions and problems for their students. In order to do this complex task, teachers must continually learn more about children's mathematical thinking and about the mathematics content they are teaching.

In making available experience drawn from a wide range of classrooms, curricula developed through classroom-based research can help illuminate student understanding. As curriculum developers carefully document the work of students and teachers who are testing their materials, they gather information about issues that may be critical for teachers who use the materials in the future. In particular, accounts of what mathematical issues arise as students of a certain age span grapple with a significant mathematical problem emerge from testing in the field. These accounts can be included in a variety of ways in curriculum materials to support teachers as they try to figure out how to encourage their own students' learning. For example, the TERC curriculum units include "Dialogue Boxes" (see Figure 2.2), discussions based on class-

Figure 2.2.

DIALOGUE BOX

What Does It Mean to Be Finished?

In this classroom, the teacher is trying to help students understand what it means to record their strategies so that someone else can understand clearly how they approached the problem. This is very difficult for many students. Because their method seems so clear to them, they think that what they wrote or drew explains their thinking even when there are gaps in their recordings. Taking the point of view of a reader of their work is a new skill for students at this age and one that they will need to work on.

In this dialogue that takes place during the activity on p. 96, the teacher is giving students feedback on the following problem:

Luis and Kathy were collecting rocks. Luis found 16 rocks and Kathy found 24. How many rocks did the children collect? (Student Sheet 19, Problem 1.)

Carla [*reading her explanation to the teacher*]: 40 rocks. I used cubes and I counted.

OK, so that tells me how many rocks they collected and it tells me that you used cubes. How did you use the cubes to help you solve the problem?

Carla: Well, I counted out 16 and then I counted 24 more and altogether that was 40.

Do you remember how you counted the cubes to get 40?

Carla: I counted the tower of 16 from 24. Like I went 25, 26, 27, 28, and I ended up with 40.

So you counted on by 1's from 24?

Carla: Yes.

That sounds like a good strategy. See if you can go back and add those ideas to your explanation. Think about how you just explained to me what you did and write it down. Jeffrey, you're next.

Jeffrey [*reading his work*]: They have 40 rocks. I used my brain.

That's a good start, Jeffrey. Can you explain more about how you used your brain?

Jeffrey: I just thought 20 + 10 is 30 and 4 + 6 is 10. So 30 and 10 is 40.

I've heard you use that strategy before. Remember when we were working on a similar problem yesterday, we wrote down lots of people's strategies. Sometimes I used words or numbers to explain what people did. And sometimes I used both. How could your record your thinking so someone reading your paper would know just what you did?

Jeffrey: I'll try numbers.

Carla [*reads her revised work to the teacher*]: 40 rocks. I used cubes and I counted. I made a tower of 16 cubes and a tower of 24 cubes. Then I counted from 24. 25, 26, 27, 28, 29, 30, 31, 32, 33, 34, 35, 36, 37, 38, 39, 40. [*Carla has also added a picture of two towers, one with 16 cubes and one with 24.*]

That tells me much more information about what you did. I can understand how you solved the problem from this information. Before you write about the next problem, think about what you did. You can even explain it to a friend or to yourself to help you start writing.

When the teacher checks in with Jeffrey he has added the following to his recording:

> 24+16=40
>
> 20+10=30 4+6=10 30+10=40
>
> i used my brane

Only by continuing to insist that students record their work fully can the teacher eventually help students imagine their audience.

Source: The *Investigations* unit, Coins, Coupons, and Combinations, by Karen Economopoulos and Susan Jo Russell.

room episodes that provide examples of how students express their mathematical ideas, what issues and confusions arise in their thinking, and how some teachers have guided these discussions. At the same time, frequent "Teacher Notes" (see Figure 2.3) provide reference material for the teacher about the mathematics they are teaching. These notes and dialogues together provide a sort of ongoing minicourse for teachers about the mathematical content and the ways in which students interact with that content. By offering significant background for teachers to use in their own reflections or in discussions with colleagues, curriculum materials can provide ways for teachers to continue to deepen their knowledge of mathematics content, of children's mathematical thinking, and of pedagogical approaches.

5. *Schoolwide collaboration is essential to the process of reform.* The workaday experience of most teachers is one of isolation: classroom doors are closed. While the few moments of daily collegial interaction allow for venting frustration over a particular problem student or a new piece of administrative folly, they don't permit serious discussion of instructional issues. In making so little provision for teachers to reflect together on their instruction, school structures support a culture of isolation consistent with traditional practice. For when instructional initiative is wired into districtwide curricular guidelines and text and workbooks, the important decisions are largely out of teachers' hands and so they don't need to trade ideas on either teaching or mathematics. But the kind of teaching now proposed—investing greater instructional responsibility in the teacher—concomitantly entails greater need for collegial cooperation. In the long run, only teachers taking similar risks and experimenting with similar approaches are in a position to support one another. They can, and must, share their reflection on classroom process (including both "successes" and "failures"), help one another plan appropriate next steps, and explore together the mathematics they teach.

No less important than these instructional issues are the institutional realities that must be brought into line with the new mathematics pedagogy—for example, the selection of texts and other teaching materials, standardized testing, parent and community outreach, and new measures of teacher effectiveness.

RESEARCH QUESTIONS

While our experience in professional development has led us to the principles stated above, it has also raised new questions for us. Our most immediate questions have brought us to design a teacher-enhancement project that would provide the context for a research program. Our questions are organized around three major concerns: (1) teachers' developing mathematical

Figure 2.3.

Teacher Note **What Should We Do with the Extras?**

Different division situations call for handling remainders in different ways. In some problems, the answer is "rounded down" and the remainder is ignored.

> There are 94 pencils and 4 students. The teacher wants to give the same number to each student. How many does each student get?

If 4 people share 94 pencils equally, each person gets 23 pencils. The remaining 2 pencils cannot be distributed evenly among the 4 people.

In other problems, the answer must be "rounded up":

> I need to put 94 pencils in boxes. I can fit 4 pencils in a box. How many boxes do I need?

If 94 pencils are to be put in boxes that hold 4, you would need 24 boxes; 23 of the boxes would be full, and the other box would hold just 2 pencils.

In still other problems, remainders are an important part of the answer:

> I won 94 dollars in a raffle and decided to share it with my family. There are 4 of us. How much do we each get?

When 4 people are sharing 94 dollars instead of 94 pencils, the remaining 2 dollars can be further divided so that each person gets 23 dollars and 50 cents.

Students may come up with still other ways of handling remainders that do not necessarily involve dividing into equal-size groups, but that make sense given the problem context.

> There were 94 students in the fifth grade and we wanted to put them in teams of 4 for the field day. How many teams were there?

The student who created this problem explained his thinking about the remainders:

> We could have done 23 teams of 4 and a team of 2, but they wouldn't win anything. We thought about having floaters who would fill in for kids absent that day, but we decide to have 22 teams of 4 and a team of 6. That team is for kids who don't want to do every event. Some people can sit out while the other people in their team take their turns. If it's money, you can split up the extra money. You can't split the kids or send them home. You have to do something with them.

As students in your class share their division situations, ask them to explain how they would handle the leftovers. By describing the remainder in the context of the problem and not just writing R 2, they are solving the problem more completely and in a way that they can follow and make sense of. They are also deepening their understanding of what it means to divide.

Source: The *Investigations* unit, Building on Numbers You Know, by Marlene Kliman, Susan Jo Russell, Cornelia Tierney, and Megan Murray.

understandings and their effect on instruction, (2) the interaction of teacher development and curriculum reform, and (3) the big ideas of the elementary curriculum.

- *Teachers' developing mathematical understandings and their effect on instruction.* How do we characterize and assess the process by which teachers develop a level of mathematical understanding adequate for facilitating students' construction of significant mathematics? How can we help teachers learn to think about mathematics in terms of big ideas? How do developing mathematical understandings impact instructional practice and goals? Research staff attempt to identify paths teachers take as they develop a practice based on a changing understanding of mathematics and consider how these changes in practice relate to changing epistemological perspectives.
- *The interaction of teacher development and curriculum reform.* What do teachers need to know and/or believe about mathematics in order to make productive use of curriculum materials for their students and for their own continuing mathematics education? In what ways can curriculum materials extend and deepen teachers' understanding of the big ideas?
- *The big ideas of the elementary mathematics curriculum.* What are the big ideas of mathematics that emerge as elementary teachers transform their instruction? Upon which of these ideas should new curriculum materials be developed? While we certainly have some notions about these issues, we expect to ground our preliminary ideas and expand and clarify them through our work with project participants and their students. The big ideas become apparent as teachers listen to students, spotting common areas of confusion, analyzing the issues that underlie that confusion, and determining which of these perplexities suggest the need for conceptual reorganization. In this process, teachers and staff developers, both collaboratively and separately, can identify big ideas as they arise in the classroom, examining these ideas as they are clarified, modified, and expanded over time.

PROJECT ACTIVITIES

The "Teaching to the Big Ideas" project is guided by principles of professional development derived from previous work and structured to address the research questions stated above. It is intended to help teachers create a classroom culture that allows big ideas to emerge and to become central themes of their instruction. Together, teachers and staff closely monitor student discussion, recording dialogue in order to identify big ideas as they arise naturally in classroom contexts. Those ideas are then analyzed to see how they shift, change, and grow as they are embedded in various mathematics topics at different grade levels. As teachers develop expertise, they become research collaborators with staff. In the last year of the project, teachers take on leadership roles to introduce these notions to colleagues in their own school systems.

The teachers who enter the project are quite heterogeneous in terms of their familiarity with the basic principles that guide its work. Many are initially unable to make sense of the notion of big ideas, for their experience in traditional instruction has not even hinted at the fact that mathematics is about ideas rather than computation. During the first year, then, these participants develop new conceptions of the nature of mathematics and begin to see the discipline as involving ideas that are formed, challenged, refined, and extended. Others may not undergo such a paradigmatic shift but do reflect deeply on mathematical ideas and student learning. This process continues in the second year as the group begins to investigate the mathematical ideas that underlie students' curiosity, interest, and/or confusion.

Years 1 and 2: Constructing a New Practice, Exploring Big Ideas

The project is structured around four annual 2-week residential summer institutes and seminars that meet approximately once every 2 weeks during the 3 intervening school years. Course activities for the institutes and seminars comprise three major strands: participants engage in mathematics lessons, analyze students' mathematical thinking, and consider issues of curriculum. Although these strands continue into years 3 and 4, they comprise the central focus of the work of the first 2 years when teachers construct a new mathematics teaching practice and begin to explore the big ideas of the elementary curriculum.

The mathematics lessons for teachers embody the principles of the new mathematics pedagogy and are directed toward mathematical issues that challenge adult learners. Two to ten 3-hour sessions are committed to explorations in each of the following areas: number systems and whole-number operations, data analysis, geometry, rational numbers, ratios, combinatorics, probability, variables, and functions. As teachers work in groups on problems, they identify their past understandings and confusions, pose further questions for themselves and their colleagues, and reach for a new level of understanding through discussions and individual work. Once an area is introduced, it is never left behind, but rather arises again and again in other contexts.

As participants explore mathematics content, the mathematics lessons provide grist for reflection: What is the nature of the mathematics you are learning? How is mathematical validity assessed? What does it mean to "think mathematically"? What is your own process of learning? What aspects of the classroom environment promoted or inhibited your learning? Following—or at times in the midst of—a mathematics lesson, the group takes time to discuss these issues. Reflection continues in the form of journal writing (which is periodically read and responded to by a member of the staff) or assigned papers. (For detailed descriptions of teachers engaged as mathematics learners, see Schifter, 1993; Schifter & Bastable, 1995; Schifter & Fosnot, 1993.)

Teachers' own mathematical explorations help them to identify big ideas. For example, many teachers who, at the beginning of a unit on fractions, are asked to draw area models to compare, say, $3/5$ and $3/8$ come up with a representation (see Figure 2.4) that appears to illustrate that $3/5 = 3/8$. They are given the opportunity to explore at length the implications of such a result in order to fully grasp why comparison of fractions presupposes that they have the same reference whole. Later on, teachers are asked to consider why the following problem is not an addition problem: *In Janice's class, $1/5$ of the boys are absent and $2/5$ of the girls are absent. What fraction of the class is absent?* After all, the analogous problem—*Find the number of absent children in the class if 1 boy and 2 girls are absent*—is solved by addition. Teachers confronted with these questions need to think through why, when adding or subtracting fractions, the reference whole must stay constant. Still later they are asked to solve a problem like the following: *Rachel has 4 (pretty small) sheet cakes, which she intends to serve to her guests at $3/5$ cake per portion. How many portions does she have?* When they first solve the problem using a diagram (Figure 2.5), many teachers believe that the answer is $6\ 2/5$. However, when they use the conventional algorithm to solve $4 \div 3/5$ they get $6\ 2/3$. Now teachers must consider the different units used for the dividend, the divisor, and the quotient.

As teachers work through these problems, they learn that a great deal of confusion can be resolved by asking the question: What is the whole to which this fraction refers? And those who understand this idea will be able to organize their instruction so that students can be repeatedly brought to confront and work it through, not only in their study of fractions but also in their work on decimals and percents, and even in algebra.

Figure 2.4. Which is greater, $3/5$ or $3/8$?

Figure 2.5. Four cakes divided into portions of $^3/_5$

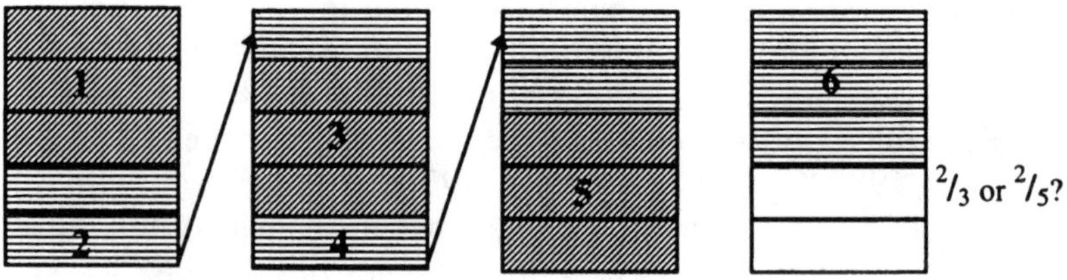

Inquiry into students' mathematical thinking begins through viewing videotapes of clinical interviews and classroom discourse and studying written materials that illustrate student work; teachers identify what the students understood and where their confusions lay. For example, one video depicts a third-grade class discussing which is larger, $^4/_4$ or $^4/_8$, and accompanying documentation includes students' notebooks in which they reflect on their classmates' conjectures and arguments, as well as the teacher's journal (Ball, 1990). With this rich set of materials, teachers analyze how these 8- and 9-year-olds confront the issue of a fraction's reference whole.

In addition to using material from outside sources, teachers write scenarios from their own teaching, including transcriptions of classroom dialogue. Our experience in previous projects has shown that the exercise of transcribing student dialogue in itself facilitates change in practice (Schifter, 1994, 1996a, 1996b). For example, one teacher reported, "When I knew I needed to write down what the children were saying, I started to pay attention in a different way. And without changing anything else, the children picked up on the fact that I was listening harder, and they started saying different things, more thoughtful things." Another teacher said, "It was only when I was writing it out in the evening that I could see what my students were really saying. They had lots of misunderstandings I just hadn't heard during class time!"

Equipped with illustrations from their own classrooms, the group comes together to look for common themes that arise in various classrooms. For example, several of the second grades have students who can add two-digit numbers like 32 + 47 but have trouble with 38 + 45. These same children, when shown, say, 53 represented with base-10 blocks as five rods and three small cubes, begin to count the tens—"10, 20, 30, 40, 50"—and, once this pattern is set in motion, continue—"60, 70, 80." As teachers consider a series of related stories, they examine the common underlying idea at issue here. That is, rather than working to help these children remember the correct procedure for regrouping for addition and the correct procedure for counting base-10 blocks—treating two separate difficulties—teachers explore whether these children recognize the relation between one group of ten and 10 ones. Do the children understand how this relationship is used in representing and calculating with two-digit numbers? By analyzing the dialogue offered by their colleagues from other grades (see, for example, the narrative included in the Conclusion to this chapter), as well as turning to published literature (e.g., Kamii, 1985; Szymaszek, 1996), the group considers what is involved in young children's construction of this big idea.

While traditional instruction promotes a view of school mathematics as whatever sequence of topics is presented in the textbook—through which one must proceed page by page—the project is designed to help teachers develop a sense of the conceptual logic of the mathematics to be taught at their grade level. Throughout the 4 years, teachers revisit the following themes: (1) the main topics to be taught in a year—which ought to receive priority? why are they important? how are different topics connected? (2) "habits of thinking" to be pursued over the year—how do children learn to think mathematically? what mathematical approaches should be emphasized? (3) the big ideas students should confront—what are the central conceptual issues that emerge as instruction focuses on student thinking? Teachers' changing notions about these questions are grounded in their own explorations of mathematics and inquiry into their students' understandings.

For the first 2 years of the project, staff visit participants' schools twice each month. The purpose of these visits is to provide support to teachers as they work to develop a classroom culture that promotes significant mathematical activity and dialogue. Each session consists of a classroom visit followed by a half-hour one-on-one discussion. At the beginning of the year, teachers choose their own goals as a starting point for changing instruction. During half-hour discussions, the staff member does not focus on classroom logistics, but rather works to pose questions that continue the process of reflection: What did you learn from this lesson? What do you want your students to learn? How will you find out what they already know? What activities will you choose and how will those activities help your students learn? How will you know what they have learned? Innovative curricular materials prepared by a team led by Susan Jo Russell (TERC, 1994) are available to project participants as another jumping off point for investigating mathematical ideas with their students.

As teachers become oriented to their new practice, the one-on-one discussions move toward close study of student thinking. In this more intimate setting, teacher and staff together analyze dialogue and written work and look for the big ideas students are confronting.

Years 3 and 4: Becoming Teacher Leaders, Documenting Big Ideas

During the first 2 years of the project, teachers construct new conceptions of pedagogical theory and practice. Many come to recognize the difference between offering their own explanations and supporting the development of their students' mathematical thinking. However, as they move into their leadership roles, translating this principle into support for their colleagues' new thinking is not automatic. Leadership teachers must begin to engage a new set of issues before they can embark on helping others transform their instruction.

In year 3, teachers address the following questions: What is it that I have learned about learning and teaching mathematics that is important for me to communicate to other teachers? How can this be communicated when they have not had the same experiences I have had? What is the process teachers go through as they work to transform their instruction and how can I support that process? They begin their study of teacher development in the summer institute by writing and analyzing their own autobiographies of change. They are then given research articles (Goldsmith & Schifter, 1993; Simon & Schifter, 1991) and papers written by other teachers (O'Reilly, 1996; Schweitzer, 1996) to discuss, first, the content of the material, and later move to a "meta" level to consider *how* the material communicates ideas, what is effective, and what is distracting or confusing.

During the academic year, participants prepare written materials designed to communicate what they have learned in the project. Papers that illustrate classroom process with specific, concrete examples—recording the dialogue of students working though mathematical issues as well as teachers' own thoughts, learnings, and decisions—provide powerful images of what is possible when students engage in significant mathematics and address dilemmas that arise as teachers work to transform their instruction. Readers are "brought into the classroom" to "see" children alive and recognizable as people and to "hear" the discussion for themselves.

Such papers can illustrate what big ideas are and how they are important to learning elementary mathematics. In year 3 of the project, teachers write narratives of classroom events to illustrate big ideas. Papers may take a number of forms. For example, a teacher might track the development of an idea among her or his students over several months. Or a group of teachers might work together to show how one idea arises in different contexts at different grades. These papers will be brought together in an anthology to be prepared for use in pre- and in-service courses.

Toward the end of year 3, participants continue with their leadership work, meeting to discuss schoolwide dissemination plans, designed collaboratively with their administrators, to be implemented the following year. While the plans necessarily vary from school to school, they each comprise at least the following features: (1) in-service sessions led by leadership teams to work on mathematics as well as pedagogical theory and practice, (2) opportunities for teachers to use and assess innovative curricular materials, (3) classroom visits by leadership teachers, (4) meetings between teachers and administrators to discuss school structures and policies, (5) parent and community outreach, and (6) an evaluation procedure.

During the fourth year, leadership teams implement dissemination plans in their schools. Each team is assigned a staff member with whom it meets once each month and who is on call to help think through any problems that arise.

CONCLUSION

The "Teaching to the Big Ideas" project outlined above has been funded by the National Science Foundation (NSF) and, at the time of writing this chapter, is in its first year of implementation. Our early thoughts about the research questions are reported in Bastable and Schifter, in press; Russell & Corwin, 1993; Russell and colleagues, 1995; Schifter (1995); Schifter & Bastable (1995).

At this stage in the project's development, all participants are examining their beliefs about the nature of mathematics and how it is learned, are thinking deeply about implications for practice, and are experimenting with new instructional goals and strategies. Some participants still find the notion of big ideas to be alien and far removed from their daily decision making; others are intrigued but confused. It is early yet. But some have already found that the notion provides a powerful construct around which to organize their mathematics programs.

For example, in a discussion with a staff member early in October, one teacher (we shall call her Emily) explained how she had been thinking about her mathematics program 1 year earlier:

> Kids are just sort of like butterflies that can land on all different kinds of ideas that are interesting and it's worth time [staying there]. And there's this . . . array of curriculum that could be anything. And the kids are growing and thinking and doing all that stuff and I'm presenting them with all kinds of different possibilities.

The image is delightful, and the approach felt appropriate to Emily during the 8-year period during which she taught kindergarten. However, it was ultimately unsatisfactory when she began to teach older students.

> When I walked into the third- and fourth-grade classroom, . . . that's . . . how I approached—on a daily basis—the learning in the classroom. And while it was interesting, and, in some chunks, very satisfying, on the whole it drove me crazy. [For these older children,] it wasn't satisfying at all.

Emily explained, "There were a lot of wonderful things to think about mathematics—[that] was more the way I looked at mathematics and my teaching of mathematics." But no idea was more wonderful, more important or central, than any other. And just as a butterfly might flit from one flower to another, so, too, might a child alight upon one idea on Tuesday and any other on Wednesday.

Now, as she has begun to work on the "Teaching to the Big Ideas" project, Emily has identified what was missing for her last year: "the depth of reaching an idea and really, really knowing what they're talking about, i.e., really, really knowing what to do with an idea or what the possibilities are." Now, as she listens to her students alight upon an idea, she looks underneath their words, trying to find what is important in what they are thinking, and then searches for a question that will push that idea further and deeper.

When asked just what it was in the project that helped her to think about her teaching differently, she said, "Conversations about those hidden . . . big ideas. The fact that . . . there are these big ideas that make a lot of difference."

For many of these teachers, the notion of big ideas is itself a big idea of teaching. They will wrestle with it, confronting the limitations of their existing conceptions, examining implications for learning and teaching. The role of project staff is to organize our instruction so that teachers can be repeatedly brought to this idea and work it through. And toward the latter part of the project, participants will share with the education community what they have learned.

ADDENDUM

This manuscript now goes to press 2 years after it was written. As we have just now completed the third year of the "Teaching to the Big Ideas" (TBI) project, teachers are preparing for the staff development programs they will be leading in their schools.

The outline of the project that is described in this chapter has been played out to powerful effect. However, one major shift that we had not initially envisioned is the nature of the materials the project is producing. As described above, the plan had been that in the third year of the project teachers would write 15- to 30-page papers about the development of mathematical ideas in their classrooms. It was intended that these papers would be used in pre- and in-service courses. Instead, the project is producing a case-based teacher development curriculum called *Developing Mathematical Ideas.*

The idea for the curriculum grew out of a discussion with our advisory board 14 months into the project. At this meeting, the advisory board challenged project staff to think in terms of helping others have the kinds of conversations we, staff and teachers, were having within the project, rather than simply presenting the results of those conversations. The challenge also involved including teacher educators and staff developers in our target audience. Furthermore, as advisers looked at the classroom scenarios we and the teachers were writing for in-project consumption, they pointed out that they could be used as the basis of case discussions in teacher education and staff development settings.

In fact, the advisory board's suggestions were so aligned with TBI objectives, intentions, and activities that, instead of pushing us into "disequilibrium," they quite dramatically brought our work into focus. We began to envision a set of modules, organized around big ideas, that would bring together the perspectives of teachers, teacher educators, and researchers. At the heart of the materials would be sets of classroom scenarios (cases) illustrating student thinking as described by their teachers. Modules would also include narratives and other support materials written by teacher educators, along with discussions of relevant research.

When TBI staff began to think about a curriculum based on teaching episodes organized around big ideas, several mathematical themes emerged; for example, developing conceptions of number as students expand the domains they work with; coordinating multiple units in the contexts of whole numbers, rational numbers, and geometry; early algebraic thinking; studying attributes and constructing arguments in geometric contexts; and analyzing data. We decided to begin by designing two modules around the themes "Building a System of Tens" and "Making Meaning for Operations." These first two modules of *Developing Mathematical Ideas* comprise a 48-hour seminar that is currently being piloted at various sites throughout the country.

The curriculum is designed to help teachers think through the major ideas of elementary school mathematics and examine how children develop those ideas. In addition to the case scenarios and discussions, the curriculum is supplemented by a variety of other activities: Teachers share and discuss samples of *their* students' work; explore mathematics in lessons led by the facilitator; plan, conduct, and analyze mathematics interviews of one of their own students; view and discuss videotapes of mathematics classrooms and mathematics interviews; write their own cases; and read an overview of related research.

The "Building a System of Tens" module begins with cases, drawn from second- and sixth-grade classrooms, that focus on the methods students develop for adding and subtracting two-digit numbers. What are the various ways children naturally tend to think about separating and combining numbers? And what is it that children must understand in order to work with numbers in these ways? These questions motivate the rest of the module. In the next three sections, the cases present children working on basic notions of the base-10 structure of number and, once some of those notions have been identified, return to consideration of addition and subtraction. How these basic notions are applied and extended to the work of the middle-grade years through multidigit multiplication and division and work with decimal fractions is the focus of the last three discussions.

The "Making Meaning for Operations" module examines the actions and situations that are modeled by the four basic operations. It begins with a view of young children's counting strategies as they work on problems that they will later solve by adding, subtracting, multiplying, or dividing. It then moves to an examination of the different types of situations that are modeled by whole-number addition/subtraction and multiplication/division. The latter part of the module revisits the operations in the context of rational numbers. What ideas, issues, and generalizations need to be refined or revised once the domain under consideration is extended to include rational numbers? For example, how does one make sense of multiplying and dividing when the numbers being operated on—fractions—already imply division?

We believe that concrete questions and classroom scenarios such as these will help to provide the scaffolding teachers need as they re-orient their teaching around big mathematical ideas.

NOTE

1. This chapter was written toward the end of the first year of the 3-year project. See the addendum at the end of the chapter for an update on the development of the project.

REFERENCES

Ball, D. L. (1990). *Mathematics and teaching through hypermedia*. East Lansing, MI: Michigan State University.

Ball, D. L. (1993a). Halves, pieces, and twoths: Constructing representational contexts in teaching fractions. In T. P. Carpenter, E. Fennema, & T. Romberg (Eds.), *Rational numbers: An integration of research* (pp. 157–196). Hillsdale, NJ: Erlbaum.

Ball, D. L. (1993b). With an eye on the mathematical horizon: Dilemmas of teaching elementary school mathematics. *Elementary School Journal, 93*(4), 373–397.

Bastable, V., & Schifter, D. (in press). Classroom stories: Examples of elementary students engaged in early algebra. In J. Kaput (Ed.), *Employing children's natural powers to build algebraic reasoning in the content of elementary mathematics.* Hillsdale, NJ: Erlbaum.

California State Department of Education. (1985). *Mathematics framework for California public schools, kindergarten through grade twelve.* Sacramento, CA: Author.

Cobb, P. (1988). The tension between theories of learning and instruction in mathematics education. *Educational Psychologist, 23*(2), 97–103.

Davis, P. J., & Hersh, R. (1980). *The mathematics experience.* Boston: Birkhauser.

Davis, R. B., Maher, C. A., & Noddings, N. (Eds.). (1990). *Constructivist views of the teaching and learning of mathematics.* Reston, VA: National Council of Teachers of Mathematics.

Ernest, P. (1991). *The philosophy of mathematics education: Studies in mathematics education.* London: Falmer.

Goldsmith, L., & Schifter, D. (1993). *Characteristics of a model for the development of mathematics teaching.* Newton, MA: Education Development Center.

Joyce, B., & Showers, B. (1988). *Student achievement through staff development.* New York: Longman.

Kamii, C. (1985). *Young children reinvent arithmetic: Implications of Piaget's theory.* New York: Teachers College Press.

Labinowicz, E. (1980). *The Piaget primer: Thinking, learning, teaching.* Menlo Park, CA: Addison-Wesley.

Lakatos, I. (1976). *Proofs and refutations.* Cambridge, UK: Cambridge University Press.

Lampert, M. (1988). The teacher's role in reinventing the meaning of mathematics knowing in the classroom. In M. J. Behr, C. B. Lacampagne, & M. M. Wheeler (Eds.), *Proceedings of the tenth annual meeting of the North American chapter of the International Group for the Psychology of Mathematics Education* (pp. 433–480). DeKalb: Northern Illinois University Press.

Lampert, M., & Ball, D. W. (1990). Using hypermedia technology to support a new pedagogy of teacher education [Issue Paper 90-5]. East Lansing, MI: National Center for Research on Teacher Education.

Lester, J. (1996). Is the algorithm all there is? In C. T. Fosnot (Ed.), *Constructivism: Foundations, perspective, and practice* (pp. 145–152). New York: Teachers College Press.

Mathematical Association of America. (1991). *A call for change: Recommendations for the mathematical preparation of teachers.* Washington, DC: Author.

Moynahan, J. (1996). "Of-ing" fractions. In D. Schifter (Ed.), *What's happening in math class? Volume 1: Envisioning new practices through teacher narratives* (pp. 24–36). New York: Teachers College Press.

National Council of Teachers of Mathematics. (1989). *Curriculum and evaluation standards for school mathematics.* Reston, VA: Author.

National Council of Teachers of Mathematics. (1991). *Professional standards for teaching mathematics.* Reston, VA: Author.

National Research Council. (1989). *Everybody counts: A report to the nation on the future of mathematics education.* Washington, DC: National Academy Press.

National Research Council. (1990). *Reshaping school mathematics: A framework for curriculum.* Washington, DC: National Academy Press.

O'Reilly, A. M. (1996). Understanding teaching/Teaching for understanding. In D. Schifter (Ed.), *What's happening in math class? Volume 2: Reconstructing professional identities* (pp. 65–73). New York: Teachers College Press.

Piaget, J. (1972). *Psychology and epistemology: Towards a theory of knowledge.* Harmondsworth: Penguin.

Piaget, J. (1977). *The principles of genetic epistemology.* London: Routledge & Kegan Paul.

Russell, S. J. (1997). The role of curriculum in teacher development. In S. Friel & G. Bright (Eds.), *Reflecting on our work: NSF teacher enhancement in mathematics K–6* (pp. 555–558). Lanham, MD: University Press of America.

Russell, S. J., & Corwin, R. B. (1993). Talking mathematics: Going slow and "letting go." *Phi Delta Kappan, 74*(7), 12.

Russell, S. J., Corwin, R. G., Friel, S., Mokros, J., & Stone, T. (1990). *Used numbers: Real data in the classroom.* Palo Alto, CA: Dale Seymour.

Russell, S. J., Schifter, D., Bastable, V., Yaffee, L., Lester, J., & Cohen, S. (1995). Learning mathematics while teaching. In B. S Nelson (Ed.), *Inquiry and the development of teaching: issues in the transformation of mathematics teaching* (pp. 9–16). Newton, MA: Center for the Development of Teaching, Education Development Center.

Russell, S. J., Tierney, C., Economopoulos, K., Mokros, J., & staff. (1995–98). *Investigations in number, data, and space.* Palo Alto, CA: Dale Seymour.

Schifter, D. (1993). Mathematics process as mathematics content: A course for teachers. *Journal of Mathematical Behavior, 12*(3), 271–283.

Schifter, D. (1994). *Voicing the new pedagogy: Teachers write about learning and teaching mathematics.* Newton, MA: Center for the Development of Teaching, Education Development Center.

Schifter, D. (1995). Teachers' changing conceptions of the nature of mathematics: Enactment in the classroom. In B. S. Nelson (Ed.), *Inquiry and the development of teaching: issues in the transformation of mathematics teaching* (pp. 17–26). Newton, MA: Center for the Development of Teaching, Education Development Center.

Schifter, D. (Ed.). (1996a). *What's happening in math class? Vol. 1: Envisioning new practices through teacher narratives.* New York: Teachers College Press.

Schifter, D. (Ed.). (1996b). *What's happening in math class? Vol. 2: Reconstructing professional identities.* New York: Teachers College Press.

Schifter, D., & Bastable, V. (1995, April). *From the teacher seminar to the classroom: The relationship between doing and teaching mathematics, an example from fractions.* Paper presented to the American Educational Research Association, San Francisco.

Schifter, D., & Fosnot, C. T. (1993). *Reconstructing mathematics education: Stories of teachers meeting the challenge of reform.* New York: Teachers College Press.

Schweitzer, K. (1996). The search for the perfect resource. In D. Schifter (Ed.), *What's happening in math class? Vol. 2: Reconstructing professional identities* (pp. 47–64). New York: Teachers College Press.

Simon, M. A. (1989, April). *The impact of intensive classroom follow-up in a constructivist mathematics teacher education program.* Paper presented at the annual meeting of the American Educational Research Association, San Francisco. (ERIC Document Reproduction Service No. ED 313 351)

Simon, M. A., & Schifter, D. E. (1991). Towards a constructivist perspective: An intervention study of mathematics teacher development. *Educational Studies in Mathematics, 22,* 309–331.

Simon, M. A., & Schifter, D. E. (1993). Toward a constructivist perspective: The impact of a mathematics teacher inservice program on students. *Educational Studies in Mathematics, 25*(4), 331–340.

Smith, G. (1993). What do I teach next? *The Constructivist: Newsletter for the Association for Constructivist Teaching, 7*(4), 1–4.

Szymaszek, J. (1996). My year of enquiry. In D. Schifter (Ed.), *What's happening in math class? Vol. 2: Reconstructing professional identities* (pp. 82–96). New York: Teachers College Press.

TERC. (1994). *Investigations in number, data, and space.* Palo Alto, CA: Dale Seymour.

Tymoczko, T. (1986). *New directions in the philosophy of mathematics.* Boston: Birkhäuser.

von Glasersfeld, E. (1983). Learning as a constructive activity. In J. C. Bergeron & N. Herscovics (Eds.), *Proceedings of the fifth annual meeting of the North American chapter of the International Group for the Psychology of Mathematics Education* (pp. 41–69). Montreal: Université de Montréal, Faculté de Science de l'Éducation.

von Glasersfeld, E. (1990). An exposition on constructivism: Why some like it radical. In R. B. Davis, C. A. Maher, & N. Noddings (Eds.), *Constructivist views on the teaching and learning of mathematics* [*Journal for Research in Mathematics Education Monograph No. 4*]. Reston, VA: National Council of Teachers of Mathematics.

Yaffee, L. (1996). Pictures at an exhibition: A mathphobic confronts fear, loathing, cosmic dread, and thirty years of math education. In D. Schifter (Ed.), *What's happening in math class?: Vol. 2. Reconstructing professional identities* (pp. 10–25). New York: Teachers College Press.

CHAPTER 3

Doing Research, Taking Action, and Changing Practice with Collaborative Support

Molly Lynn Watt and Daniel Lynn Watt

The very nature of teaching implies resolving problems, constructing theory, learning continuously in a lifelong spiral of improving and deepening practice. What teachers need to know changes according to the individual students who present themselves, the particular context of the school, the best knowledge of each discipline, professional standards, and policy directives. This complex array is never the same 2 years in a row, nor does it present itself neatly according to some master long-range plan. Teachers, as professionals, need spaces in which to collaborate, to leverage their understandings, and to invent answers. Most solutions come in the form of small changes, intermediate steps, just noticeable differences, which eventually pull on the fabric of practice, creating something much fuller, much deeper, a better fit for the students. Courses and in-service trainings can address simpler components of practice. But none can adequately address the complexity of practice in all of its messy manifestations. That takes something more.

INTRODUCING ACTION RESEARCH

Action research is an evolving discipline, a form of professional inquiry in which the action researchers are recognized as key to identifying and creating improvement: Those responsible for changing practice do the research. The definition of action research used in this chapter is a systematic inquiry by collaborative, self-critical communities of teachers, which takes place in schools. It is pursued out of a desire or need to improve educational knowledge and practices. It is accomplished through a recursive cycle of (1) identifying a problem area, (2) studying it by gathering data, and (3) reflecting on the data in order to make teaching decisions grounded in evidence rather than in hunches. Taking action is a moral imperative for the action researcher and an integral part of the research.

This 50-year-old methodology introduced first in the United States by sociologist Kurt Lewin (1946) is used widely in the United States, Australia, and the United Kingdom, and it has a track record for successfully supporting change (King & Lonnquist, in press). The definition of action research provides a sense of promise but does not provide a vision of how an action research collaborative functions. This chapter provides some illumination on how research and action are linked. It describes the components we have found necessary to support effective collaboration by teachers and demonstrates the use of one formal process used to facilitate the work. It illustrates with examples from work with teacher researchers how small studies interspersed with little revisions in practice can add up over time to conceptual paradigm shifts and truly better ways of working. And it shows how research studies undertaken by individual teachers can influence others, within the collaborative and beyond it.

IDENTIFYING THE COMPONENTS OF COLLABORATIVE WORK

This chapter draws on 15 years of work in collaborative action research. As teachers we were action researchers in our own classrooms, first participating in study groups, institutes, and collaboratives that others led or coordinated. Later we were facilitators of action research collaboratives. In 1986, National Science Foundation (NSF) funding supported us to develop a methodology able to be replicated and to lead a network of action research collaboratives, working most closely with their facilitating teacher leaders. This work has since been incorporated into more systemic initiatives and larger reform efforts, but whether on a small or grand scale, certain elements for supporting success are non-negotiable. These have evolved into a theory that we use to create contexts for collaborative action research to support ongoing improvement and change of practice. The seven components of our action research theory are:

- Action research takes place within a collaborative context.
- It is carried out by those having a common vision and/or domain of interest.
- Participants are committed to shared cultural norms.
- Data are gathered to focus inquiry and analysis.
- Structured conversations are used to facilitate reflection, documentation, and description.

- Participants utilize knowledge in their own practice.
- Participants share what they have learned in more public ways—outside the group—to make a difference to the larger community.

A collaborative context creates collegial nourishment for overly busy professional teachers and a safe haven (Louis, 1996) for taking an honest look into deeper aspects of practice, including focusing on discrepancies between ideals and practice, hopes and outcomes, goals and implementation. It is in the collaborative context that critical analysis, insights, and knowledge of practice by colleagues can play a supportive role for forward momentum (Elliot, 1991; Somekh, 1988). It is important to note that a collaborative context as we define it means that all are co-researchers, each taking on the stance of colleague and learner. No one is simply an observer, and none are exempted because of their role as experts. For instance, although group facilitators may in some cases have legitimate claims to more skills, content knowledge, or authority, their role is to assist the group through facilitating the work while simultaneously studying some aspect of their practice as facilitator.

A common vision and/or domain of inquiry for the collaborative provides a sense of being part of an effort larger than one's own classroom. This serves to leverage the group's shared inquiry by drawing on a wealth of professional resources, literature, research, theory, policy, and standards created by the educational community outside the collaborative. This outside knowledge informs and deepens the inside knowledge of the group. Each teacher's focus for study falls within the same larger domain. Therefore the complexity of moving the vision into practice becomes apparent to teachers by conducting individual studies and supporting their colleagues' studies.

Shared cultural norms are essential to creating a safe haven for honest participation. It is important to make these norms explicit and to negotiate them within the group. Any member of the collaborative can invoke them to support the group in maintaining processes for safe inquiry and a comfortable and democratic context for working. These shared norms bring people into a research frame of mind by fostering inquiry, rather than encouraging the usual discourse of teacher meetings.

Some cultural norms we have used as starting points for negotiation with groups are:

- Respect each other as professional colleagues.
- Recognize that everyone has knowledge, strategies, resources, and practical experiences to share.
- Engage in inquiry: "I'm curious about . . ."; "I wonder. . . ."
- Encourage real questions.
- Encourage specific, context-rich sharing.

- Avoid judgmental comments.
- Talk about other people—students, parents, colleagues—as respectfully as if they were present.
- Use an action research approach to experimenting and constructing knowledge.
- Take an active role in supporting the action research efforts of your colleagues.
- Keep the content of the meetings confidential within the group, unless specifically negotiated for sharing outside the group.

Some leaders prefer to start with norms about the group's commitments: "We start promptly and stay to the end of the meeting." "Everyone has something to contribute." "Group members have the right to use each other's data." Cultural norms surface assumptions, reduce misunderstandings, and increase commitment to fair group process.

The data gathered by group members and shared at meetings illuminate thinking, create understanding, and ensure success in implementation. Data vary in form: We define data as something tangible, something that can be seen, heard, or touched (e.g., examples of student work or audiotapes of classroom dialogue) and therefore analyzed in a collaborative context. Data ground the research, surface the dissonances, inform decision making, and substantiate reporting.

Structured conversations assist a group in moving beyond normal teachers' room talk. They are formalized with ground rules and rotating roles with designated responsibilities. These provide a scaffolding for describing and inquiring before asserting and assisting. The processes are systematic, and documentation is made and shared among participants. Each process, therefore, becomes a collaborative ministudy for the group, assisting participants in creating new conceptual understandings related to the common domain or vision.

Utilization of the knowledge constructed through action research is the purpose for undertaking the study. The results of a study usually include insights into practice, and therefore it is a moral imperative for an educator entrusted with the lives of children to implement them as soon as they become apparent. Action researchers studying their own practices are in ideal positions to use what they learn, circumventing the traditional difficulties of researchers who must somehow transmit research findings to practitioners, who are then expected to apply these often distant-seeming findings to their own daily practice.

Sharing outside the group is an important way to increase the influence of a study, which creates not only applications but also new knowledge. Deciding on appropriate audiences and forms for sharing the knowledge is one of the ways action research becomes transformational. The audience that would find the knowledge most useful may include teachers in one's own school district, a principal, a parent group, a school board, those involved in a local systemic change initiative, or a national professional group. The presentation must be made in a form that will speak to the specific audience: a letter, a workshop, a videotape, a report with graphics, a journal article—whatever form will convey the work most effectively. The responsibility to share with an audience changes the stance of teachers. Constructing knowledge and changing their own practice environments brings new power to teachers and greater professionalism to their role.

THE SIGNIFICANCE OF LOGO AS A DOMAIN FOR ACTION RESEARCH

The development and spread of the Logo computer language anticipated the spirit of the educational reforms of the 1990s by more than 15 years. The constructivist approach to learning developed by MIT Professor Seymour Papert and colleagues in the MIT Logo Group (Papert, 1971, 1980) in the early to mid-1970s is similar to constructivist approaches embedded in the National Council of Teachers of Mathematics (NCTM) Standards (NCTM, 1989, 1991, 1995), the National Science Standards (National Research Council, 1994), and Science for All Americans (American Association for the Advancement of Science, 1989). Papert and colleagues created a computer-based learning environment that would simultaneously foster the learning of important concepts of mathematics and computer science and the learning of generalizable problem-solving strategies. Papert believed this environment could transform the learning of mathematics from the formal procedures for memorizing algorithms he observed in most schools to the constructivist approach now widely espoused.

The rapid introduction of Logo into classrooms in the early 1980s, without an adequately developed culture of support, led to serious questions about whether Papert's vision could ever be achieved in classroom settings. The major incentive for establishing the Logo Action Research Collaborative came directly from teachers who were implementing Logo in the schools. Many classroom teachers liked Logo and felt it was important. Yet they felt administrative pressure to justify their enthusiasm and to defend the inclusion of Logo in the curriculum. They frequently asked questions such as, "Where can I find research to prove that Logo is good for my students?" Yet when the question was returned to them, "What are *your* students learning with Logo?", most were unsure and offered vague responses such as: "It just seems to be worthwhile learning"; "My students smile a lot and talk a lot about how to solve programming projects"; and "They seem generally involved."

At the same time, these teachers also recognized that their statements about Logo's benefits did not apply to all of their students. To move toward a vision of Logo as an open-ended environment in which all learners can take greater responsibility for their own learning requires teachers who understand important aspects of Logo learning. Teachers need to possess a collection of strategies to challenge students' curiosity, support students' project development, and probe students' understanding (Watt & Watt, 1986). Regardless of their technical expertise, most Logo teachers have not had the opportunity to participate in a culture of collaborative inquiry as learners themselves. Therefore it is a problem for them to facilitate their students through inquiry learning experiences.

PRESENTING TWO ILLUSTRATIVE EXAMPLES OF USING DATA TO CHANGE PRACTICE

The Logo Action Research Collaborative (LARC) was initiated in 1986 as an exploratory effort to support teachers using Logo in building professional cultures for studying and assessing Logo learning in order to deepen their understandings and improve their practice.[1] The process of supporting a year-long action research cycle and the benefits for participating teachers and their students are described more fully elsewhere (Watt & Watt, 1982, 1991, 1993; Watt, Watt, McKiernan, & Schwartz, in press; Youngerman, 1993). In the rest of this chapter we present data from two studies, illustrating how two teachers were able to raise troubling issues about teaching and learning in their own practices. Studies also show how the collaborative processes supported the entire group in understanding the data presented, how the teachers developed strategies to support the students in question, and, most importantly, how studying one student's work in rich detail led both teachers to revise their teaching practices for all their students.[2]

Both illustrative examples involve teachers working with fourth-grade students in a suburban school district outside Boston. Each teacher in the Logo Action Research Collaborative chooses two students to follow through the year: one student the teacher is particularly interested in for his or her own reasons, and a second student who offers a contrast to the first. Teachers record day-to-day observations of the students, formulate their own research questions, and prepare a report on their observations and the effects of their interventions.

The first study follows Kathy,[3] a student whose understanding of Logo appeared to be stalled and who seemed to be ignoring her teacher's suggestions. When her teacher, Stephen Wall, brought examples of her work to the research group for collaborative analysis, he was able to gain essential insights about the knowledge Kathy was using and thereby build from her strengths to support her to think more powerfully and systematically about her work. The second example concerns Douglas, an extremely able student whose knowledge of Logo surpassed his teacher's. When Douglas got stuck on a complex programming problem, his teacher, Susan Frank, called on the collaborative research group for assistance in understanding how to help him progress. The group as a whole took on the challenge. First, they entered Douglas's thinking, deconstructing his work in order to understand the way he was thinking about it. Then they attempted to solve the problem using strategies that were consistent with Douglas's ways of working, in order to be able to make suggestions that could help him solve the problem on his own, in his own style.

How can Kathy make progress? Working with a Student Who Does Not Seem to Be Learning

Stephen Wall chose Kathy as one of his two students because he was concerned that mid-way through her second year of Logo instruction she did not seem to be making progress or using ideas and strategies that he was teaching her. Stephen recorded in his journal that Kathy was "considered to be rather average in overall ability. I considered her ability to work in the Logo environment to be one of the lowest in the class. She was always very tentative in her approach to using Logo, and she always solicited a great deal of help from me as she worked on her Logo projects. It was my hope that by focusing attention specifically on her, I would be able to help her overcome some of her problems with Logo."

Stephen's broader action research questions were closely related to what he was trying to learn by following Kathy's progress, and they informed his observations of her work throughout the year:

- How do students use what they are given in teacher-directed lessons?
- Is there a change in programming style over time?
- How much help do students solicit, and what type of support do I have to provide?

In Stephen's school system, the Logo curriculum starts in the third grade: Students practice moving like a turtle robot and use basic Logo commands to move a turtle cursor around the computer screen. In the fourth grade, children are taught to write procedures and subprocedures—simple computer programs—while constructing their own mathematical computer graphics projects. (As a reference for readers who are unfamiliar with Logo, we have provided a series of "Logo Notes" throughout the chapter. These Notes contain explanations of Logo features and terms that appear in the student work and teacher dialogues presented in this chapter.)

> Logo Note: The Logo Turtle
> *The Logo turtle is typically used to create mathematical computer graphics images on a computer screen. It does so by moving FORWARD (FD) and BACK (BK) a variable distance according to commands typed by a user. The turtle turns to its own RIGHT (RT) or LEFT (LT) a given number of degrees. When its pen is down, it draws a line on the screen as it moves.*

Stephen brought a printout of Kathy's procedure, House.6 (see Figure 3.1), to share with our research group in early March of her fourth-grade year, fully a year and a half after she started to use Logo. He seemed to be somewhat discouraged about Kathy's work. He reported that he had been teaching students to divide long procedures into subprocedures since early in the year and that Kathy's work did not reflect that part of his teaching at all.

> Logo Note: Procedures and Subprocedures
> *A* procedure *is a series of typed commands, preceded by a name (e.g., TO HOUSE.6 [see Figure 3.1]) and completed with the command END. A procedure that is used as a command in another procedure is called a* subprocedure. *The use of subprocedures is a convenient, understandable way to divide a complex program into manageable, understandable parts. Learning to use subprocedures with appropriate names is one of the major goals of early Logo instruction, because it is an example of a well-known general problem-solving heuristic—divide a large problem into smaller subproblems. A* superprocedure *is a single procedure that includes several other procedures as subprocedures.*

The group used a collaborative process to understand Kathy's work. Starting with a printout of Kathy's picture and procedure, the group brainstormed answers to three questions in sequence: First: What knowledge is Kathy using? Then: What potentially useful knowledge is Kathy not using? Followed by: What teaching intervention would you take, as Kathy's teacher, to support her in using Logo more powerfully? Why and how would you take it? A structured format for using this collaborative process in a formal way is described later in this chapter.

Step 1: What Knowledge Is Kathy Using? The group spent over an hour analyzing the printout shown in Figure 3.1, making a point of not overlooking the obvious or dismissing any knowledge as trivial. This created as com-

Figure 3.1.

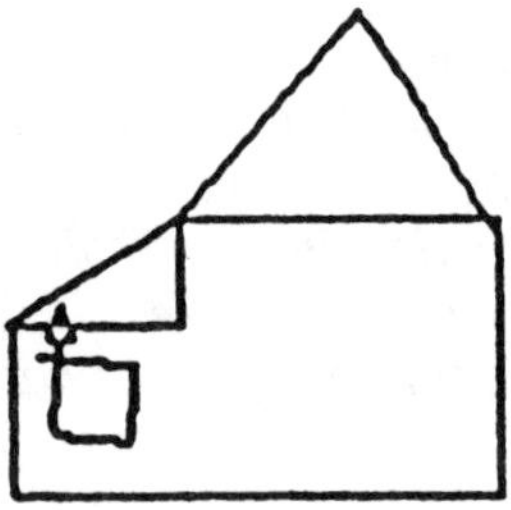

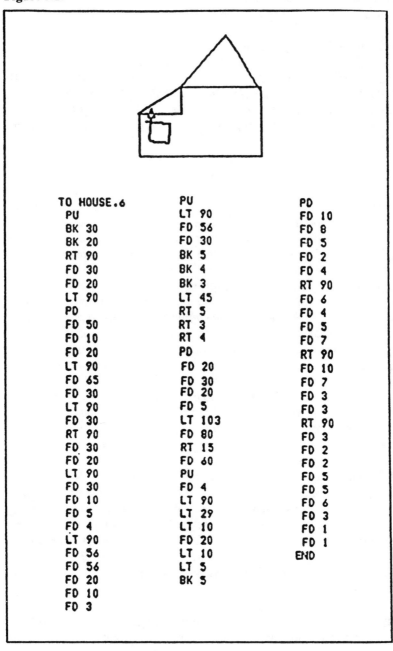

```
TO HOUSE.6
 PU
 BK 30
 BK 20
 RT 90
 FD 30
 FD 20
 LT 90
 PD
 FD 50
 FD 10
 FD 20
 LT 90
 FD 65
 FD 30
 LT 90
 FD 30
 RT 90
 FD 30
 FD 20
 LT 90
 FD 30
 FD 10
 FD 5
 FD 4
 LT 90
 FD 56
 FD 56
 FD 20
 FD 10
 FD 3
PU
LT 90
FD 56
FD 30
BK 5
BK 4
BK 3
LT 45
RT 5
RT 3
RT 4
PD
 FD 20
 FD 30
 FD 20
 FD 5
 LT 103
 FD 80
 RT 15
 FD 60
 PU
 FD 4
 LT 90
 LT 29
 LT 10
 FD 20
 LT 10
 LT 5
 BK 5
PD
FD 10
FD 8
FD 5
FD 2
FD 4
RT 90
FD 6
FD 4
FD 5
FD 7
RT 90
FD 10
FD 7
FD 3
FD 3
RT 90
FD 3
FD 2
FD 2
FD 5
FD 5
FD 6
FD 3
FD 1
FD 1
END
```

plete a picture as possible of what Kathy understood. The group discovered that Kathy was using a lot of Logo knowledge in her work, more than Stephen had realized in his own first assessment. Some of the knowledge Kathy was using in her project as identified by the group included:[4]

- Something about what a house looks like
- Basic turtle commands
- How to use a turtle to create a picture
- How to use penup and pendown to place the turtle without leaving a trace on the screen
- How to position the turtle on the screen to center a drawing
- How to use 90-degree turns to make square corners
- How to estimate turns that are not 90 degrees
- How to observe the turtle's position and make fine adjustments
- How to solve problems by trial and error, making successive approximations
- How to use BACK and FORWARD as inverses
- How to use RIGHT and LEFT as inverses
- How to write and edit a simple, sequential procedure

Step 2: What Potentially Useful Knowledge Is Kathy Not Using? Next the group identified some knowledge Kathy hadn't used but might find useful. This is an important intermediate step before deciding on a teaching intervention. Kathy might have been able to work more powerfully if she had known:

- How to orient the turtle so that the window in her house would look square
- How to combine similar commands to make her procedures easier to read and to identify mathematical patterns (e.g., replace FD 10, FD 20 by one command, FD 30)
- How to use REPEAT (for a rectangle or square)
- How to use subprocedures to divide her work into smaller pieces

Logo Note: The REPEAT Command

REPEAT is a Logo command that causes a bracketed sequence of commands to be repeated a specific number of times. For example, REPEAT 4 [FORWARD 50 RIGHT 90] draws a square with sides 50 units long.

Step 3: If You Were Kathy's Teacher, What One Intervention Would You Take? How and Why? It can be daunting to anyone to receive a long list of all the changes one might make. Each teacher is asked to recommend one intervention at a time to make a real difference to the learner in solving his or her own problem that fits the problem-solving approach the learner is already using. Some of the suggestions made to Stephen for helping Kathy included:

- Show her how to combine commands, so that she can make opposite sides of her building exactly the same length.
- Remind her how to use the REPEAT command to make a square or rectangle more easily.
- Suggest that she make separate subprocedures for each part of the house so that she can divide her problem into parts and more easily debug (correct) parts that don't work the way she likes.
- Ask her to draw a sketch for the house on graph paper and use the number of squares to plan how long each side of the house should be.

Here are some excerpts from Stephen's written observations of his work with Kathy over the following weeks.

> 3/13 OBSERVATION: The basic approach of both Kathy and her partner has been to work in the immediate mode, one partner writing down all of the steps that seem to work, the other typing in the commands. After they get so far, they switch to the editor and enter these same commands into one long procedure. What is interesting is that absolutely no attempts have been made to compensate or make adjustments for any slight errors made while investigating in the immediate mode. An example of this is not changing FD 10 FD 20 FD 5 FD 2 FD 3 typed in the immediate mode to FD 40 in the editor. . . .
>
> Kathy did solicit help during the observation period. . . . Kathy was not satisfied with the way her window came out and she couldn't figure out how to make it look like a rectangle. She said that it also kept coming out looking a little lopsided. I asked her what she wanted to do and she said she wanted to make a normal-looking rectangle for a window. She didn't seem to be aware that the turtle was turned to perhaps 2 degrees right before she made the window. I suggested that she check the turtle's heading [by using the commands PRINT HEADING]. She saw then that the turtle's heading was off a bit and then actually asked me what she should do to fix it. I told her that she might try making the turtle's heading 0 before making the window. It took her two tries before she got it right.

Stephen's first comment focused on his observation that Kathy and her partner did not combine steps or eliminate unnecessary ones. This confirmed one of the concerns that had been raised in the collaborative assessment process. His second observation shows how he talked with Kathy and found out that she was dissatisfied with her window: She wanted it to look like a rectangle, not "lopsided." When Kathy asked for help, he was ready to show her one new piece of Logo knowledge and how it would help her solve her problem. Significantly, Kathy could not have *discovered* this information; someone needed to show her. Once Kathy knew that there was a way to find the turtle's precise heading and then make it exactly 0, she could solve her problem.

> Logo Note: Turtle Headings
> *The turtle's heading is a number between 0 and 360 indicating the degrees of turtle's absolute direction on the screen, measured clockwise from a vertical axis. A heading of 0 means the turtle is pointing to the top of the screen. When the turtle's heading is exactly 0, 90, 180, or 270, it draws smooth vertical and horizontal lines on the screen. Otherwise it draws jagged lines. Kathy's difficulty was that because of the limits of screen resolution the turtle looked as if it had a heading of 0 when it actually had a heading of 2 degrees. Jagged lines showed where she was expecting smooth ones.*

> 3/16 OBSERVATION AND INTERVENTION: I felt compelled while watching Kathy today to say something about writing her commands in a more concise way when taking commands from immediate mode and putting them in the editor. She almost immediately complied but did not wish to go back through the entire procedure and make the necessary changes. I told her it was necessary from this point on that both she and her partner make a more serious effort to do this in every procedure they make. Kathy was just beginning to type in the commands that made the rectangular window when I heard her say to her partner, "Let's use a REPEAT to make this." They got the turtle in position to make the door and helped each other with a REPEAT that made the door. They started talking about making two square windows and where they should place them when the time was up.

> 3/18 and 3/20 Kathy was out sick.

> 3/23 OBSERVATION: Kathy and partner were able to make the two square windows they had talked about making. As I looked at their procedures, I noticed that when they made the square windows, they were not written as REPEATS. They tried placing the windows in three different locations before they seemed satisfied with what I hope is their final location.

On 3/16 Stephen observed that Kathy knew about the REPEAT command. However, after missing school for a week, she did not use REPEAT, even though it would have been appropriate for what she was doing and might have made her work easier. She did, however, continue to combine small steps before entering them into the editor, and eventually complete House.6 (see Fig. 3.2).

Through Stephen's close work with Kathy he began to notice that other students were having some of the same difficulties using the idea of subprocedures. He began to pay closer attention to the Logo knowledge his other students were and were not using:

> I noticed on 3/25 that only about half the students in the class were attempting to use super- and subprocedures when working on Logo projects of their own choosing. When I asked the class about their reasons for continuing to write the long "spaghetti" way, I was basically told they felt more comfortable doing it that way. There were about six students who said that even though I had explained it before and even made them try using them, they still didn't understand it. I explained to them that I felt they were ready to start using this higher-level approach to Logo programming and problem solving, and we decided as a class some review might be helpful. I honestly believe that if most, or even all, of the students are going to begin using this method of writing procedures, intervention now is necessary.
>
> On 3/27 I conducted a thorough review with the whole class of the method of planning, sketching, then deciding on subprocedures that will be used. . . . I then explained the next project that I wanted them

Figure 3.2.

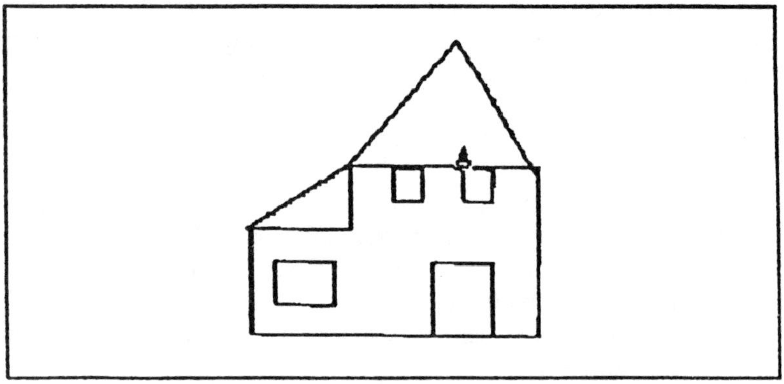

> to work on. It involved planning with their partner, sketching, and using a superprocedure and subprocedures to make a picture of their own choosing . . .

Kathy and her partner decided to draw a schoolhouse (see Figure 3.3, Kathy's sketch of the schoolhouse she planned to draw). Stephen reminded them at several points to combine steps such as RIGHT 30 and RIGHT 60 into RIGHT 90. Before Kathy and her partner went to the computer, Stephen reviewed the idea of using a superprocedure, using the same examples he'd used in the whole-class lesson. These teacher interventions were different from the earlier ones in that they were made *before* rather than after the students started programming.

As Kathy worked on her schoolhouse project over the next month, she incorporated many of her teacher's suggestions. Working from a sketch, she labeled and named each part of the drawing and wrote separate subprocedures for each part. She also used REPEAT to draw regular geometric shapes (see Figure 3.4). Stephen's attention shifted to other aspects of her work. Here are his observations of Kathy's work recorded on 5/4:

> . . . I honestly don't believe she needs as much help as she asks for. I asked her why she always asked for help. She said she wanted to make sure she was doing things the right way and didn't want to make too many mistakes. . . . I told her I didn't mind trying to help them, but I wanted them to try something several times before they decide they are

Figure 3.3.

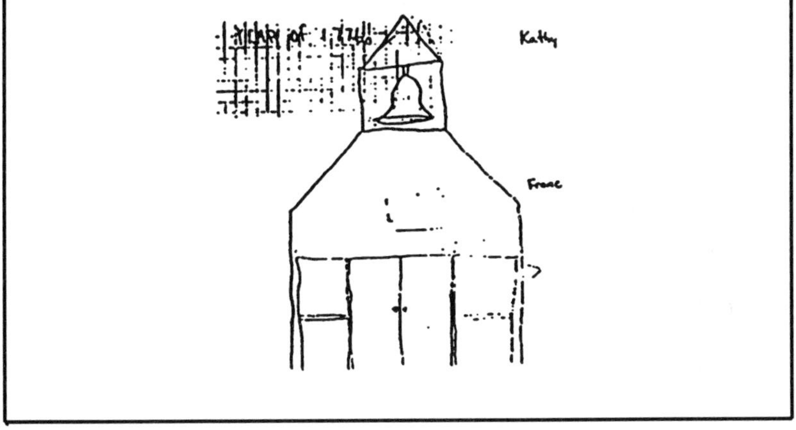

Figure 3.4.

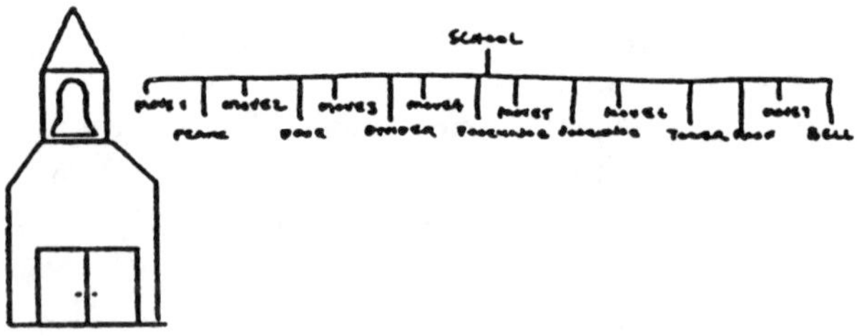


```
TO SCHOOL
 HT
 MOVE1
 FRAME
 MOVE2
 DOOR
 MOVE3
 DIVIDER
 MOVE4
 DOORKNOB
 MOVE5
 DOORKNOB
 MOVE6
 TOWER
 ROOF
 MOVE7
 BELL
END

TO MOVE1
 FULLSCREEN
 PU
 BK 80
 RT 90
 FD 50
 LT 90
 PD
END

TO FRAME
 FD 90
 LT 50
 FD 40
 LT 40
 FD 50
 LT 50
 FD 37
 LT 40
 FD 90
 LT 90
 FD 110
END

TO MOVE2
 PU
 LT 180
 FD 20
 RT 90
END

TO DOOR
 PD
 FD 50
 LT 90
 FD 70
 LT 90
 FD 50
END

TO MOVE3
 PU
 LT 90
 FD 35
 LT 90
 PD
END

TO DIVIDER
 FD 50
END

TO MOVE4
 PU
 BK 30
 RT 90
 FD 5
 PD
END

TO DOORKNOB
 FD 1
END

TO MOVE5
 PU
 BK 12
 PD
END

TO MOVE6
 PU
 LT 90
 FD 100
 LT 90
 FD 25
 RT 90
 PD
END

TO TOWER
 REPEAT 4 [FD 45 RT 90]
 FD 45
END

TO ROOF
 RT 30
 REPEAT 3 [FD 45 RT 120]
END

TO MOVE7
 PU
 FD 34
 RT 20
 FD 10
 RT 130
 FD 60
 RT 90
 FD 12
 RT 90
 BK 9
 PD
END

TO BELL
 FD 15
 REPEAT 6 [FD 5 RT 30]
 FD 15
 LT 15
 REPEAT 3 [FD 5 LT 15]
 LT 30
 RT 180
 FD 33
 RT 30
 LT 30
 RT 121
 FD 6
 FD 5
END
```

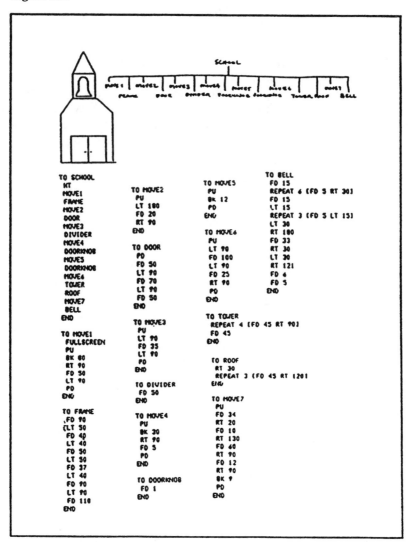

stuck and really need some assistance. I said they could ask me for help if they wanted to make something and really didn't even know how to even start making it . . .

Stephen's notes tell us that Kathy and her partner went on to complete their schoolhouse with a rather sophisticated bell shape, after several more interventions from Stephen. These interventions were subtler than previous ones. They were given in the form of questions and suggestions: "Can you find a way to draw a smaller circle, by changing the numbers in your procedure and watching what happens?" "Can you figure out how to make just half of a circle? Then you will know almost all you need to make the bell!" (Kathy's final result is shown in Figure 3.4.)

In his final report, Stephen stated that:

> After that conversation [about trying things herself], Kathy was a changed person. She did continue asking for my help, but with less frequency, and only when she had tried, and still couldn't figure out what to do. I saw her making mistakes, and working on them until she had resolved them. I felt I had finally made the big breakthrough with her that I was hoping for.

As we have seen, Stephen Wall succeeded in creating an effective relationship with Kathy, whose "ability to work in the Logo environment" he originally considered to be "one of the lowest in the class." He accomplished this change through being a diagnostic teacher and investigating his own questions in his own classroom.

Through professional engagement in classroom action research, which included the critical support from colleagues, Stephen transformed an experience that could have been merely confusing or frustrating into an opportunity to investigate his own questions and to make sense out of his own teaching and the learning of students in his classroom. In this example, we have seen how Stephen engaged Kathy in working more effectively and powerfully with Logo and how his work with her led him to focus on an important idea that had been missed by most of his students—an omission that had gone unnoticed by him. By sharing his documentation and insights publicly, he also made a professional contribution to the wider community of Logo-using educators.

Through his larger action research study, Stephen came to grips with his original concerns about the place of Logo in his fourth-grade curriculum. He turned his skepticism about some of the specific content and time allotted for Logo in the district's curriculum into action by spending the next summer working with colleagues to strengthen the curriculum. He concluded his research with this statement: "I am now able to justify in my own mind why the teaching and learning of Logo is important. If taught the right way, students learn to think both logically and creatively. Not only do they have the opportunity to learn about math, problem solving and programming, but more importantly, they begin to learn about their own thinking."[5]

How can Susan help Douglas make progress?
When Teacher and Student Are Stumped

The national agenda for school reform places an increasing emphasis on the teaching and learning of problem solving and on the professional development of teachers. Yet most teachers have had little, if any, education for teaching problem solving. Most teachers assign students problems that have answers that are already known. Then they teach the specific steps and procedures involved in solving them. Yet real-world problems do not have known solutions—they may even be unsolvable. And real-world problem solvers use methods that may lead to dead-ends, forcing them to start over. Unfortunately, teachers have not had many opportunities to solve complex mathematical problems. Nor does their training provide much experience in teaching students to solve problems whose solutions are not already known. How can teachers intervene effectively to help students solve problems when the student's knowledge of programming surpasses the teacher's?

The example that follows centers on a collaborative process developed to deal with situations in which neither the teacher nor the student has the answer to a problem the student is trying to solve. Susan Frank was extremely skilled at setting up a rich, experiential learning classroom for her students. Although Susan had taken several Logo in-service training workshops each year for 6 years, she did not consider herself a programmer in Logo. She taught Logo in a fourth-grade class using six computers located in the back of the classroom. Students clustered at the computers to work on their own projects while Susan taught a regular math curriculum to the rest of the class.

Susan brought Douglas's problem (Figure 3.5) to share with the collaborative action research group because she was stumped. She did not know how to help Douglas solve his own problem, and she needed suggestions.

Douglas wrote a program that did something interesting, yet he was not satisfied with it. His procedure did not distribute the designs—which the group came to call "whirligigs"—evenly in each section of the divided circle.

The research group committed 2 hours to working through Susan's problem. They divided into three small working groups and set up a three-stage process based on the format for collaborative assessment of student work.

Stage 1. Starting with a printout of Douglas's picture and procedure, the group worked through the three questions of the collaborative assessment process: (1) What knowledge is Douglas using? (2) What potentially useful knowledge is Douglas not using? (3) What would you, as teacher, suggest to Douglas to help him solve his problem?

Stage 2. After each group brainstormed lists of responses to each question, the group worked collaboratively on the computer to solve Douglas's

Figure 3.5.

[NOTE SPACINGS BETWEEN LINES ARE TO EMPHASIZE NESTED REPEATS IN LINES 4 AND 5. LINE 5 TAKES UP TWO LINES OF THE PAGE!]

```
TO PENTACIRCLE

HT

PU LT 90 FD 50 RT 90 PD

REPEAT 360 [FD 1.5 RT 1]

REPEAT 5 [RT 90 FD 85.1734 BK 85 LT 90 REPEAT 72 [FD 1.5 RT 1]]

PU RT 90 REPEAT 5 [FD 30 LT 90 FD 40 PD REPEAT 30 [REPEAT 2
[FD 1.5 RT 1] FD 15 BK 35 LT 90] PU LT 180 FD 30 RT 180 LT 72]

END
```

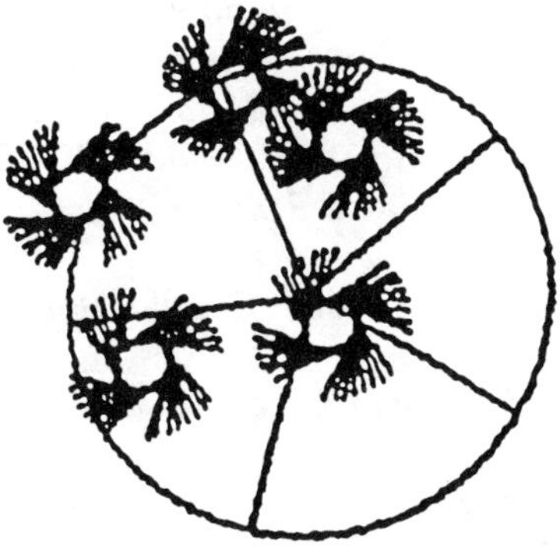

problem themselves. While working, they kept in mind his knowledge and his particular ways of working, so that their solutions might help Susan coach Douglas in solving the problem. This process was documented by each small group. It should be noted that some members of the group were excellent programmers. Yet no one found Douglas's program easy to understand or his problem simple to resolve.

Stage 3. The third aspect of the process was recursive. The group asked itself the three original questions again, but this time the answers were based on the experience of attempting to solve the programming problem themselves.

Here are some of the items listed in stage 1, answering the three questions before working on the problem:

What knowledge is Douglas using?

- Knowledge of basic commands
- REPEAT commands and nested REPEAT commands
- How to write a procedure
- How to move a turtle without leaving a trace
- How to make the turtle draw a circle
- Some understanding of decimals, in particular the number 85.1734
- The geometry needed to divide a circle into five equal segments.

Logo Note: A Total Turtle Trip

A sequence of turtle commands that brings the turtle back to its starting position and heading must include a total rotation of 360 degrees. This mathematical idea is sometimes called a "total turtle trip" in Logo, and a procedure that employs a total turtle trip is referred to as "state-transparent." Douglas used his knowledge of a total turtle trip to make the turtle draw a circle, using REPEAT 360 [FORWARD 1.5 RIGHT 1]. He used the same knowledge to divide the circle into five equal sectors—each sector included a 72-degree arc—using a nested REPEAT command: REPEAT 5 [RIGHT 90 FORWARD 85.1734 BACK 85 LEFT 90 REPEAT 72 [FORWARD 1.5 RIGHT 1]].

What potentially useful knowledge is Douglas not using?

- Subprocedures to divide the problem into manageable parts
- The idea of a separate "move procedure" to move the turtle over before drawing the whirligig design
- Placing a different Logo command on each line to make a procedure easier to read
- Effective ways to place the turtle properly on the screen to draw his design in the desired orientation
- The SETXY command that moves the turtle to any point on the screen using coordinates
- Full understanding of a total turtle trip
- Using the TRACE command to step through a procedure one command at a time in order to debug it

Logo Note: Untangling Douglas's Difficult Problem

Douglas used the total turtle trip idea and nested REPEAT commands to draw the circle and divide it into five equal sectors. He ran into trouble, however, when he attempted to place each whirligig into a separate sector of the circle using the same nested REPEAT command,

REPEAT 5 ["do something" LEFT 72]. Douglas thought that that complex command would distribute the five whirligigs evenly around the 360-degree circle. What he apparently did not realize was that the commands that created the whirligig drawing included a net rotation of only 210 degrees. When this was followed by LEFT 72, it produced a rotation of 282 degrees. And when this process was repeated five times, it produced a total rotation of 1,470 degrees, which is not an exact multiple of 360. Hence the whirligigs were not evenly distributed around the circle, despite Douglas's use of REPEAT 5 ["do something" LEFT 72]. To accomplish Douglas's intention, each of the whirligig drawings should have had a net rotation of 360 degrees. That would have made them "state-transparent"—ending and beginning in the same position and with the same orientation.

What would you suggest to Douglas to help him solve his problem?

- Use subprocedures to divide the problem clearly into separate parts.
- Make separate move procedures to move the turtle before and after drawing each whirligig.
- Use decimals to figure out midpoints of the radius to place figures more accurately.
- Use variables to get the circle bigger so the whirligigs will fit.
- Redesign the entire program: Make one pie wedge and whirligig design correctly; then turn the turtle to reproduce the same wedge five times.
- Use TRACE for debugging; also use the SETXY and SETHEADING commands.

For an hour, all three groups reworked the program. The programming was tough and no group finished the process, but each was engaged fully in the challenge. Each group approached the problem in a different way, yet each attempted to solve it in a way that took Douglas's thinking into account.

Jane's group reported:

> We really tried not to change too much of his program, but to break it down into pieces. . . . We had problems because we were thinking about it opposite to the way he was thinking about it. He was thinking about moving the turtle from the outside in and we were thinking about it from the inside out.

Bob's group reported:

> Our overall strategy was to leave it basically the way it was. We introduced subprocedures and superprocedure. We liked the way he drew the circle. We got rid of the nested REPEATs and knocked off some of the decimals. We decided he didn't really understand decimals. . . . We centered the circle. Our ultimate strategy to put one whirligig in each piece, was to make a move procedure to center the turtle in a good position . . .

Anne's group thought about how to break the program down into super- and subprocedures and then how to place a simpler, state-transparent design in each section. They also thought about giving Douglas some tool procedures that could move the turtle automatically back to its starting point after making each whirligig design.

After working directly with Douglas's program, the whole group repeated the collaborative assessment process. Their hands-on experience focused the sharing on powerful mathematical ideas useful for Logo programming.

What potentially useful knowledge is Douglas not using?

- State-transparent turtle procedures
- Using the total turtle trip idea correctly to complete the design
- Creating move procedures distinct from turtle drawing procedures
- Using subprocedures
- Writing understandable code

This time the group made many teaching suggestions to Susan. And most of the ideas had to do with good programming and good problem-solving practices such as: Keep it simple; use smaller procedures; make the moves distinct from the drawing; use state-transparent subdesigns; use a simpler design, such as a square, before using the whirligig shape.

Susan reported that she took some of the ideas back to her classroom and offered them to Douglas. However, to the group's bemusement, Douglas no longer wanted to change his program. He had learned to love it the way it was and chose to publish this design in a class Logo book.

Does this mean that the process was a waste of time? Quite the contrary. Teachers reported learning more sophisticated Logo programming, better diagnostic teaching, and more about coaching students on their own projects. Susan realized that she already knew enough strategies to help Douglas; she just hadn't realized how helpful general problem-solving coaching would be. All realized that examining Douglas's work carefully helped focus on how the powerful ideas in Logo allow students to carry out projects more effectively. Also, because the same ideas make procedures more readable, their use makes it easier for students to collaborate with each other and for teachers to coach students through their difficulties. Susan said that she will emphasize state-transparency, superprocedures, and subprocedures with all of her students. And she has many suggestions for next steps in working with Douglas on future projects. The research group chose Douglas' problem as their T-shirt logo.

In this example, problem solving took place on two different levels. First, there was the mathematical problem Douglas was trying to solve. And then there was the pedagogical problem teachers were trying to solve: How could Susan help Douglas solve his problem, while teaching him something more about problem solving, in a situation in which she did not know the answer to the original problem herself? While carrying out the process, the group recognized that it had made use of George Polya's problem-solving process and problem-solving heuristics (Polya, 1957) without realizing it. They struggled to find what was known and what was unknown: in the mathematical sense, in the cognitive sense (by Douglas), and in the pedagogical sense (by the teachers). They thought of similar problems that they had already solved, found general rules to apply, divided the problem into simpler parts, and named each part. Finally, as they worked, they looked back and reflected on what they had done. Having worked through the problem themselves, they added it to their repertoire of problems seen before and of Logo programming difficulties seen before. Thus investigating one problem in great detail supported the building of professional knowledge by all the teachers involved.

RATIONALE AND GUIDELINES FOR THE COLLABORATIVE ASSESSMENT OF STUDENT WORK

This process, which was first developed to assist the LARC in understanding Kathy's and Douglas's fourth-grade Logo programming needs, has evolved into a robust and well-defined formal method for collaborative assessment of student work in order to make teaching decisions that fit. It is reproduced here to illustrate one formal process that readers may adapt to their own work. It is presented deliberately in a straightforward manner to be easily used and understood. Each page of the format has notes at the bottom to assist the group in sharing responsibility for facilitating the process. The process is formal, and its formality provides an overarching authority for the person taking the chair's role—which, though often difficult for colleagues to assume with each other, is necessary for moving the conversation forward.

Rationale

The process allows practitioners to share puzzling data about their students in a no-fault environment and supports the presenter in reflecting, identifying, and making effective teaching interventions with students. At the same time, it provides critical friends a way to offer ideas that can be heard. While participating in the process, all find themselves rethinking their own approaches to looking at students' work. Ongoing task groups and research collaboratives have found this process an invaluable tool for assessing student work and planning teaching interventions.

How It Works

The idea for a collaborative assessment process is similar to an author's circle in the writing process, which was developed to allow the author to get specific help from colleagues for a particular writing issue. The surround and data are presented as a context for the particular puzzle.

The Presenter. The presenter brings real data from one or more students and a particular question or concern to the whole group in order to deepen understanding about a particular student and to take appropriate steps to further the student's learning. A good example is one that is deeply connected to the goals the teacher has for the student and that is somehow perplexing or puzzling. The process is a formal one that requires colleagues to focus on the relevant issues raised by the data themselves without becoming sidetracked by oversimplifying or generalizing inappropriately. During step 3 of the process, participants make specific suggestions; however, the presenter may listen without evaluating or refuting. (This allows the other members of the collaborative to consider each suggestion offered as it applies not only to the presenter's practice but to their own.) After reflecting on the insights and suggestions offered, the presenter thanks the group without making any evaluation of the suggestions or commitments to next steps. It is entirely up to the presenter to decide which of the suggestions, if any, to follow at a time removed from the group.

The Chairperson. The chairperson is a member of the group who facilitates the process. It is the responsibility of the chair to use the process to keep the group focused on the data; maintain a professional atmosphere; and support the presenter, who may be feeling vulnerable about presenting a real dilemma or puzzle. The chair may meet with the presenter prior to the meeting to review the student work and decide which examples to present. At the meeting, the chair sets the tone and sits next to the presenter to provide visible support and the possibility of consultation. The chair informs the group of the presenter's questions and concerns. The presenter shares information that will give the group a context for the work being assessed. The chair then leads the group through the process by following the format, guiding participants to provide appropriate feedback for each step of the process, and determining when to move on from one step to another. It may be helpful to summarize the main points of the preceding step before stating the guiding question for the next step.

The Recorder. The recorder takes notes on the entire process, copies them, and distributes them to all immediately following the process. This allows the presenter and the group members to listen rather than trying to remember suggestions. The list of suggestions includes the name of the person who made the suggestion; for example, "Sheila: I'd do ______ in this way ______ because ______." Including the person's name is important since often people want to know more about the suggestion at a later time. The ideas invariably turn out to be useful to others even though they were given to address a particular question.

The records of the sessions provide documentation of the whole group's collaborative work as critical friends using systematic inquiry; the records may become data on the group's collaboration.

Other Guidelines

- Each student whose work is presented is discussed as respectfully as if the student or the student's parents were present and within the specific teaching/learning dilemma raised.
- Evaluation or discussion of suggestions is not permitted during the process, as these tend to limit people's openness to the shared insights the process is used to evoke.
- A discussion needs to follow the process, as people usually find that the ideas provoke thinking about implications for their own practices. It is important to take time for conversations about issues surfaced during the process about content, rationale, theory, pedagogy, resources, and so forth.
- The content and details of the process and the notes are confidential to members of the group, unless specifically negotiated otherwise.

The format for facilitating and recording the collaborative assessment process is presented in the Appendix.

REFLECTING BACK

This chapter illuminates the relationship between doing research and taking action and describes some of the theory and structures we developed and used in creating and facilitating action research collaboratives. The two excerpts from teacher research make several points. Stephen Wall, a confident teacher and Logo programmer, underestimated the Logo knowledge used by his student, Kathy, a cautious Logo programmer. On the other hand, Susan Frank, an experienced teacher and a novice Logo programmer, overestimated the sophistication of the programming accomplished by her student, Douglas, a bold and eager Logo programmer. By examining their student's work deeply, each reconceptualized their original assessment of that work and identified important teaching interventions that supported learning progress. They based their teaching on new understandings of important issues in Logo programming, mathematical ideas, and diagnostic teaching. Their Logo classes began to look more like their writing workshops, with opportunities for peer coaching, portfolio development, and focus on specific issues of Logo syntax punctuating the free-form project development. They integrated these ways of working with the district's Logo curriculum, creating a better fit between teaching and learning.

Stephen Wall's and Susan Frank's illustrative examples are excerpts from their larger, year-long studies. They were chosen for their specificity and comprehensiveness, as well as to illustrate a replicable approach for starting action research by shadowing a student. Two major ripples from these studies were that Stephen Wall revised the district curriculum with colleagues the following summer, strengthening it through the insights gleaned from the LARC work. And the examples of the data collected and the documentation by Stephen and Susan became part of the resources used at the LARC Leadership Institute for new leaders, who in turn use them to assist teacher researchers in understanding what following a student might look like as they are about to embark on their own research study.

This chapter demonstrates that the research and action necessary to lifelong improvement of educational practice is a rigorous endeavor that can be undertaken by professional educators anywhere. However, it requires thoughtful attention to creating the context, facilitating the collaboration, and engaging over extended periods of time to realize the tremendous benefits that bring quality through deep understanding to the fabric of education.

Appendix

Collaborative Assessment of Student Work

The process and the notes are confidential to members of the group.

Use a black pen and write clearly to save recopying before duplicating for the group!

Presenter:

Chairperson:

Recorder:

Date of Meeting:

Brief description of the work (copy attached):

Feedback requested by presenter:

Presenter: ______________________________ Date: ____________

Step 1. What knowledge is ____________ using?

Notes:

- Start from the most apparent or obvious knowledge shown in the data. All student work takes a great deal of prior skill and knowledge. Starting with the obvious ensures that we create a full picture of this student's capabilities and knowledge.
- Include only items which can be documented by looking at the data themselves. Locating comments in the data allows all participants to share insights, not just the presenter.
- Try to avoid interpretations, generalizations, or hypotheses that are not clearly visible in the data. This lays the groundwork for broadening the range of possible interpretations later.

Step 2. What potentially useful knowledge is ____________ *not* using?

Notes:

- Include skills that the student has not used; mathematical or scientific concepts; problem solving and planning processes that might have made the work easier or might help the student generalize from this work.
- Include ideas that might make the work or the student's thinking more powerful, and that you have reason to believe would be accessible to this student.
- The ideas listed DO NOT IMPLY that the student does not know or has not previously learned the concept or process suggested—simply that their use cannot be documented from the data presented.

Presenter:___________________________________ Date: _____________

Step 3. If you were _____________ 's teacher, what is one teaching intervention you would now take? How would you do it, and why?

Notes:

- Number and record each suggestion, the person making it, the method, and the reason.
- Base suggestions on observations of this student's work and on the knowledge listed on the previous page as not being used by the student. Address the concerns articulated by the presenter at the beginning of the session, but do not limit suggestions to those concerns.
- The presenter may not comment on any suggestion during this phase of the process. It is up to the presenter, as a professional, to reflect on the list later and decide how the suggestions can be adapted to his or her practice.

Step 4. Notes and Discussion: What aspects of content knowledge and pedagogy came up in this case? As educators, what do we want to learn more about as a result of considering this case?

Notes:

- The process is not complete for the participants without time for discussing thoughts, new ideas, and concepts that were suggested. This discussion becomes a powerful way for participants to share their best professional practices and expert knowledge and to learn from one another. New content and pedagogical knowledge are gained by all according to their professional interest. In addition, the discussion may raise real issues for further study by individuals or the whole group.

NOTES

The work reported here was supported in part by the NSF under grants #MDR 8651600 and TPE 8855541 and ESI 9253030. The ideas expressed are those of the authors and do not necessarily represent the views of the NSF.

1. During the first two pilot cycles (1986–87, 1989–90) of the LARC, the project developed a set of materials and activities to support the implementation of action research activities with a focus on Logo learning. During 1990–91, it disseminated these materials to 90 teachers at nine sites around the United States, where school district personnel led collaborative action research groups with teachers in their own districts representing all grade levels—preschool through high school. Groups of teacher researchers in Boston, Brookline, and Concord, Massachusetts, were led by past project participants. Six additional groups were led by experienced Logo teachers and teacher educators in Bellevue, Washington; Brattleboro, Vermont; Chapel Hill, North Carolina; Chicago, Illinois; Ladue, Missouri; and Madison, Wisconsin.

2. Some of the material in these examples originally appeared in different form in *The Computing Teacher* (Watt, 1988/89, 1989) and in *Logo Learning: Strategies for Assessing Content and Process* (Watt & Watt, 1992). They are used with permission of the publisher, the International Society for Technology in Education.

3. Pseudonyms are used to protect the privacy of all students and teachers whose work is brought to the group.

4. In using the collaborative assessment process, it is important to take as much time as possible to gather insights and suggestions at each step of the process. In the interest of brevity and clarity, we have selected just a few of the insights listed by participants to include with the examples in this chapter.

5. We are grateful to all of the teachers who participated in this project, particularly for their courage in sharing real teaching dilemmas. The processes we developed to support these teachers have evolved over the years into the format provided later in the paper, and have been used by thousands of teachers since.

REFERENCES

American Association for the Advancement of Science. (1989). *Science for all Americans: A project 2061 report on literacy goals in science, mathematics, and technology*. Washington, DC: Author.

Elliot, J. (1991). *Action research for educational change*. Buckingham, UK: Open University Press

King, J., & Lonnquist, M. P. (in press). Learning from the literature: A review of fifty years of writing on action research. In M. Watt (Ed.), *Action research and the reform of mathematics and science education*. New York: Teachers College Press.

Lewin, K. (1946). Action research and minority problems. *Journal of Social Issues, 2*(4), 34–46.

Louis, M. R. (1996). Creating safe havens at work. In D. T. Hall (Ed.), *The career is dead: Long live the career.* San Francisco: Jossey-Bass.

National Council of Teachers of Mathematics. (1989). *Curriculum and evaluation standards for school mathematics.* Reston, VA: Author.

National Council of Teachers of Mathematics. (1991). *Professional standards for teaching mathematics.* Reston, VA: Author.

National Council of Teachers of Mathematics. (1995). *Assessment standards for teaching mathematics.* Reston, VA: Author.

National Research Council. (1994). *National Science Education Standards.* Washington, DC: Author.

Papert, S. (1971). *Teaching children to be mathematicians versus teaching them about mathematics* [Logo Memo #4]. Cambridge, MA: MIT Logo Group.

Papert, S. (1980). *Mindstorms.* New York: Basic Books.

Polya, G. (1957). *How to solve it: A new aspect of mathematical method* (Second ed.). Garden City, NJ: Doubleday.

Somekh, B. (1988, March). *The role of action research in collaborative inquiry and school improvement.* Paper presented at CARN conference, Cambridge, UK.

Watt, M. (1988/1989). A reflective teacher's interventions with a tentative learner of Logo: A case study. *The Computing Teacher, 16*(4), 51–55.

Watt, M. (1989). When teacher and student are stumped. *The Computing Teacher, 16*(8), 30–32.

Watt, M., & Watt, D. (1982). Design criteria for collaborative classroom research. In T. Amabile & M. Stubbs (Eds.), *Psychological research in the classroom: Issues for educators and researcher.* New York: Pergamon.

Watt, M., & Watt, D. (1986). *Teaching with Logo: Building blocks for learning.* Menlo Park, CA: Addison-Wesley.

Watt, M., & Watt, D. (1991, April). *Classroom action research: A professional development opportunity for experienced teachers.* Paper presented at the annual meeting of the American Educational Research Association, Chicago, IL.

Watt, D., & Watt, M. (1992). *Logo learning: Strategies for assessing content and process.* Eugene, OR: International Society for Technology in Education.

Watt, M., & Watt, D. (1993). Action Research, teacher research: The case of the Logo Action Research Collaborative. *Educational Action Research Journal, 1*(1), 35–63.

Watt, M., Watt, D., McKiernan, J., & Schwartz, E. (in press). The Logo Action Research Collaborative: A case study from four perspectives. In M. Watt (Ed.), *Action research and the reform of mathematics and science education.* New York: Teachers College Press.

Youngerman, N. (1993). An action research collaborative from a leader's perspective. In D. L. Watt & M. L. Watt (Eds.), *New paradigms in classroom research on Logo learning* (pp. 127–139) (NECC Monograph). Eugene, OR: International Society for Technology in Education.

CHAPTER 4

Crafting a Sharper Lens

Classroom Assessment in Mathematics

MARK DRISCOLL

"Looks like people have been busy, or is that paper mostly blank?" Theresa was pointing to the piles of student work on the table. Her five teammates chuckled and made nervous jokes about whose papers were neater, more colorful, or more plentiful. Theresa threw her hands in the air in mock disapproval: "I don't think the purpose of the project has sunk in yet!" Then, seriously: "I know this isn't easy—putting tasks and student work out to be scrutinized. It's hard, but let's try to remember our number one ground rule: We're talking primarily about the students' work, the students' understanding, and not about the quality of teaching. Later, when we feel we have a good grasp on students' difficulty with a particular task, then we can put our heads together to plan instruction."

"Well," said Marty, pointing to one of the piles of paper, "I'm going to need some fresh ideas on teaching division of fractions, because this was a real bust."

Frank made a face: "I don't think there *are* any fresh ideas on teaching division of fractions. I usually hold my nose, go through the chapter, and try not to look back." To add emphasis, he held his nose, a gesture that brought a smile to Lois's face: "Oh, great message to be giving your kids, Frank!"

"Again," said Theresa, "let's put a hold on the teaching concerns until we get clear on the assessment data. Marty, talk about what task you gave the kids, why you gave it, what you expected, and what you got back from them."

Helping teachers shift from a focus on themselves to a focus on student understanding represents a radical shift from the way in which staff development is usually conceived and carried out. Traditionally, the emphasis in staff development has been on inducing teachers to alter their classroom behavior.

Yet fundamentally this is putting the cart before the horse. Teachers are exhorted to learn and practice new teaching methods without first being encouraged to assess their students' understanding and skills and, only then, shaping their pedagogical strategies in response to what they observe of student work.

Yet in their observations of elementary teachers' growth, Schifter and Fosnot (1993) have described what appears to be a developmental sequence of stages, marked by teachers' increasing focus on their students' learning rather than on their own instructional behavior. The most able teachers tend to analyze student work, confront student misconceptions, and revise lessons more often than their colleagues. In addition, the most effective teachers tend to think of mathematics in terms of the "big ideas" of the subject, not just in terms of isolated topics. They pay attention, for example, to proportional reasoning, not just to fractions; to equivalence and generalizing from patterns, not just to solving linear equations.

A significant challenge for staff developers is to discover ways to deepen teachers' appreciation for what is worthwhile in mathematics and to do so in ways that can take into account the full context of student understanding and experience. Ideally, staff developers should help teachers craft a sharper lens on their work. Such a lens should help them view mathematical tasks more critically in light of their deepening knowledge of their students and, conversely, to see their students more clearly in the light of their growing appreciation of what makes a mathematical task "worthwhile."

This chapter recounts one model for staff development that my colleagues and I designed to help teachers craft just such a lens. It is a model premised on the central importance of *assessment* but that defines "assessment" in ways that differ substantially from older, more prevalent definitions. The chapter explains why we expected assessment to be an important point of leverage for teacher change; offers criteria for good assessment tasks; illustrates what happens when teachers are encouraged to develop, use, and analyze such tasks; and identifies some of the issues staff developers and teachers are likely to confront if they adopt this model.

HISTORY AND RATIONALE: A MANDATE FOR CHANGE

In 1991, the National Council of Teachers of Mathematics (NCTM) released its *Professional Standards for Teaching Mathematics* as a complement to the 1989 volume *Curriculum and Evaluation Standards for School Mathematics.* The earlier document had addressed the need for radically changed programs in school mathematics, and so-called teaching standards then sought to delineate new roles for individual teachers and for professional communities of teachers. In part because of the unprecedented grassroots development behind both documents, they have become highly visible in the education reform movement. Their popularity and wide support, however, veil some very serious attendant challenges.

For example, consider the difficulty of truly fulfilling the spirit of the first of NCTM's (1991) "teaching standards," quoted in part below:

> Teachers must also consider the students in deciding on the appropriateness of a particular [mathematical] task. They must consider what they know about their particular students as well as what they know more generally about students from psychological, cultural, sociological, and political perspectives. (p. 27)

The document goes on to address the role of teachers in selecting and employing "worthwhile mathematical tasks." Traditionally, this term has offered little room for invention and local adaptation. Others besides teachers—usually textbook authors—have been the arbiters of what are worthwhile tasks and in what sequence they are best administered. Now, however, teachers are being asked to tie both content and instruction to the ***contexts of individual classrooms***, not in a superficial way that makes use of activities with presumed topical relevance for students, but in a way that includes views of student needs from "psychological, cultural, sociological, and political perspectives."

The most fundamental challenges associated with these documents is the challenge to understand and internalize the depth of their meaning and the need to develop processes to support change among teachers. These challenges are not trivial ones. To fully accept the NCTM recommendations is to oblige oneself to shift from a replacing-parts mindset about change to one that is oriented to full-scale restructuring.

RESPONDING TO THE CHALLENGE: FOCUSING ON ASSESSMENT

In reflecting on these challenges, my colleagues and I saw that one appropriate response for school systems would be to create a community of teachers dedicated to transforming their approaches to classroom assessment. Our rationale for designing professional development around classroom assessment was twofold.

First, we believed then, as we do now, that current assessment systems have failed to address inequities in education—particularly in urban education, which has been the focus of our work. In general, assessments provide a very narrow range of information. Instead of providing schools with needed diagnostic supports and tools for inquiring into teaching and learning, external assessments are primarily sorting mechanisms for comparing schools with one another. At the same time, classroom assessments by teachers generally do not aim well at student learning, have a relatively low status in the world of educational data, and vary considerably in quality, in good part because they receive scant attention in teachers' professional development [Stiggins, Conklin, & Bridgeford, 1986]. Most important, present assessment systems fail to provide effective links among learning goals, instruction, and assessment data. Inevitably, if there is not significant attention to assessment as a tool for inquiring into teaching and learning, assessment systems will perpetuate educational inequities because teachers and schools will be left without adequate direction for improvement.

Second, we recognized that to be more effective, future assessment systems ought to rely extensively on teacher-gathered data. By 1991, NCTM's curriculum, evaluation, and teaching standards had made it clear that assessment systems relying primarily on narrow, norm-referenced mathematics assessments were bankrupt and that shifts toward multiple, standards-referenced assessments were needed. Based on our prior work in teacher change (see, e.g., Education Development Center [EDC], 1990a, 1990b), we believed that teachers should be in the foreground, not the background, of reform efforts. We hypothesized that shifts in assessment practices could be enhanced by improving the capacity of mathematics teachers to see the links among curriculum, instruction, and assessment in the classroom. We were convinced of the need for and feasibility of designing a systemically sound approach for teachers to monitor consistency among assessment, instruction, and curriculum. In particular, we wanted to engage teachers in tracking and aligning information and decisions through a three-way feedback loop (see Figure 4.1).

Traditionally, assessment is the afterthought in this feedback loop. However, we reasoned that assessment, properly understood, could be a powerful tool for enabling teachers to move along the continuum Schifter and Fosnot had described. We saw assessment as a fertile ground for teacher development

Figure 4.1.

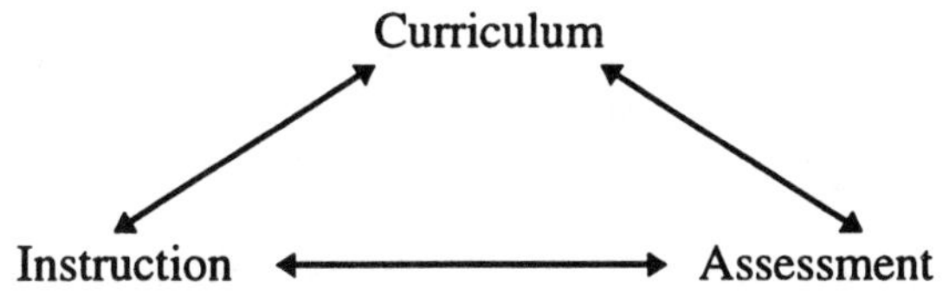

because, when structured appropriately, assessment activities can engage teachers in exactly the kind of active observation and reflection characteristic of constuctivist pedagogy. By revealing students' knowledge and misconceptions, good assessment tasks can provide teachers with a powerful tool for actively reshaping their instruction to fit their students' needs. Moreover, we hoped that teachers would come to see teaching as essentially a process of assessment. We hoped that they would no longer view assessment as a separate end-stage activity used to check knowledge gains *after* instruction, but rather as an ongoing interactive process *of* instruction.

Traditionally, however, assessment has meant looking at student work to measure the extent to which the students "have mastered it." Assessment has focused on measuring, scoring, and reporting to students, parents, and the broader community. There have been very few opportunities to use assessment to look more qualitatively at students' understandings and misconceptions. Even where these opportunities have existed, it has been rare that teachers consciously designed assessment activities and used them to guide their choice of teaching objectives and instructional strategies.

In our effort to meet the challenges set forth by the NCTM standards, we chose to focus on the power inherent in defining assessment in its fuller, less traditional sense. Accordingly, we developed a working definition for this new sort of assessment:

> Assessment is the process of gathering evidence about students' knowledge, skills, and disposition toward mathematics and of making inferences based on that evidence for a variety of purposes, including better understanding of students' needs and more appropriate instructional goals and curriculum design.

As this definition indicates, our goal was to fashion a means for helping teachers to develop assessment activities that would help them understand what students do and do not understand. Second, we wanted teachers to develop assessment tasks that would prompt them to begin thinking in terms of the big mathematical ideas they wanted their students to learn.

Our emphasis on helping teachers design and employ their own assessment activities and then using the information to refashion instruction is in sharp contrast to the traditional emphasis in staff development on merely inducing teachers to alter their classroom behavior. Indeed, we recognized that we were attempting to do something that would not only be very different, but also very difficult. In agreeing to work in this new way, teachers would eventually face hurdles they had not encountered before. It would be our job to structure a process to ease their transition, facilitating their movement from reliance on *assessment as judgment* to *assessment as diagnosis*.

A New Model to Encourage New Kinds of Assessment

To meet these objectives, we designed a model that calls for collaboration among teachers, district mathematics supervisors, and staff at Education Development Center, who act as a liaison among participating schools by providing direct assistance and support to the mathematics supervisors. Entitled the "Classroom Assessment in Mathematics (CAM) Network Project," our work was first funded as a National Eisenhower Project by the Department of Education in 1991. Between 1991 and 1993, the model was field-tested in six Urban Mathematics Collaborative (UMC) cities: Dayton, Memphis, Milwaukee, Pittsburgh, San Diego, and San Francisco.

The CAM model shares many of the same values espoused by the collaboratives, which were conceived by the Ford Foundation in 1985. In particular, two essential commitments are: (1) to improve urban mathematics education through innovative, teacher-driven professional development programs and (2) to focus these programs not on remediation and perceived teacher deficits but rather on the cutting edge of the mathematics reform movement.

We also designed the structure of the CAM project to be consistent with what has been learned from UMC research (e.g., EDC, 1990a, 1990b; Webb, Pittelman, Romberg, Pitman, & Williams, 1988) and other research efforts that have characterized the essential features of productive professional development efforts (e.g., Lichtenstein, McLaughlin, & Knudson, 1992; Little, 1990; Miller & Dorney, 1992). These features include:

- Sustained follow-up, including time for coaching and regular peer interaction
- Greater control by teachers over staff development resources, such as time and materials
- Sensitivity to context, so that teachers and administrators can adapt innovations to meet their own local needs
- Collegial networks that favor experimentation and innovation.

We proposed a structure for CAM in which teachers would engage as a group in a set of *workshop investigations* in assessment, then be supported in their individual *ongoing investigations* in assessment. Within that structure, the key features of the project are:

- *Three national assessment workshops* for the CAM teachers and supervisors, one at the beginning (5 days); one at the end of the first year (3 days); and one at the end of the second year (2 days). The workshops combined teacher activities, such as developing assessment tasks and scoring student work, with interactions with assessment consultants.

- At least *four middle-grade teachers* (*a pair in each of two schools*) *in each of six UMC cities* who, with one release period a day, design and employ alternative approaches to classroom assessment. Within each school, the teacher pairs have the opportunity to collaborate on design. The teachers run the gamut from several who have served as pilot teachers for innovative curriculum projects to teachers who, prior to CAM, were totally dedicated to a textbook and worksheet approach to instruction.
- *Local teams* comprising the four teachers and their district mathematics supervisor, who meet at least once a month to gather information about the teacher experiments, to provide guidance on revisions, and to select samples to be sent to EDC.
- *Regular communication* among the local teams and sharing of sample assessments and commentary, facilitated by EDC staff through an electronic conferencing system, monthly mailings, site visits, and a project newsletter.
- A synthesis of the various project investigations and teacher commentary to form *a staff development guide* for other school districts around the country.

Thus the project, with teachers and supervisors working concurrently in six cities, is conceived as a system having two interconnected feedback loops. Local team meetings allow individual teachers to get feedback and guidance on task construction and revision. The national database and communication from EDC allow teams to adapt or embellish tasks submitted by teams from other cities and to benefit from the commentary of their colleagues regarding the tasks.

Building Three Core Capacities

Throughout the project, we have been interested in helping teachers develop three core capacities. We want teachers to understand how assessments can be used:

1. To evaluate what students do and do not know and how they learn
2. To select and invent curriculum and instructional strategies that are more finely tuned to meet student needs
3. To probe what mathematics learning should be valued—to discern what, in NCTM's phrase, is "worthwhile mathematics."

Assessing What's Valued; Valuing What's Assessed: Theresa and Marty's Story

Following are two brief cases from the project, adapted from interviews with CAM teachers and mathematics supervisors, that illustrate how the teachers have engaged in and been supported in building these three capacities. The first case focuses primarily on the first and third core capacities, using assessments to evaluate what students do and do not know about mathematics and exploring the issue of what kind of mathematics is worth learning. The second case focuses on the second objective, demonstrating how an assessment orientation leads to revisions in pedagogy and curriculum design. The second case also illustrates the difficulty in attempting to truly engage with the NCTM standards' call for more attention to the cultural, political, and uniquely individual characteristics of urban students living in poverty.

For the first case, we pick up the story of Theresa and Marty with which we began this chapter. As the reader may recall, Marty felt that his lesson on teaching division of fractions was "a real bust," but Theresa, a project facilitator and the mathematics supervisor in Marty's district, was trying to refocus his attention away from himself and onto the ways in which Marty's students had handled the task he had given them and what he could learn about them from how they had approached the problem.

> "Again," said Theresa, "let's put a hold on the teaching concerns until we get clear on the assessment data. Marty, talk about what task you gave the kids, why you gave it, what you expected, and what you got back from them."
>
> In response to Theresa's invitation and her reframing of the discussion, Marty explains: "We had just completed the section on dividing fractions last week. I waited a few days into the next chapter and, without telling them anything about it, I gave the kids a task that involved dividing fractions. I wanted to see if they could apply the rule for dividing fractions—you know, invert and multiply."
>
> Frank, Marty's teaching partner, leaned forward: "What was the task?"
>
> Marty started circulating a few of the papers: "I told them: 'You have two candles, one is 6 inches tall and the other is 12 inches tall. If the 6-inch candle burns ¼ of an inch every hour and the 12-inch candle burns ½ inch every hour, which candle will last longer? Show and explain all of your work.'
>
> "By the way," Marty continued, "a good number said they didn't know what a candle was. I anticipated this and had one with me and, when they saw it, there was a lot of: 'Oh, so *that's* a candle.'"
>
> Lois shook her head slowly: "Yeah, it's easy to make wrong assumptions about cultural knowledge and background experiences."
>
> Theresa, who with Maria had been skimming Marty's students' work, held up a handful of the papers: "But, Marty, from your opening comment, I expected a disaster. There seems to be a lot of interesting work here. What bothered you?"

Then Marty revealed the reason for his discomfort: "Not one of the students used the rule for dividing fractions! It was as if we never covered the topic."

Theresa started laying the papers on the table so they could examine them: "OK, let's look and see what the students did do. Here are two that seem different from each other. What's going on here, do you think?" (See Figure 4.2)

Maria pointed enthusiastically to one of the papers: "Well, this child made a table and compared the change every 4 hours to show they'd both burn out after 24 hours. That's nice, Marty."

Frank pointed to the other paper: "And this kid found how many quarter-inches are in 6 inches, and how many half-inches are in 12 inches, and compared. I guess he divided."

Theresa was nodding and, like the others, leaning with interest over the two papers: "Yes, the one made a rate table; the other did a direct division. Both of them seemed to be thinking proportionally."

Marty appeared irritated by the enthusiastic response: "But, I didn't get what I wanted! And not just in these two. If you look, you'll see the other papers are similar."

Lois sat back: "You mean they didn't use the division rule? Is that important? The kids showed they know how to do the task, didn't they?"

"*Isn't* it important?" asked Marty. "The book devotes a bunch of pages to it."

"Yeah," Frank said, "but is it important that they know the invert-and-multiply rule when they're 25 years old? That's my rule of thumb on what's important."

Theresa went to the chalkboard: "Deciding what's important is key to what we are about in this project—what's the important mathematics we want the students to understand? Then, the other half of our focus—what understanding does their work show?"

She picked up a piece of chalk and wrote two column headings: "Understandings Revealed" and "Difficulties." Under the first heading, she wrote: "Rate of change; the concept of division (involving fractions)."

"Now, these are two understandings we find are there, at least for individual students. What else did you see?"

Maria replied: "Well, the one child showed an understanding of how to use tables to order and extend the information given."

Under the first column, Theresa added "making tables" and "organizing information."

Figure 4.2.

They'll both burn down at the same time because there are 4 1/4s in a whole and there are 6 wholes and $6 \times 4 = 24$. And in 12 inches there are 2 1/2s in every whole and 12 wholes $12 \times 2 = 24$. They both burn in approximately 24 hours.

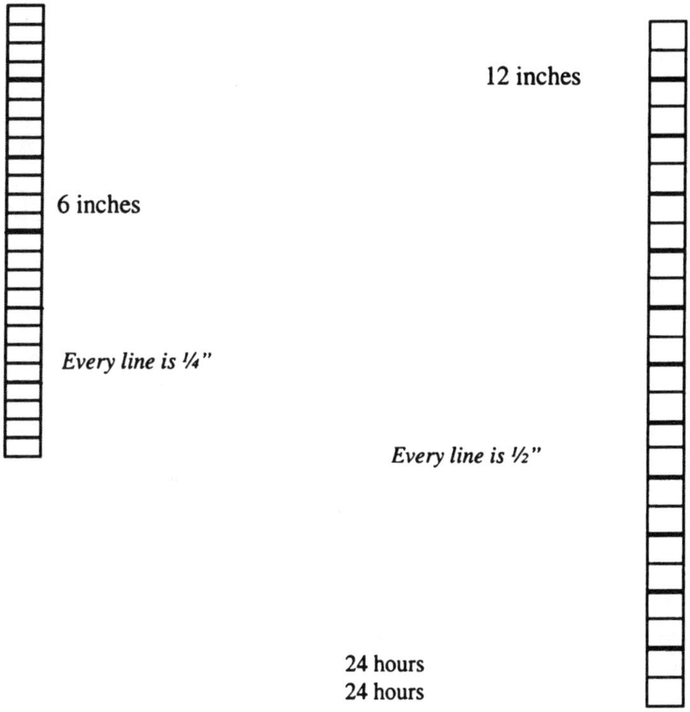

They'll both burn the same amount. They both take the same amount of time. After every four hours the 12-inch candle will burn twice as much as the 6-inch candle. So after 24 hours they'll both be gone. So neither one will burn longer; they are both the same. Every four hours the 12-inch candle burns down two inches and the 6-inch candle goes down one inch every four hours.

Hours	*12"*	*6"*
4	2	1
8	4	2
12	6	3
16	8	4
20	10	5
24	12	6

"I want us to keep going on this list as we analyze each of the papers, to get a snapshot of what understandings the group revealed. Then, in this other column, we make a list of what misunderstandings and learning difficulties appear."

Pointing to the other side of the board, Theresa added: "Where does the division-of-fractions rule belong? On the learning difficulty list? What do you think, Marty?"

Marty looked uncertain: "I don't know. Can we make a list of 'things forgotten'? That's where I'm afraid division-of-fractions has gone."

Everyone laughed—a brief, but evidently welcome, moment of relief—after which Lois returned to the question: "But we don't know anything about their understanding of the rule because the activity didn't ask for that specifically, and the task could be solved without the rule. In fact, Marty, I'd say you should be pleased with the knowledge of the concept of division shown by your students, at least these two we've looked at."

This time, Marty looked really stuck, so Theresa said: "Let's put aside for the moment the question of how important in the big picture this division-of-fractions rule is. Later, if you'd like, we can put together a task that could assess how well the students understand that particular rule. In the meantime, let's continue to look at what the rest of Marty's students did on the task, and add to the lists on the board."

At that, Theresa rejoined the group at the table, where Maria was already dividing the pile of papers into smaller piles and handing them around.

The team interactions in Marty's case, like many in CAM, raise issues about what is worthwhile mathematics to teach and to assess. No one in the story—in particular, Marty—had any epiphanies about the issue. Change in the project comes through a dynamic, iterative process of task selection–examination of student work–task revision, all supported by adequate time for reflection and discussion. In the complex world of urban mathematics teaching, the meaning of "worthwhile" has to be negotiated from a web of information, itself drawn from the students' diverse backgrounds, the content of mandated textbooks, and the aspirations and values of earnest teachers undertaking "reform."

Although we do not see consensus emerge about what constitutes worthwhile mathematics, the vignette does highlight the crucial role the mathematics supervisor plays by asking carefully selected questions and constantly reframing teachers' orientations so that they do not lose sight of the main point: observation of student work and reflection on what that work reveals about student understanding. Notice the key statements and questions Theresa used:

"Let's put a hold on the teaching concerns until we get clear on the assessment data"
"Talk about what task you gave the kids, why you gave, what you expected, and what you got back from them."
"There seems to be a lot of interesting work here."
"What bothered you?"
"OK, let's look and see what the students did here."
"What's going on here, do you think?"

All these statements and questions invite the teachers to look more closely at what student work reveals about student understanding. Theresa's questions and statements keep the teachers focused on active observation. In addition, compiling a list of "Student Understandings" and "Difficulties" further prompted the teachers to focus on what they were seeing in the student work, and this strategy was a subtle way for Theresa to insist that changes in pedagogy and task construction follow from those observations. In our view, this kind of emphasis on description followed by analysis and reflection is key to the promotion of change in teachers' development.

Marty and Theresa's case also lightly touched on the challenges of working with urban students whose cultural knowledge is often quite different from suburban and rural children's and also different from their teachers' knowledge and assumptions. The fact that some kids did not know what a candle is did not surprise Marty, who was used to teaching in an urban setting, but might have caught other less experienced or more naive teachers off guard. Even when teachers are prepared for these differences, the divide between the life experiences of students from different backgrounds can be daunting, as can poor students' lack of equal access to resources such as home computers and expensive art materials.

Good Work Gets Better: Howard's and Gwen's Story

The next case we are about to take up illustrates some of the problems stated above. It also illustrates the important interplay between assessment and eventual redesign of instructional strategies so that they can better meet students' needs.

> Sipping his coffee and inching his way around the classroom, Howard was bewildered. He glanced at one student poster, then another, and shook his head. The graphs were fine. Better, in fact, than he had expected they would be in depicting the survey data his students had collected. Some students even used double bar graphs to divide boys

and girls; others worked carefully to scale on their bar graphs—one unit equaling five students or ten students.

But the student paragraphs that were arranged next to the posters missed the mark totally—they didn't do at all what they were supposed to do: describe the typical Steele School sixth-grader. In fact, they hardly did any of the interpretation that Howard had hoped for—no comparisons, no descriptions of unusual results, no references to percentages. Not even a mention of *mean* or *median*, two concepts the class had recently covered. Where did they go astray? Why couldn't they write the paragraphs if they understood the mathematics?

Another problem dogged Howard in this, his first venture into alternative assessment through mathematics poster presentations. Of the eight students who didn't turn in a poster, seven were Chapter 1 [now called Title 1] students. He thought about this for a few seconds, jotted a note to himself for Wednesday's meeting, and turned off the classroom light.

At Wednesday's CAM team meeting, Howard told his story to Betty and Jules, his sixth-grade team partners, and to Warren, the Chapter 1 teacher. "Same in my class," said Jules. "The lack of writing, I mean. I didn't check on the Chapter 1 kids."

"Well, I did," said Betty. "A few of them didn't turn in anything. A few others were off the mark on both the graph and the explanations, and the others were off the mark on the explanations. But so were all but one or two students in the class!"

"With my kids," said Warren, "I know that they had no idea of how to start writing down anything about the survey. I don't think they had a clue what you wanted them to write."

"Nor how you wanted it to look, maybe," interjected Gwen, the principal, as she approached some of the posters spread on the desk, next to the box of doughnuts. "I didn't mean to interrupt, but this was such a heated discussion, I thought I'd stick my nose in . . . Some of these look so polished. . . . Did they work on them at home?"

"Some did," answered Howard, and Betty and Jules nodded. "Not my kids," said Warren. "I don't think a single one took a poster home."

"Well, that could be part of the problem," offered Gwen, as she moved from the posters to the doughnuts. "At least it could explain why some are missing. It certainly could explain the difference in quality of presentation—some having a computer at home, or tagboard, or different-colored markers, and others having nothing. We have a lot of those things, and more, in the resource room—yardsticks, T-squares —all the makings for a good visual presentation. Why don't you try again but, this time, let's keep the resource room open before and after school. . . . Is that the only jelly doughnut, Betty?"

Howard lit up: "Wait a minute. . . . Let's go a step further. If none of us talked with our classes about what we expected in the way the poster presentations *looked*—that's what you're saying, right, Gwen? That some of the kids might have been turned off because they didn't have an equal chance to make their posters attractive to look at? . . . Then neither did we . . . or at least I . . . tell them what the written interpretations should look like."

Betty started to get animated, too, and waved her jelly doughnut in the air: "Yeah, we could talk to them about the quality of writing . . . or, better yet, we could show them a range of examples and have *them* talk about quality—what's clear, what isn't; what matches the graphs; what doesn't . . ." Suddenly, the hand and jelly doughnut stopped waving, and Betty's tone grew less enthusiastic: "Hold on, though, I don't want them tearing up each other's work."

"Oh, you could set rules on that, I'm sure," said Gwen, "but it seems to me that you don't even have to. Since each of you three did the same task, you could trade sets of student responses . . . Howard could photocopy and use a set of yours, Betty, you could use a set from Jules, and so on. And have your students look over the work from another class."

Jules, balancing his chair back on two legs and arching his brow, was doubtful: "Then what do we do after we discuss the quality of the presentation . . . have them do the poster boards over again? It's messy and isn't it going to deflate them a bit?" The question reignited Howard: "We don't have to! And you're right, Jules, we don't want them to lose sight of the fact that we think the quality of their graphing is *fine*—it's the interpretation and presentation we have to concentrate on . . . But, you know what we can do? . . . We can generate a set of data on Steele faculty—just like the kids did for the sixth-graders—and we can have them do another poster presentation."

Betty finished brushing sugar granules into a small, neat pile by her coffee cup, then beamed: "OK. Let's do it. What do we go after in the survey . . . types of cars, faculty age ranges?" Exiting the room just as quietly as she entered it, Gwen waved good-bye: "You're on to some exciting stuff. Good luck. Don't forget to leave the resource room open for help."

A week later, at the team meeting, there was an air of guarded self-congratulation, as Howard, Betty, Jules, and Warren scanned the several dozen posters spread across the table. Betty was almost singing as she fingered through them: "O-o-h, look at this one. 'Twice as many teechers at Steele grew up in big familys than as the only child. Maybe they became teechers becuz they are used to bein around kids.' That's great! To do it, she had to pick a cutoff for "large family" then aggregate the numbers of large-family teachers. Then she proposed an explanation. I think they're catching on!"

Howard's smile faded a bit: "Yeah, I'm pleased . . . I mean, the writing is lots better . . . most talked about mean and median, and some went way beyond, but I was disappointed that a bunch still didn't turn anything in." "Right," nodded Warren," I'm disappointed, too . . . I thought the message got through to most . . . but I have an idea. Do you think the three of you could come up with a checklist—a spec sheet, really—of the kinds of things you want them to put in their written explanations? If you could . . . I mean, I know some kids I work with could really use that kind of organizational help."

"That," said Howard, his smile regaining its luster, "is a fantastic idea."

Howard's story illuminates the fact that we learned to place importance on a disciplined flow from assessment to instruction back to assessment, and how this iterative process can empower both teachers and students. A careful look at the role that Gwen, the principal, played also shows that—as in the previous story of Theresa and Marty—with just the right set of questions or statements, a staff supervisor can have a subtle yet profound influence on teachers' insights and development. Like Theresa, Gwen chose a few simple points of leverage. For example, she offered an explanation for why the Chapter 1 kids might not have been able to do the assignment and offered a simple solution—keeping the resource room open before and after school—to create easier access to the computer and art supplies. She also built on the teachers' idea of having the kids assess each other's work, suggesting that the teachers' swap student work so that kids would not be assessing the work of the students in their own classrooms.

Both cases demonstrate how perceptions about assessment shifted during the course of the project: All of us in the project began to appreciate the power of assessment as an ongoing process to raise questions for professional inquiry. How important *is* the division-of-fractions algorithm? Do students understand the connection between data and its interpretation? How *can* equitable resources be made available so that Chapter 1 students have the opportunity to perform up to standards? In contrast with more typical staff development programs, CAM has made inquiry into questions such as these the very fiber of the teachers' professional development experiences.

Our use of the two stories also demonstrates something important about the power of story itself to motivate teacher change and to create a professional community among otherwise isolated individuals. In part because of the distances that separate project participants, we have been bound together by the fabric of teacher stories. Stories have brought us together in our struggles, have driven efforts to change, and have helped to crystallize important change. They have proved to be a learning tool as well as a humanizing force. Marty's story has been recounted numerous times when questions about important mathematics arise; similarly, Howard's story has provided useful reminders about attending to students' opportunities to perform and learn. There is good epistemological sense in this flowering of narrative: CAM has stressed the integrative power of teachers actively linking assessment with learning and teaching; one of the mechanisms of this integration is narrative, because of its power to raise complex issues in an accessible and economical way. As CAM evolves to its next stages, we will look for ways to capitalize on the force of narrative in professional development and teacher support.

USING ASSESSMENT TO PROMOTE STAFF DEVELOPMENT: SOME LESSONS LEARNED

Within the framework of the three core capacities mentioned previously, we have focused on helping teachers select or design tasks for gathering evidence and on using that evidence to draw valid inferences. The assessment tasks that the teachers have used fall mainly into three categories: *questions* they ask their students (open-ended or single-answer, oral or written in the form of quizzes or tests); *observations* of student work (individual or group work); *student products* (such as projects, journals, impromptu writing assignments, homework, portfolios). Yet, regardless of the particular tasks on which the teachers settle, we have found that there are three main issues it is important for staff supervisors to address: developing "good taste;" drawing valid inferences; and balancing attention to student understanding with attention to student mastery.

Developing "Good Taste": Recognizing Worthwhile Tasks

Considerable attention in the project has been paid to our developing good taste in choosing assessment tasks. Good taste evolves from persistent attention to the question: What are some characteristics of good assessment tasks? Ideally, assessment tasks should reveal the thinking—and misunderstandings—students bring to the tasks. Thus, in any representative collection of tasks, there should be particular attention paid to typical conceptual stumbling blocks for students, such as the concept of unit in rational numbers (i.e., the reference whole that the fraction is a part of). In addition, tasks should help students grapple with important mathematical ideas, such as proportional reasoning and the concept of function. Worthwhile tasks should be educative for the students, with multiple entry points for students with varying backgrounds; they should reflect what is valued in mathematics learning; they should be sensitive to the contexts in which they are being used; and they should aim *directly* at knowledge that is valued.

Part of our training in CAM has emphasized techniques in developing and adapting worthwhile tasks. Thus, in Howard's case, the task required that students collect and display descriptive statistics and then interpret those data in meaningful ways. On many levels this task scores well as a "worthwhile task." It requires students not only to organize a descriptive display of data but also to apply critical thinking skills to understand what the information is really telling them. Yet, as the case vignette makes clear, it did not offer "multiple entry" points for all students and did not, at least in its first instantiation, fully take into account the problems some students might have in gaining access to the materials necessary for doing an adequate job. Thus it was conceptually a sound task, but one in need of further revision to become even more worthwhile.

Sometimes, however, a task falls far short of the mark, and teachers must be helped to articulate why the task is not worthwhile and to decide whether to jettison the task or revise it in some fundamental way. Furthermore, it isn't always possible to anticipate exactly where students will head with a task, as the following example demonstrates.

The San Francisco CAM team wanted to assess eighth graders' understanding of fractional parts of regions and their use of alternate representations (e.g., decimals, percents). They liked an item from the California State Department of Education that they had used in an assessment workshop (see Example A, Figure 4.3), because it had elicited rich and varied responses. But they thought the context, a painted board game, was unrealistic and boring. To instill more relevance and life in the task, they changed the context to restaurant smoking areas (Example B, Figure 4.3) and attempted to make the task more open-ended by asking about perceived risk.

The new task engaged students, but the teachers were surprised to find that it prompted responses that contained little information about fractions and alternate representations. Students had engaged in solving the risk question, focusing on context, with little consideration for mathematics. As summarized in the team's monthly report to EDC:

> After realizing that there were many possible correct answers, according to how the problem was interpreted, we looked at what the possible answers were. Some students felt that one out of the four

Figure 4.3.

DIRECTIONS TO THE STUDENT: This is an open-ended question. Your answer will be judged on how well you show your understanding of mathematics and on how well you can explain it to others. Please write your response in the space below the question and on the next page, if necessary.

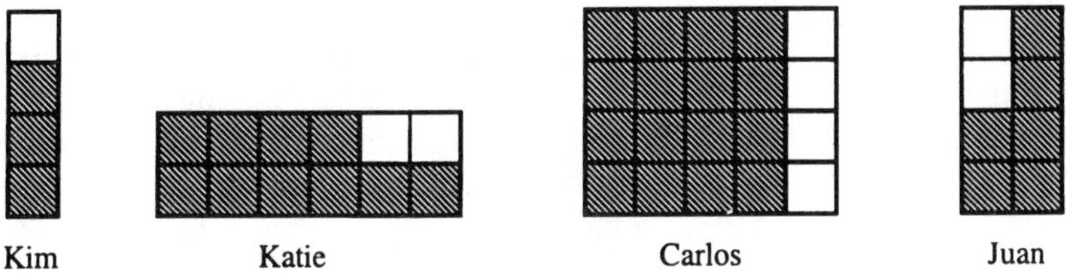

Example A: Game Context

Four friends are making game boards of different sizes and shapes. They each painted part of their game board (shaded area), as you can see from the pictures above.

Katie says that she has the greatest fractional part of her game board unpainted. Kim, Juan, and Carlos disagree with Katie. Please settle the argument and help each student to understand your answer. Use a diagram if it will help you to explain.

Example B: Restaurant Context

These are floor plans of four different restaurants. You have been offered a job waiting on tables at these four different restaurants. A recent study shows secondhand smoke from restaurant patrons dramatically increases the risk of lung cancer in restaurant workers. Which restaurant will offer you the least risk? Explain.

(The shaded area represents non-smoking area.)

rooms set aside for smoking would pose the least risk, because that would make for the fewest smoking rooms of all the restaurants. Others figured the percentage of each restaurant that was designated "smoking" and answered that the restaurant with the smallest percent would pose the least risk. A few students answered using false probability: "I would have a 25% chance of getting lung cancer in this restaurant as opposed to a 17% chance in the other."

The teachers' group concluded that, since their goal had been to elicit convincing comparisons of fractions and/or percents, it might have been better to ask the students to back up or refute the claim of one of the restaurants that it had the smallest percentage of space devoted to smoking. Later, the Pittsburgh team tried that alteration and were able to verify that the revised task was more reliable in eliciting comparisons of percentages.

Drawing Valid Inferences

In order to be an effective tool for diagnosing students' skills and improving instruction, the assessment process has to be complete, meaning that it is not sufficient to gather evidence without careful attention to making valid inferences based on that evidence. Therefore we developed several devices and structures that supervisors and group leaders could use to help teachers make and critically examine inferences. One such structure is ongoing experimental discussion groups, where teachers can inquire together and examine their inferences collectively. The cases of both Marty and Howard reveal the variety of inferences that have been examined in the project. These include:

1. *Inferences about evidence in student work of important mathematics learning* (e.g., several of Marty's colleagues saw evidence in the student work of an understanding of the concept of division)
2. *Inferences about students' opportunity to learn what has been or will be assessed* (e.g., Howard and his colleagues tested their hypothesis about absence of work by the Chapter 1 students)
3. *Inferences about the alignment of the prompt in a task with the purpose of the task* (e.g., Lois commented that the student work revealed nothing about their understanding of the division-of-fractions rule, because the activity didn't prompt them to communicate that knowledge)
4. *Inferences about evidence in student work of possible misconceptions or misunderstandings* (e.g., Howard inferred that many of his students were unaware of, or didn't understand, his standards for written interpretations)

Another device that has encouraged critical examination of inferences is the regular, structured teacher report, wherein we explicitly ask the teachers to reflect on their tasks and student work submitted that month. Such reports help teachers focus on what works or doesn't work, and why. For example, in one report a Milwaukee teacher, whom I will call Ellen, told how she adapted a task for her eighth-grade algebra students:

> A man needed his lawn cut for a big party he was giving that evening. The lawn was very large. He called an employment agency and Tomika, Tiffany, and Harold were sent to him.
>
> I can do the job in 6 hours, Tomika said.
>
> But I can do the whole lawn in 4 hours, Tiffany said.
>
> Wait! I'll do it in 3 hours, Harold said.
>
> The owner did not know whom to hire. Since it was late and the job needed to be done in 1 hour, the owner said, "I will hire all three of you."

Your job is to decide whether Tomika, Tiffany, and Harold would be able to finish the job in 1 hour or not.

Write your solution, and include a drawing.

Ellen used the task to see how well her students understood fractions when their use is not explicitly prompted. She reported: "We had not been studying fractions per se, but this class was used to reading/studying new situations and writing their solutions . . . I didn't expect the results I got." Generally, the results indicated that the students were thinking in the right direction about proportioning the work but didn't express the proportions numerically, that is, as rational numbers. As a consequence, much of the reasoning was vague and incomplete.

Together with the full class, Ellen analyzed four of the solutions and helped the group to develop a better solution. She then drew some inferences for her instruction: "This book doesn't deal with fractions . . . It is an algebra book. I am thinking of a few units to begin next year before starting this text. One of the units will be on fractional thinking, not fractional arithmetic. They seem to know the arithmetic but connections are not being made."

Inferences such as Ellen's are a part of most teachers' planning in response to student work. What is distinctive about our approach is the explicit nature of drawing inferences. Through its structured team meetings and teacher reports, CAM has elevated the process of drawing inferences to a more visible plane and attempted to make it part of the fiber of staff development for teachers.

Balancing Attention to Student Understanding with Attention to Student Mastery

In our view, teachers who analyze student work need to address two distinct, though related, sets of questions:

- *What does this student work reveal about the student's understanding related to the task?* Are there evident misconceptions at play here? Are there any misunderstandings connected to the instruction leading to this task? What are the next instructional steps to take?
- *What does this student work reveal about the extent to which the student has achieved the desired outcome?* What is the measure of the quality of the student performance? How close to standards is the performance? Do the standards and the task itself reflect all that is valued in the desired outcome? To what extent do current curriculum materials and instructional methods support students in attaining the desired outcomes?

In many ways, the story of CAM is the story of our efforts to balance our attention to these two kinds of questions, focusing both on understanding and on mastery. The balance is essential if we are to improve instruction in line with the NCTM standards. A teacher who sees the purpose of a task to be purely evaluative will likely react to a faulty student answer by correcting the student or merely rewording, rather than rethinking, the question. On the other hand, a teacher whose understanding of "assessment" extends beyond simple evaluation of student mastery is likely to ask a series of questions structured to uncover the student's thinking. Using assessment activities as a kind of dialogue to uncover student thinking is at the heart of the student-centered approach to instruction that NCTM advocates.

The early days of the project were a lesson to us in how extensively perspectives on assessment have been knocked out of balance by a system in which quantitative measures of student behavior are given excessive weight. Traditionally, assessment has meant looking at student work to measure the extent to which the students "have mastered it" and to separate students according to the side of the line on which they fall. Assessment has not been about looking more qualitatively at what understanding or breakdowns in understanding the student work reveals—and how instruction can respond. This latter point—that assessment can be a tool for instruction—has been an especially empowering realization for the CAM teachers. As a Milwaukee teacher wrote in her project reflections:

> Assessing not only means finding out what a student understands and doesn't understand, but it also informs my instruction. "Not everything that counts can be counted and not everything that can be counted counts."—I read [that] this was posted on Albert Einstein's office wall.

Yet teachers need help in coming to this realization, and staff supervisors and group leaders can play an exceedingly useful role here.

During the course of the project, I was able to visit sites and participate in CAM team meetings. At one of these meetings, relatively early in the project, I listened as each of the six teachers, in turn, summarized their students' responses to an assessment task. Alice reported that she had given her students, who had already "covered" fractions and decimals with her, the task shown in Figure 4.4:

In her account of the student responses, Alice said that she had been surprised at how confused her students (a "smart" group) had been with the task; that when she prompted them further by telling them they should "think fractions," they performed much better. She seemed focused on the fact that the students "didn't get it" but did not go further in her analysis. I was intrigued

Figure 4.4.

Directions: Label each number line.
Tell everything you know about each number line.

6___?___?___?___?___?___?___?___?___?___7

0__________?__________?__________1

by this account and waited for others in the group to ask what I wanted to ask, namely: "Why do you think the original task caused such confusion? Might they not have internalized that fractions are numbers, with number-line relationships to whole numbers?" But no one asked, and the discussion moved on to the next teacher.

For me, this story illustrates how easy it is to underestimate the deep connections between mathematics instruction and standardized testing, connections that run so deep that the working vision of assessment among most CAM teachers at the start of the project was ***summary*** evaluation. A teacher who sees the purpose of a question to be purely evaluative will likely react to a faulty student answer by rewording the question or correcting the student. Therefore it is important to formally build key questions into the structure of CAM team meetings. The group leader needs to be sure that participants do not only ask "Did they get it?" but also "What misconceptions or misunderstandings are revealed by this student's work?" "What inferences about this student's thinking can we draw from the way she has approached the problem?" Without someone being sure that these kinds of questions are raised, team meeting and assessment work in general cannot fulfill their promise.

LIMITATIONS, CONSTRAINTS, AND NEW DIRECTIONS

The CAM Network Project was an ambitious project on several counts. It aimed to take the NCTM Standards seriously by empowering teachers to reframe their understanding and beliefs about classroom assessment and worthwhile mathematical tasks. It explored—and hoped to define—conditions for taking a constructivist approach to staff development. At the same time, it intended to provide balanced and helpful support for teachers with the time, resources, and opportunities for collaboration necessary to perform and learn from experiments in alternative assessment.

Inevitably, such aspirations led to our confronting several important limitations and constraints on our ability to fully realize this vision. The first relates to the impact of context on equity and students' opportunities to learn. The second has to do with the need for appropriate teacher support.

Equity and Access: The Politics of Reform

CAM teachers worked in classrooms with students from diverse ethnic and class backgrounds who spoke many different languages. In the face of such diversity and, particularly, in the context of urban poverty, opportunities to learn and to demonstrate knowledge are highly complex and problematic. Teachers have become concerned that students vary widely in family and other out-of-school experiences that could prepare them for open-ended and inquiry-based instruction. In our final national workshop, in August 1993, they expressed the fear that, in our rush to reform mathematics education in urban schools, we might reinvent the old social arithmetic of haves and have-nots.

In a written reflection prepared for that last conference, one of the San Francisco CAM teachers framed the issue this way:

> We find ourselves expanding the curriculum from the textbook-oriented, low-level skills that emphasized computation and some problem solving to include "complete work." Units challenge students to use math ideas, problem solving, tools and techniques, and communication—both individually and collaboratively. Not only has the content of our classrooms changed, but also the method we use has shifted away from a teacher-oriented class to a more student-centered class where students construct their own understanding of concepts.

The challenge to fold students' "complete work" into their assessment frameworks led CAM teachers to attend more to issues of context and equity—in particular, to how contextual variables impact on students' opportunities to learn. A striking recognition of this came in a question from several of the San Francisco teachers, which was raised in their team meeting and eventually became a focal point for the third national CAM workshop: *Is constructivism just a middle-class luxury?* With rapid classroom changes being urged, if not thrust on them, the teachers worriedly conjecture that there are critical class-background differences dividing students, related to learning and guidance outside of school, and that classroom interventions alone may not be sufficient to provide the appropriate opportunities to learn in open-ended and inquiry-driven settings.

The issue reaches to the core of urban teaching and extends beyond the classroom and school to the broader contexts in which the students live. To a large extent, the teachers who raised the issue have met the NCTM challenge and considered "what they know about their particular students as well as what they know more generally about students from psychological, cultural, sociological, and political perspectives." But in doing so, they may have drifted beyond their capacities to reform students' opportunities to learn mathematics and illuminated the mandate for a full systemic response with more than just the rhetoric of reform.

Support for Teacher Experimentation and Development

The EDC/district combination offered a blanket of support for the teachers' work by providing time for planning; regular team meetings; district encouragement and the direct support and involvement of the mathematics supervisors; three national conferences focusing on important classroom assessment issues; information, encouragement, and other resources through the electronic network and through mailings. It was our intention to let this blanket protect the teachers in their experimentation—in particular, from expectations for rapid change and improvement. Toward that end, we gave them considerable space to "mess around," especially in year 1.

Judging from CAM's final evaluation report (Cutler & LaBue, 1993), all of the CAM teachers benefited considerably from the freedom to experiment in the first year—especially in their appreciation and understanding of assessment's ability to inform instruction. However, according to the project evaluators, despite the teachers' expanding appreciation of assessment as a tool for constant improvement of instruction, there was considerable variation in the amount of instructional change actually effected by the teachers. As a result, the evaluators recommend that extensions of CAM add another component: teacher–teacher mentoring and classroom coaching, which could capitalize on the changing appreciation of assessment as a tool for improvement as well as on the evident mutual trust and sense of community that characterize the CAM teams.

On the national level, we have been working from EDC to establish a full system of *support* for the teachers and their teams. We have wanted it to be a system in the full meaning of the term—that is, a dynamic structure that fuses EDC's knowledge base on assessment and instruction with the growing knowledge base in each CAM site and that moves information fluidly throughout the districts, with timely feedback.

The teachers have made excellent use of the feedback and the collaboration—their impressive accomplishments are testimony to that. However, we have found that—even in the six cooperative CAM districts—time and supportive leadership for teachers occasionally fall victim to shrinking budgets and realigned political agendas. Such systemic snags, in turn, have slowed the flow of information from the district teams to EDC and then back again to the six districts.

A systemic approach like ours to the challenges of urban mathematics education makes sense because it is premised on the belief that the cross-district collaboration yields a whole much greater than the sum of its parts. In addition, it makes sense because it moves those of us in education away from the pursuit of simple answers to complex questions and toward a framework for seeing patterns and interrelationships and for incorporating regular feedback of new learnings into the professional development of teachers.

But the effectiveness of a cross-district system like ours is deeply dependent on the reliability and responsiveness of the individual school systems. In any continuation of CAM or in similar endeavors, the currencies of time, resources, and supportive leadership must be reliably secure, so that participating teachers can reap the full benefit of this innovative model of staff development.

ACKNOWLEDGMENTS

In the writing of this chapter, I had the invaluable help of my two CAM Project co-directors, Diane Briars and Maria Santos, who provided key anecdotes and helped me to organize this description of our project.

REFERENCES

Cutler, A. B., & LaBue, M. A. (1993). Classroom assessment in mathematics network: Final evaluation report. Education Matters, Inc., December.

Duckworth, E. (1987). *The having of wonderful ideas and other essays on teaching and learning.* New York: Teachers College Press.

Education Development Center (EDC). (1990a). *The urban mathematics collaboratives: A handbook.* Newton, MA: Author.

Education Development Center (EDC). (1990b). *The urban mathematics collaboratives: A sourcebook.* Newton, MA: Author

Lichtenstein, G., McLaughlin, M., & Knudsen, J. (1992). Teacher empowerment and professional knowledge. *1991 NSSE yearbook.* Chicago: University of Chicago Press.

Little, J. W. (1990). Conditions of professional development in secondary schools. In M. W. McLaughlin, J. E. Talbert, & N. Bascia (Eds.), *The context of teaching in secondary schools: Teachers' realities* (pp. 187–223). New York: Teachers College Press.

Miller, B., & Dorney, J. (1992). *The impact of teacher leadership workshops.* Unpublished paper, Education Development Center, Newton, MA.

National Council of Teachers of Mathematics. (1989). *Curriculum and evaluation standards for school mathematics.* Reston, VA: Author.

National Council of Teachers of Mathematics. (1991). *Professional standards for teaching mathematics.* Reston, VA: Author.

Schifter, D., & Fosnot, C. T. (1993). *Reconstructing mathematics education: Stories of teachers meeting the challenge of reform.* New York: Teachers College Press.

Stiggins, R., Conklin, N., & Bridgeford, N. (1986). Classroom assessment: A key to effective education. *Journal of Educational Measurement, 5*(2), 5–17.

Webb, N. L., Pittelman, S. D., Romberg, T. A., Pitman, A. J., & Williams, S. R. (1988). *The Urban Mathematics Collaborative Project: Report to the Ford Foundation on the 1986–87 school year* (Program Report 88–1). Madison: University of Wisconsin, School of Education, Wisconsin Center for Education Research.

CHAPTER 5

Talking in School

Constructive Conversations for Written Language

MAUREEN KEOHANE RILEY AND CATHERINE COBB MOROCCO

Collaboration, like conversation, means that others are involved in your inquiry and that others live in your text in intimate and connected ways. (Harste, 1994)

In our everyday lives, we build intimacy and gain new insights through conversation. For those same reasons, conversation should have a central place in learning in school. Throughout this century, Piaget, Dewey, Bruner, Vygotsky, and Bakhtin have explained why children learn best when they are actively and curiously involved and why dialogue is central to that activity. Recent thinkers too (Bruffee, 1986; Englert & Palincsar, 1991) suggest that knowledge is socially constructed as members of a literacy community negotiate ideas and build consensus and shared meaning. All of this strong theoretical and intuitive support for the role of conversation in learning should make talk a core activity in school and yet, in many of our classrooms, we see young children sitting quietly to learn.

During the first exploratory 18 months of a 4-year study of teacher planning in third- and fourth-grade classrooms, a project called Teacher as Composer (TAC), we found this image a familiar one. Where there were conversations around learning, we observed that teachers directed much of the talking and that the talk was often aimed at helping children move through lesson procedures or take in new information. Children engaged in natural conversation in the classroom, but mainly while they were in transition between learning activities, rather than within the academic context. Students' written products generally were prescribed and did not focus on their own topics and ideas; students with special needs were particularly unproductive.

The language use in these classrooms reflected a view of learning as a process of transmitting knowledge from teacher to child. The teacher initiated most of the conversations, the student responded, and the teacher provided feedback and evaluation (Brown, Bransford, Ferrara, & Campione, 1983; Sternberg & Martin, 1988; Stubbs, 1976). A very different pattern occurs outside of school in other adult–child relationships. Mothers create genuinely reciprocal exchanges; classic examples are mother–child play with peek-a-boo or the reading of nursery rhymes in which agent and object role become reversed (Bruner, 1978; Cazden, 1973; Rome-Flanders & Ricard, 1992). We saw in our research sites the need for teachers to elicit children's ideas and to organize and support learning activities in which children are active participants in the conversation (Wood, Bruner, & Ross, 1976). A better balance between receptive (reading/listening) and expressive (talking/writing) language use would promote the expression and development of children's ideas.

Following our exploratory study, we spent 30 months working with eight classroom teachers and five specialists who assist them in the classroom on integrating conversation with reading and particularly with writing instruction. As a teacher-researcher group, we settled on the goal of improving students' writing because teachers found writing instruction to be the most perplexing part of their language arts work and a major area of failure for many of their students. While most of the teachers were still required to use basals for reading instruction, they had considerable flexibility in their writing programs. Several of the teachers had been through in-service sessions on process writing—single, fairly traditional workshops with little direct application to their own classrooms or follow-up support. Most were familiar with new practices, such as peer conferencing, but had only a partial grasp of the ideas that underlie many of the new practices in writing instruction. They tended to see writing as a way to practice the subskills of written language, rather than as a process of building meaning. Some of the teachers assumed that the management challenges of having children engage in more varied and extended writing activities would be overwhelming.

The program we jointly constructed with the teachers involved them in four cycles of unit planning, implementation, and analysis, with each cycle taking about 3 months. We felt that teachers needed to become immersed in writing units that were clearly problem-centered and focused on students' thinking—a radical change in the purpose of writing for most of the teachers, whose typical writing assignments were built around story starters or encyclopedia-based reports. The units were organized around varied reading and writing genres: personal narrative and supported argument in the expository mode. Students listened to literature that modeled and stimulated their writing in the particular genre. They listened to the teacher read aloud historical fiction and then developed arguments that focused on the theme of "making hard choices" around dilemmas in the story. The teachers, who came from eight classrooms in three different school districts (two suburban and one urban), met periodically for day-long workshops. With EDC staff, teachers designed common units and developed specific lessons, tailoring them to their particular students' strengths and needs.

Between workshops, teachers taught the units, in some cases with classroom teacher and specialist planning and teaching together. The research staff observed several lessons of each teacher in each unit cycle; we drew on our observations to select events—mainly instances of difficult-to-reach children successfully engaging in active learning experiences—for further analysis in the whole-group workshops. Care was taken that each teacher was represented in our analysis of positive examples; the episodes were used to highlight the factors underlying the successful engagement. Researchers interviewed students following the lessons to determine what aspects of the experience had engaged their attention. Outcomes of these interviews, as well as student products, were included in the workshop and strengthened the conversations about students' engagement and productivity.

The focus of this chapter is teachers' conceptual change over 2½ years around several ideas: writing is a process of social construction of meaning; certain kinds of conversation can facilitate that process; and teachers have critical, highly intentional roles to play in facilitating students' talking and thinking for writing. The chapter describes the features of "constructive conversation" and the intervention strategies we used to encourage this conversation with adults and children. Case studies of two teachers illustrate the kinds of pivotal growth points and growth processes we observed across the teacher group as a whole. The two teachers grew in different ways in their understanding of the role of conversation in writing because they started at different places, had different personal and teaching styles, and negotiated different system constraints.

CONSTRUCTIVE CONVERSATION

Conversation around a shared problem can serve as a natural scaffolding to move students from private thoughts to shared ideas. The presence of "the other" compels the speaker to assemble and formulate ideas in ways that reach out and communicate meaningfully to others.

From our prior research and from the literature on classroom discourse, we identified several elements of "constructive conversation"—talking that engages learners in building complex ideas together and lays the groundwork for the writing process. These features are similar to ones discussed in studies of instructional conversation (Goldenberg & Gallimore, 1991; Saunders, Goldenberg, & Hamann, 1992) as well as in research on classroom discourse in science (Fleer, 1992), reading (Englert, Tarrant, Mariage, & Oxer, 1994; Palincsar & Brown, 1984), and literature study (Gamoran & Nystrand, 1992).

Each feature involves challenging choices and requires facilitation on the part of teachers.

- *Compelling communication problem.* Students begin to build ideas together when they share a common communication purpose that requires complex thinking. The teacher's job is to pose, or help students discover, an authentic problem—one with which students and others outside the school actually wrestle. The problem should have sufficient complexity to require new thinking.
- *Interesting and relevant content.* Interest creates both affective and cognitive energy. Rich literature embeds the complex problem in a context about which students possess prior knowledge and interest. New information and details in the literature stimulate new associations that sustain attention and support the building of new ideas.
- *Inclusive and collaborative formats.* Pairs and small groups place students in the role of speaker and initiator with much greater frequency. Formats such as alternating talking and listening in pairs or giving each child in a small group 1 minute to give his or her viewpoint help students manage the inclusion of different learning styles and backgrounds and focus the conversation.
- *Genre-related communication processes.* Teachers anticipate the specific kinds of problem solving involved in writing in a particular genre. They provide different kinds of "scaffolding," temporary and adjustable supports, that highlight the distinctive components of the genre and activate the related kinds of thinking required for students' reading, talking, and writing in that genre.
- *Opportunities to elicit prior knowledge and build further background knowledge.* Constructive conversation draws on what students know and distributes that knowledge among members of the group. This helps all students extend the knowledge base they bring to the reading and writing. The teacher introduces additional related resources.
- *Responsive/interactive discourse.* Constructive conversations are shared and reciprocal rather than directed or initiated solely by the teacher or any one member. The teacher's role is to ask authentic questions, seeking to know as a naive fellow investigator and "follow[ing] from behind the children's conceptual thinking" rather than leading their thinking (Biddulph & Osborne, 1984, in Fleer, 1992, p. 393).
- *Gradual release and distributed expertise.* Over time, teachers progressively "hand-over" to children more of the responsibility for the process (Fleer, 1992). This gradual release of skills in conversational abilities of listening, questioning, and building interpretations is essential to students' becoming self-directed members of learning communities (Palincsar & Brown, 1984).

These elements, and the craft of applying them in classroom literacy experiences, are at the core of writing instruction and promote accomplished language arts teaching at the elementary level and probably at higher levels of schooling.

OVERVIEW OF THE INTERVENTION STRATEGY

Our approach to supporting teachers in expanding the role of constructive conversation in their writing programs was to engage them in designing a series of integrated reading/writing units together. The process incorporated and was intended to explicate the principles and concepts of active, meaningful learning. On the practical side, the units reflected themes and literature selections that teachers judged would fit broad curriculum mandates in their districts so as not to add to the weighty responsibility to "cover the content." Five elements of our approach contributed to the conceptual change we observed with teachers.

1. Immerse Teachers in the Genre Through Analogue Experiences. We involved teachers in intellectually engaging experiences with writing, and talking about writing, with other adults. We termed these "analogue experiences" (Riley, Morocco, Gordon, & Howard, 1993) because these adult, integrated reading/writing/discussion challenges involved teachers in the very kinds of thinking and writing that they needed to plan for their students. We hypothesized that if teachers experienced the power of the principles and practices themselves, they would be more likely to apply them with their students. We designed substantive learning experiences using adult literature and engaging teachers in writing about adult experiences and themes, rather than initially reading children's books or thinking immediately about students' activities and responses.

In the first unit development cycle, teachers focused on personal narrative because it fit easily into their existing language arts curricula and provided a relatively secure starting point for the students with reading and writing difficulties. To build a collective understanding of the kind of memory and organization of thought this requires for students, we established several *inclusive and collaborative formats* for teachers to use in writing and discussing their own personal narratives.

The research staff facilitated responsive and interactive discourse focused on identifying the specific *characteristics* of personal narrative as a genre and the parallel kinds of thinking demanded by each of these features. Teachers made connections between their writing experiences and their work with students. For example, with personal narrative, one teacher found to her chagrin that her story "went on and on just like my student's," appreciating the very real challenge of what we as a group had identified as one of the components—the need to select a restricted time frame, which we called bracketing an event from the stream of memories.

Teachers drew on these first-hand experiences over subsequent weeks as they all tried more conversational ways of involving and supporting their students' engagement in personal narrative writing.

2. Building Thinking Frames. We encouraged teachers to talk about their thinking processes during writing. As teachers talked about scanning memories, censoring certain writing topics, and recalling small details and particular feelings associated with their stories, we kept track of these processes on large chart paper. This constellation of thought processes related to the purpose of their writing, and the components—such as "bracketed event," first-person perspective, tension and resolution, an episode with beginning, middle, and end—were organized into the *personal narrative genre thinking frame* (Riley et al., 1993).

Later units took the step forward to expository writing and focused on decision making and the building of an argument. In an analogue experience, designed around expository writing, teachers read a powerful adult short story, "Jury of Her Peers," involving a moral dilemma about domestic violence in the early part of this century but highly relevant to women's issues today. In varied groupings to promote conversation, the teachers engaged fully in this emotionally charged story. In the constructive conversations, they strongly argued their points of view—analyzing the events, identifying subtle details, and weighing the facts. In building their argument, they found themselves raising and discussing moral values and legal issues. Again, we highlighted the constructive features of the conversation: the emerging components of the genre and related kinds of thinking. Together we created another framework, this time for expository writing—specifically, the building of an argument (Riley & Howard, 1994). See Figure 5.1.

Following the adult analogues, teachers designed writing lessons for students that were parallel to their own literacy experiences in the workshops. They evaluated the selection of the children's literature for the essential features—high interest and relevance—as well as the potential of the novels (*Sign of the Beaver* and, later, *Groundhog's Horse*) to provide the complex problems needed to stimulate decision making and argument. Teachers anticipated the writing demands, the distinctive features of the genre, and the kinds of thinking involved as they planned ways to support students' conversation and writing.

3. Designing for and Monitoring Focal Students. Teachers selected at least one low-achieving and one moderately high-achieving student to keep in mind as they developed the units. This strategy enables teachers to carry

Figure 5.1. Expository Writing—Making Hard Choices/Taking Sides

Genre Features	Thinking Processes
Point of View	Perspective Taking
Explanation, Argument	Developing an argument
Reasons, Facts, Details, Circumstances	Causes: Hypothesizing, Comparing, Weighing
Consequences	Effects: Reflecting, Comparing, Weighing
Prediction	Hypothesizing, Inferencing
Values, Rules	Applying, Rejecting
Resolution	Deciding, Judging
Clear, Cohesive Audience Perspective	Thinking Logically

out a closer ongoing assessment of students' writing abilities and writing processes than they had exhibited in our baseline study (Morocco, Riley, Gordon, & Howard, 1996; Watt & Watt, 1995). The workshop staff introduced several "tracking tools" that teachers could use to follow their students' progress in the unit. One was a tool for predicting how well particular students would handle the thinking and writing challenges involved in a lesson. This device encouraged teachers to conjecture about their students' strengths and needs in relation to the experience. They closely observe and note the student's talking during the supported conversations and later analyze the talking and writing for evidence of the thinking and genre components. Another tool to elicit children's thinking was an interviewing protocol for talking with students about how they came to the ideas in their writing.

4. Analyzing Success. The early planning cycles involved highly detailed planning for low-achieving students around these principles of writing instruction found effective with highly diverse groups of students (Englert & Mariage, 1991; Morocco, Dalton, & Tivnan, 1992). As a result, teachers experienced a high level of success with students who generally wrote little or nothing and for whom they had low expectations. Teachers' surprise at their success motivated them to analyze their lesson designs, particularly their interactions with their students; they reassessed their assumptions about their students' intellectual abilities and potential as writers (Riley, 1994b). We find that teachers cope with persistent failure with certain students by attributing the failure to factors beyond the classroom, such as emotional or motivational issues related to economic stress or family concerns. Teachers may be more willing to look at the impact of their own role and their teaching around *successful* teaching experiences, particularly experiences with students who do not usually succeed. This view is consistent with a substantial body of theory and research on the role of dissonance or disequilibrium in stimulating the inquiry and reflection that result in learning (Linn, 1987; Poplin, 1988).

5. Scaffolding Design and Analysis. Creating the conditions for teacher success required that we build in considerable support for teachers (Morocco & Zorfass, 1996). The analogue experiences described above were one form of support. We also paired teachers who expressed interest in each other's work and presented selected research on writing and cognition to provide teachers language for talking about teaching and learning from fresh perspectives. These supports were consistent with the notion of scaffolding in cognitive research—just enough temporary and adjustable support to enable a learner to carry out a task that would otherwise be too complex.

By the fourth design cycle, teachers worked more independently, which was consistent with our goal of gradual release of support. They chose to work on a common problem and with common literature selections in order to be able to share and analyze their individual experiences. They selected a final version of writing about hard choices, a kind of expository writing they had predicted at the outset was too difficult for fourth-graders. Because teachers had by then internalized many principals of active learning in their planning, we played more of an observer role, providing technical assistance as they requested it.

DOCUMENTING THE INTERVENTION

We used several forms of documentation throughout the 30-month intervention, building on baseline observation and interview data gathered in the initial, exploratory 18 months. We interviewed teachers after each cycle about their beliefs about writing, the reasoning behind specific facilitation decisions, and their perceptions of students' abilities and learning. Project staff tape-recorded and transcribed and analyzed interviews, workshops, and the observed lessons. Portfolios were developed for teachers and focal students.

The case studies that follow highlight changes in two teachers' mindset about conversation and writing, as well as changes in their approach to writing instruction. Together the two teachers illustrate the individual and iterative nature of the learning process where complex content and the internalization of new learning principles and practices are involved.

MERIN

Merin joined the project as one of the most highly respected teachers in her school. Traditional in her approach, she was dedicated to responding to the needs of all of her fourth-grade students. Reserved and personally intense, she was meticulous in her planning and assessment of students' progress.

Baseline Study: Merin's Language Arts Program

In the spring and fall of 1990, when we first began to work with Merin, she had three different reading levels in her room, each using a different language arts basal text. Students typically sat in close proximity to other members of their reading group, but they often worked on subskills lessons side by side without interacting. When they met as groups, they took turns reading aloud. Merin devoted extensive time and thought to the placement of students in their groups. Her assessments were thoughtful—based on her careful reading of past evaluations, several skills tests of her own choosing, and observations of students over several weeks. Students did all their reading instruction in those groups; they listened for enjoyment to Merin read aloud trade books after lunch.

Nested within this basal-focused language arts program, Merin's writing instruction consisted mainly of writing short pieces around assigned topics related to national holidays. She generally gave the students a topic for these "creative writing" activities, for example, "a scary ghost story," "something to be thankful for." Students all received the same story starters on mimeograph paper, which might have a picture and lines for writing. She engaged the class in discussion about the picture, mainly to get students to generate vocabulary words, which she wrote on the board to waylay spelling problems. While these assignments capitalized on the excitement of holidays, they did not require complex thinking. Students tended to use stock images and language—"thankful family" (Thanksgiving), "scary graveyard" (Halloween).

Beyond these creative writing activities, as Merin referred to them, her students occasionally practiced letter writing to pen pals or to Chambers of Commerce to request information about cities they were discussing in social studies. Occasionally they wrote a "group story": Merin wrote a few opening lines on big chart paper and students came up, one at a time, during the day to add to it. They occasionally wrote short reports on social studies topics; in a Native American unit, some children located information about Navajo clothing; others wrote about food or games.

Outside of language arts, Merin engaged students in some collaborative work, supported with writing. As part of a pilot science program with a local museum, her students conducted water experiments in pairs and made journal entries about their observations. Merin was intrigued by how actively they talked about science concepts during these activities, noticing that "even the learning-disabled students could do it because there wasn't a concern for spelling."

Intervention

First Encounter. In the spring of 1991, when the TAC teachers began collaborative unit planning, Merin's school was beginning to emphasize process approaches to writing, and Merin had begun to include more writing in her program. The TAC workshops on personal narrative writing interested her because of the continuity she saw with the very new demands in her system, and they provided her support to experiment with these new ways of teaching writing. During the opening workshop she wrote a story about an accident she had while on a tour of Peru. She and her partner laughed and talked excitedly as Merin recounted the adventure. The two teachers told the group they were "on a roll" talking about Merin's story; subsequently Merin elaborated her story to include some details her partner had elicited from her and had found hilarious.

While writing this story was fun for Merin, it was disconnected from the way writing happened in her own classroom. Nevertheless, she went along with the TAC group assignment to engage her students in writing stories on topics of their own choice because she had so much enjoyed reconstructing her own experience in Peru. She said she was willing to try something new if it would help students who struggle with writing to generate more. Merin carried over the workshop experience into her planning by trying out a conversation format similar to one we had used in the workshop: pairing students to talk about their lists of potential writing topics. Consistent with her typically meticulous approach to planning, she thought a great deal about how to pair students for this conversation. She paired Meredith, a student who rushes through her work and writes very little, with Rachel, a student who is methodical and might slow Meredith down.

With her usual style of making most of the choices for her students, she wrote out a set of criteria for selecting a final writing topic on a large chart before class. Once in the class, however, she put it aside and held a conversation with her students that was much more like the part of her own TAC adult workshop where the teachers and researchers had constructed writing guidelines together.

T: Are there some ideas that you think might help you decide which one you'll write about? What would help you decide?

S: One that's most exciting?

T: OK, one that would be really exciting for someone to read? Good idea (***lists students' ideas on the board***)
S: Most funny?
T: To whom?
S: Most interesting.

Merin pointed out to the students that they were focusing on the reader's point of view in these criteria. "What about the writer? What about someone else? Who else is important?" she asked, and they added to the list, "the one that the writer likes the most."

She organized students into partners to talk about their three topics, using their selection criteria to narrow down to one topic. She gave them a procedure: (1) Tell your partner a little bit about three experiences you circled and ask your partner which ideas she or he would most want to read about and why; (2) identify the idea you like best and explain to your partner why; and (3) star the idea you plan to write about.

She was surprised that most of her students could talk so easily about their ideas, using the conversation format and the criteria they had generated for themselves. She noticed how closely they held to the topics they cared most about. Meredith's list of topics included her first day at Disney World, first time skiing downhill, or first dance recital. When Rachel said she wanted to know more about Disney World, Meredith responded thoughtfully that she preferred to write about the ski trip. Rachel was certain that she would write about "a favorite fish that died," although Meredith had expressed interest in all of her topics.

At this point, Merin saw student conversation mainly as a new way to lighten her load, rather than a fundamental aspect of writing. She explained that partner conversations helped her manage the greater amount of writing that her students were doing due to her involvement with the TAC project and the increasing emphasis on writing in her system. But, conducive to change in mindset, she saw some student capabilities she had not seen before. She had not expected the classroom conversations to have such a marked effect on the quality of her students' ideas and was surprised at the richness of the students' own topics and their ability to select thoughtfully among them. She saw that working with Rachel had, in fact, slowed Meredith down. When we asked why she decided to have her students build the criteria for selecting topics when she had so carefully prepared a set to give to them, she said, "It just came to me. Let them come up with the ideas." She took a risk in letting go of her directive approach in this activity.

Conflict. An interview with Merin at the beginning of the second year of the intervention, just before the beginning of the second unit design cycle, confirmed our sense that change would be difficult for Merin. At that point, Merin said she felt overwhelmed by changing district policies around curriculum and instruction, as well as by the new approaches of our TAC program. The flexible, heterogeneous student grouping that she experimented with lightly as a part of the TAC program had become a districtwide mandate for reading, and she found the transition "very difficult, very difficult. I'm not having the time to do the things that I like to do. I'm under pressure all the time, and I can't get through this and do my things."

One of her "things" was the holiday writing activities. She reiterated all the skills students practice in the Halloween assignment: "editing, reading the story out loud, looking for spelling mistakes, capitals, seeing if all the ideas are down." Her difficulties were exacerbated by her attempt to take on all the materials and activities in the new curriculum while also holding onto all her familiar routines.

Her former assessment system was becoming less relevant. It was geared to sorting students according to needs around basic reading subskills, while her new literature-based reading series was organized around higher-level reading processes. She was unsure of her role when students were working in heterogeneous groups, feeling "out of charge" and unsure how to assess what the children were accomplishing or how to intervene to "teach." "I don't feel like I know my kids this year. I'm more with the class, introducing the story, and then having them work with partners, and I'm walking around watching them." Turning the lead over to the students was a major shift that upset her sense of control, particularly with the focus on higher-order thinking, hypothesizing, inferencing, and so forth. She did not know how to intervene in this less predictable and less familiar format.

Experimentation. In the second cycle of curriculum design, the highly animated TAC workshops around the "Jury of Her Peers" and *Sign of the Beaver* gave new meaning to instructional conversations for Merin and nudged her further toward a different relationship with writing. In experimenting in her own classroom with the common lesson the teachers designed for *Sign of the Beaver*, Merin initially wanted to avoid having her students talk with each other about Matt's (the main character) dilemma until they developed their individual arguments. One of Matt's dilemmas was whether to stay alone in his family cabin any longer, since his father was long overdue and his Indian friend, Atean, has offered him family and protection in his village. When she saw that students were having difficulty thinking out the problem on their own, she prompted them to "write about any reasons why you think that Matt should go with the Indians. Number them as you go along so you can see how many reasons you have." When few students started to write, she prompted them again, "Remember the time of year it is getting to be . . . how long he has been alone . . ." When students continued to look blank, Merin shifted her approach, asking them to "see if you can lengthen that list by talking to the person who is next to you." Her students immediately began talking about Matt and his dilemma; lively conversation continued and then quieted as the students broke off and began writing energetically. She explained to the observer after class that she changed her plans because "so many were sitting there and not getting anywhere."

Following this success, Merin began to experiment more deliberately with having students talk and share their ideas. Reflecting the thinking frame, she noticed that the discussions were affecting their reasoning; she asked her students to notice, and even write about, how their own ideas were changing. "If you want to change your mind, write, 'I changed my mind, now I think . . .' Write why. The reasons that made you change your mind." She struggled to find her role in this kind of writing experience and felt the tension between the visible benefits of involving students in this way and the intensive demands on her time and energy. "It's a lot of work going through it this way. It's much easier to have them do the first draft, then correct the mechanical kinds of things and go on to another." Yet, fortunately, Merin was intrigued with the focus on children's thinking, including having the students become aware of their own thinking. "Just to get them thinking in terms of the material that they've written down—seeing they have their ideas down rather than just mechanical kinds of things. It's a whole different way of looking at writing."

Shifting Mindset. Merin's new direction solidified when she saw her most "difficult-to-teach" student who was "just about a nonwriter" benefit from a more conversational, collaborative approach to writing. This focal student, Sam, had above-average intellectual abilities and a tangled combination of attention difficulties, an exceptionally high activity level, and family health and emotional problems. Merin found that it's "hard to get him really motivated for anything, and writing is that much more work." She used tracking tools developed in the TAC workshops to think about Sam, observe him during some of the *Sign of the Beaver* lessons, and talk to him personally about this writing.

Before a second writing assignment about the novel, she organized her students in pairs and groups of three to talk about whether Matt should abandon his cabin for the security of his friend Atean's village, with the risk of never seeing his family again. She saw Sam talk with the other students in his group and afterwards saw that he had written much more than he ever had on any previous assignment. In her first experience with directly interviewing a student about his or her work, Merin asked Sam why he had been able to write so much. Sam said that talking with other students helped him and that he was "really interested in this story." Merin saw that Sam also loved the chance to talk with her about his writing; she "never thought he would be so warm and responsive." His success brought home to her the power of writing in a context in which children can think and talk about provocative issues of high interest to them and with others as interested listeners.

Intentionality. An echo of earlier themes of loss and confusion marked Merin's March interview just before she left the project and school to manage a chronic health problem. "So sometimes I just feel tongue-tied when I try to talk about it, because I feel like I haven't been doing anything. I think it's going to take me a couple of years of doing it like this to really get hold of it, so I'm at a loss." She described herself as "fumbling through the year." Yet she also saw that she was consciously changing her role. She had decided to lessen her control over students' writing and enjoyed structuring opportunities for students to think aloud together and seek out the human dilemmas they could relate to and reason about. She reflected that these difficult changes were worth it because the lessons "really are successful where they [the students] are actively involved, when they really tap the sources that are inside of them." She agreed in workshop discussion with another teacher that, now, the students "wanted to correct the products they felt proud of" and that, as a result, they "were actually working on more mechanics."

Merin rejoined the group in the fourth and final TAC cycle with much greater enthusiasm than she had expressed when she initially joined the project. As a group, the teachers focused on building students' background knowledge about Native American cultures for the novel about a Cherokee family in *Groundhog's Horse.* Merin incorporated many of the ideas into her lessons, where conversations about writing were now pervasive. In her interest in promoting active learning, she now sometimes engaged students in almost too many activities; sometimes lessons were "overengineered" with detailed procedures. She saw herself as the manager of those conversations and the key person in helping children expand their ideas. Clearly, she remained in the role of director, but only sometimes initiator, and she was providing a greater range of flexibility and opportunity for personal choice. Her thoroughness in providing background resources for information sharing and inventive maps to support students' listening to the complex story line in the novel demonstrated her strong investment in meaningfulness and comprehension.

Throughout this cycle and in Merin's final interview in June, there was little trace of nostalgia for her old ways of teaching writing as skill-based exercises. She was highly focused on describing her various roles in the activities—in particular, her individual conferences with children. These personalized conversations with students about their writing became an established aspect of Merin's teaching during this final cycle. We observed her interview 10 different students while her practice teacher worked with the rest of the class. Although she sometimes interrupted students before they could think fully about her questions, her intention in these conversations was clearly to "uptake" students' ideas and encourage them to extend their thinking.

Writing shifted from skill-building exercises to opportunities for animated conversations about ideas in Merin's classroom. A next step for Merin would be growth in facilitating the writing conversations among students in groups with activity structures that promote greater independence. To expand on her successful individual interviewing skills, she needed to extend this mode to her role as facilitator of group conversation. A specific step would be to provide her students with strategies for questioning and extending one another's ideas as members of a classroom writing community.

DIANA

Baseline Study: Diana's Language Arts Program

Through observations and interviews during the exploratory year of the project, we identified Diana as the teacher most skillful at building meaning and purpose into the learning experiences of her students. Diana was accomplishing this in her busy, urban, fourth-grade classroom with 29 students. A number of her students spoke languages other than English as their first language: Laotian, Cambodian, Vietnamese, Creole, Portuguese, and Spanish. Many of the children were experiencing economic and family stress; and a higher than usual number of students with special needs were referred to Diana because, as her principal told us, she was "so good with them." Despite the challenges, the tone of the classroom reflected Diana's style: "Remarkably comfortable, orderly and what one would have to describe as joyful" (observer's notes).

In her regular schedule, there was very little time or opportunity for professional camaraderie or reflection. "If I walk over to the teachers' room for lunch, I can't fit in a bathroom break." The large urban system in which Diana taught differed from Merin's suburban system in a number of ways. While Merin was feeling overwhelmed by the systemwide curriculum initiatives, Diana's move toward more meaningful, integrated curriculum was self-initiated. When Diana entered the TAC project, she was already engaged in an early stage of experimentation with "new literacy" practices. She was intuitively honoring many of the features of constructive conversation in the area of reading, and she and the children were particularly enjoying that subject area. "I want the children to enjoy reading and learn to love literature. I also read to them every day after lunch and they love it." Diana also was openly grappling with transition in curriculum and instruction as was Merin, but with very different issues.

> I've been trying to do more literature-based reading with them. I have spent some of my own money. I've raided my own children's bookcases and use them [books] so that they [students] have some exposure to them because a lot of them don't go to a library.

She described the existing reading curriculum in her system as "topsy-turvy . . . everyone more or less does with the materials they have. I have an old Scott Foresman series that I've been using." She planned not to abandon the direct skill instruction and practice provided in the basal format. She was at a growth point and asking what-do-I-take-with-me on her step forward. She described her lowest achievers as a very low group but quickly added, "but every group has read at least two complete books." Her enthusiasm shone through as she expressed how much the children enjoyed having read a "whole book." She went on to describe a $1,700 grant that she and the magnet school coordinator had sought out on their own and won for the following year.

Surprisingly, Diana did not approach writing, as she did reading, as a process of social construction of meaning, and neither she nor the children were experiencing success in this area. She described her writing program as a "disaster." "Their writing is the worst I've ever seen in my life. It's such a struggle, like pulling teeth, even with the top group." When we requested children's writing samples, Diana did not have any; she mentioned only a letter they had written and that it had gone home a long time before. As we had observed in Merin's class, letter writing and short compositions on holiday topics were the kinds of writing experiences Diana did with her class—and, as she explained, not very often. In marked contrast to her description of her reading program, when discussing her writing instruction, Diana described a bottom-up, part-to-whole approach to writing.

> We still have to go through a few more parts of speech. We have gone through verbs, nouns. We still have adjectives and adverbs that we are trying to work on. Once we finish that we are going to get into a little more writing.

When we tried to enter into discussions with Diana about the effectiveness of her literature-based reading approach in contrast to her writing program, her responses demonstrated a more intuitive than reflective approach: "Sometimes things just end up [successful] without really thinking about it." We came to see this as Diana's style; at meetings with other teachers, she did not readily engage in reflection or analysis. For Diana, we identified a goal of moving toward a deeper understanding, a meta-awareness, of the principles underpinning the constructivist practices she applied so ably in her reading instruction. In our evolving schema, we saw meta-awareness and intentionality as our highest "level." We predicted that this would allow Diana to generalize the power of the principles to other subject areas, in particular to her most frustrating subject area, writing instruction.

One active learning practice that Diana's school system did support was cooperative learning. A consultant-trainer modeled the practice in her class in a single session; Diana was then to implement the practice. Discussion of the rationale behind this "new" practice was not a part of the in-service. The power of students having conversations to extend and clarify their thinking or to enrich each others' ideas for reading and writing was not part of the session. Diana discussed the in-service solely in terms of peer editing. It was surprising to us that Merin, and several other teachers in the project, also saw peer editing as the primary role for students in cooperative learning groups for writing. Diana essentially closed out the idea of cooperative groups for writing because the editing posed a risk to students' self-esteem:

> I don't think I would ask another group to help edit because it would almost be like they would be looking down on them [the low group] . . . They just don't have the finesse; it's destructive, just can't work well.

Academic discussions in Diana's room almost exclusively involved the whole class. Though lively and rich, the verbal interaction moved pivotally around Diana, following the conventional model: Teacher initiates, student responds, and the teacher picks up the lead again. Diana did orchestrate the discussions with her large, diverse class with exceptional skill. She was sensitive and responsive to individuals, and full of fun; the class laughed often. She maintained the attention and cooperation of this high-energy group with apparent ease. (This was not the case for other professionals on the few occasions we saw them take over for Diana.)

The large-group discussions typically involved high-level concepts. During one reading–writing lesson observation, the class compared the images they visualized as they listened to Diana read the novel *Island of the Blue Dolphins* to the images they saw in a video of the novel. The children concluded that they preferred listening to the book and "*making up*" their own images, especially "what the characters looked like." They noted that in the video many "good parts of the story were left out," some of their "favorite parts." As she read aloud, Diana developed vocabulary in relaxed and meaningful ways. She asked a Latino child to explain the word "mesa" as she drew both a table and the land structure on the board. The richness of the content and the quality of the exchanges made it clear that the children were benefiting from these large-group sessions. Yet, given the class size, a majority of the students were inevitably in a listening, receptive mode most of the time.

A decrease in participation and productivity was striking when the lesson shifted from reading to writing about the story. "Students wrote very little, and the students with special needs wrote nothing at all" (observer's notes). Diana said that she felt stymied when it came to "getting them to write almost anything at all." Another goal for Diana was that she come to appreciate the power of conversation as a bridge for children, from receiving and comprehending the story to organizing and expressing their own thoughts about it. As with Merin, a goal was to encourage small conversational writing groups, and in this area Diana had less experience than Merin. Diana avoided small-group work because she felt it would be *chaotic* with so many students and with so many who "go off so easily if I don't keep my eye right on them."

Intervention

First Encounter. Diana's participation in the workshops started out slowly. Considering her buoyant personality and competence as a teacher, she was surprisingly quiet in early discussions. She showed more enthusiasm for the practical ideas other teachers shared than for the pedagogical rationale. She was not particularly optimistic about her students' ability to perform in the area of written language. She sensitively listed her concerns: Many of her students were coping with social and emotional burdens, stressful economic conditions, learning English. Writing, she thought, presented such "a high demand on them." When writing a personal narrative was set as the project's goal for the first writing unit, Diana's response was, "My goal for this class is to get them to write a coherent paragraph, let alone a story."

It was not until the analogue experience we called Conferencing About Personal Narrative with Ms. Smith and Ms. Jones (Riley et al., 1993) that we saw Diana come alive. The goal of this analogue was to highlight the effectiveness of ownership, of supporting students' own ideas as the springboard for further idea building. Some teachers, as unsuspecting participants, experienced feedback on their writing from other teachers playing the role of two artfully devised styles of feedback/conferencers: the facilitative Ms. Smith and Ms. Jones, who politely but intensely imposes her ideas, taking away the writer's opportunity to build on what he or she knows and cares about. We hoped to engender that feeling of discouragement, of being at a loss as to where to go with another person's ideas. Diana became visibly upset as she listened to Ms. Jones give feedback to one of the teachers. "I wanted to tell her how awful she was, so bossy to be making all those suggestions. I had all I could do to hold back." Later she reflected:

> I realized, it [the analogue] hit me. Without meaning to, that's what we do to kids . . . because they think anything the teacher says is right,

> so that if you're saying, "Don't you think you should say this" . . . you're invalidating what they're putting down on paper . . . "Let's just change this sentence and fix it up here and just write this" . . . you've changed it so that it's not theirs anymore, and they don't care. They've lost interest in their writing because you've rewritten it.

The impact of this analogue on Diana became evident in the subsequent pre-observation interview. She planned to spend more time "searching out" the students' interests and own ideas for topics. She wanted to monitor her own conversations with them, to "follow their lead."

Shifting Mindset. Diana took this step forward, but as with Merin, we saw that change was an iterative process. In her next interview, as she described her holiday writing lesson, we heard Diana's new thinking mixed in with the old. She combined an emphasis on parts of speech with a search for the children's genuine interest:

> As far as letting them have complete authorship, I think I'm more aware of that . . . I'm letting it be their own work . . . We talked about [Halloween] adjectives, words describing the night, the costumes . . . verbs that described what they would do . . . nouns, things they would see. For phrases, one of them was "Now you must die." I almost tried to steer them to a little happier [one], but they voted on it and that's what they wanted, so I let them go with it . . . [It was] sensitive because one boy's father was murdered a couple of years ago and the twins' mother died lately . . . I watched out for them, but they were fine so I went with it and they really used it.

Later, in analyzing her student's writing sample, Diana expressed a level of meta-awareness as well as personal reflection as she took on the perspective also of teacher developer.

> That's what I would focus in on here, go in on his own idea . . . the greatest value I've gotten so far is letting them have the work. I'm more aware of that. I think it's a real big thing. I think it really should be stressed to teachers, and I don't think it is.

It was clear to all of these experienced teachers, however, that to find the individual interests of a large classroom of children was not a simple process. They concluded that students needed more time and support in the beginning stage of the writing process. We saw this shift, away from the story starters and the one-session composition, as an important indicator of growth. In the workshop, teachers eagerly shared with each other practical approaches (we called them "facilitators") to support the broader search for topics. Diana expressed it best when she said, "I guess you just keep piling up facilitators 'til they get there."

In addition to her usual group brainstorming, Diana's next writing plan included two strategies suggested by Rachel, a teacher from another system whom she especially enjoyed pairing with at workshops. One was a variation of peer collaboration that Rachel called "peer talking"; the other, for the yet unmotivated, simply involved flipping through magazines in search of ideas.

Diana explained that peer talking was something that "maybe could work" with her "very energetic" class. Her concern about groups was that her students would "get off the subject and get into a battle." In peer talking, one talks for 30 seconds about a possible topic while the other listens but is not supposed to speak; the two switch roles on cue. She thoughtfully paired one of her focal students, John, with another boy she described as "very easy-going." Diana discussed good listening behaviors—"Look at the other person while s/he is speaking, nod" and so forth. She rearranged all the seating. She placed the pairs at a distance from other pairs and partners close to each other, face-to-face. She commented to the observer, "I'm surprised how well they're handling it"; a little later she changed the format and "let the conversations go." Diana was no longer doing all the initiating; her carefully designed structure had the students initiating and leading their own discussions.

Her prediction in the pre-observation interview for John was that he would not be successful: "Chances are he'll come up with something having nothing to do with what he should be doing." John had seen a picture of an airplane in the magazine; he shared with his partner an episode from the Persian Gulf War he had seen on television and went on to write about it. In the follow-up interview Diana was anxious to reflect and analyze: "It worked. I'm amazed. Really, I never thought he'd write this much . . . apparently the war was very personal to him." Here we see Diana growing in appreciation of her students' abilities, broadening her view of peer conferencing, and reflecting a major intervention strategy of the project—that teachers' unexpected success with their own instruction would encourage analysis.

Intentionality. Diana had become a delighted observer of the student collaboration, but she was not yet actively extending the children's thinking during the conversations. Diana took the step forward to intentionally intervene in her next lesson by making use of the genre thinking frame for personal narrative, which delineates the critical components of personal narrative and the related thinking challenges to be activated and supported. First, she chose to read, as a model of the genre, *Alexander and the Terrible, Horrible, No Good, Very Bad Day*; the children would write about a terrible day of their own. Throughout an animated reading of the story, Diana drew the children's attention to central components of personal narrative. She highlighted Alexander's voice and introduced the concept of first person. After the story, she again emphasized components of the genre as she modeled her experiences with bad days, "bracketed event—brief story with a beginning, middle and end" and so forth.

As the children's stories poured out in the large group, Diana again reinforced components from the genre thinking frame. Later in a workshop, Diana contrasted this experience with how stymied she had felt with topics selected by her students, such as "Good Dinner Last Night" in which the child described only the food she had eaten. "I've thought it [the genre] through now, I have an idea of what's missing, what they need, how to be helpful."

The pre-writing phase for this writing experience was much longer and more elaborated than any Diana had used. The conversation then continued as she moved to small groups; Diana built in student conversations now as a matter of course. The students responded to the stories with both seriousness and laughter. The classroom was alive with conversation and story. "Every student in the class participated for a sustained period of academic learning time" (observer's notes). All of the students wrote, including three boys whom Diana had described up to that point as "nonwriters."

> I couldn't believe it, Adam here never writes anything and Paul usually just finds a way out of the room, to the lavatory or something. I mean these are good stories, I mean with good ideas and they follow the format. I love that book, and they were really able to listen to each other and get their ideas out. It really helped with the writing I'd say, the sharing and the story. I am afraid having bad days is really relevant to a lot of them, (*laughs*) me too.

Here we see Diana successfully facilitating students' talking, thinking, and writing. Her design sustained the powerful conversations—moving private thoughts to the plane of communication, from the receptive mode to the expressive. Diana's activating structure helped shape the conversation to correspond with the genre. Importantly, we hear Diana's understanding of the rationale behind collaborative learning. In her own terms (listening, getting ideas out, good ideas, sharing, story, helped with the writing), she is defining the social construction of meaning, with conversation as the bridge to the more exacting form of written language and resulting in productive student outcomes.

Metacognition and Generalization. Diana was thriving in the supportive and safe learning community of teachers and developers and was becoming increasingly interactive and metacognitive about her experiences. The project devised multiple opportunities for experimentation. In our next cycle on expository writing for argument and decision making, Diana moved forward again. She reflected on the workshop, specifically on the facilitating format of the meeting—the "Jury of Her Peers" analogue experience.

> I liked the way you did it with us. I really enjoyed the discussion [about the short story "Jury of Her Peers"] because I thought it was very helpful. It clarified some things and it did change my mind. I was unsure, and then it helped sway me so that I was more clear about my own theme. Getting some more points of view . . . once I listened to other people, and talking myself, actually verbalizing it, I ended up, "OK, now I know how I feel."

Initially in the discussion, Diana went directly to a solution, to tell the authorities, because it was the "right thing to do, you have to, it would be illegal not to." Later, she stated, "I'm surprised at myself that I didn't consider how they would treat women in that era! Sarah brought that up. That really changed my mind." Following this experience, she took a risk and planned larger conversation groups for the students' writing about hard decisions.

> It will be interesting to see if it works with them because they are so talkative. I was going to do groups of three, but I think I will keep it in their [new] cooperative learning groups [of four] and have them discuss their feelings and what they wrote down. Because *I know that when we [the teachers] did it, it gave us different ideas, and we had different points of view.*

Later in the interview, Diana again raised her concerns about her group structures for conversation:

> This could be a mistake. It might be better having them in groups of two, but I am going to see how this works with groups of four because they are so noisy and so talkative and they might not be willing to wait their turn and they might be more distracted. I was thinking of Caesar [focal student]. Caesar is one that doesn't follow directions when you think you've explained everything . . . and alas, we will see if Steven and Martin do it. I am going to take a chance.

Diana's hesitation here and the differences in teachers' pacing for change in general need to be considered in relation to the variations in settings. The observer's notes mention the frequent energy level in the class of 29 students and describe an incident when the class erupted into chaos when the lunch-time monitors came in to take over the class. Diana was cautious about structure, but there is an optimism about the groups and a clear emphasis on the need for sufficient time for thinking.

> It's kind of hard, because they need time to kind of think and then start writing. I'll give them a little more time, maybe 5 minutes for the discussion and if the discussions are going great, I may even give them a couple of minutes more, but I will judge that.

Throughout the exploratory phase of the project, we found an absence of teachers' thinking about children's thinking (Morocco et al., 1996). Lesson observation notes report that Diana's 5-minute time limit here actually extended much longer. Even the 5-minute plan with discussion groups of four was a major step forward when compared with her first plan—groups of two, with 30-second intervals to speak, and no exchanges. The observer's notes for this lesson also describe another important growth area for Diana. During this cycle, we had introduced the concept of "assessment as assistance" (Riley, 1994a). The format involves a conversational exchange between teacher and students that raises the students' awareness of genre components through the teacher's supportive comments and questioning. In this way the teacher calls their attention to features of the writing *while students are in the process of writing*, rather than later through a *correction* process.

In place of her usual supportive but general comments, in this second writing lesson Diana went around guided by the hard choices genre thinking frames both *assessing* what the students' writing needed and *assisting* them with selective comments and questions. To support elaboration of detail in a student's writing, Diana said, "Oh, I'd love to hear more about how Matt was feeling when he said that to the stranger." At one point, Diana noticed that her focal child, Martin, was very quiet in his group, so she crouched down beside him at eye level and engaged him in conversation. It was obvious by his facial expressions that he was responding to her but taking long periods of time to think. (Diana described getting "knee lock" from crouching and waiting so long for him to speak.)

Diana shared afterwards that she felt very uncomfortable in this role, partially because she was uncertain whether she could enter and exit without "spoiling the group conversation." Particularly Martin, she thought, could "withdraw entirely, which he does, if he feels pressured." Her concerns illustrate the complexity of honoring the principles of active learning in the real world, but Diana's "knee lock" intervention succeeded.

> Martin is not one who would really write anything, unless you wanted to really force him to. He's so withdrawn, depressed really. I was

> asking him about his feelings, having him be Matt. How would you feel? What would you see if you were Matt? He got into it, slowly, but he really got into it and wrote about all that. I was so pleased, happy actually; I worry about him, so it was wonderful to see him involved.

Diana was enjoying her ability to facilitate the creating of mutual constructions between her and her students, as well as the student conversations that bridge to written language. She was delighted when she later read the observer's follow-up interviews with the focal children. She could see that Martin had been actively listening in his group—as she had in the workshop—and had extended his thinking by listening to others. Putting himself in Matt's shoes, Martin explained that he had refused to let the stranger in until one of his classmates reminded him that Matt had his father's gun in the cabin—and, on that basis, he changed his decision, and went on to write about that.

> *Interviewer:* And who mentioned the gun?
> *Martin:* John did.
> *Interviewer:* And what did that do for you?
> *Martin:* Then I wrote down the, I wrote down what I was going to do . . . I wrote down, I wrote down when, if when I tell him to go, he wouldn't go. And then I would have took out the gun and threatened him.

This observer–child interview was another strategy by which project staff gathered data to elicit children's thinking, to learn why or how the children became stimulated to think or to write.

More and more, Diana was expressing her interest in these how's and why's—the relationships between children's thinking and writing and the principles and concepts underpinning the active learning practices. Through increased reflection and deeper understanding, she generalized this constructivist approach to her writing curriculum. She enhanced her assessment and instructional skills to reveal and develop her students' language and writing abilities. Impressively, she accomplished this in as challenging a setting as we had observed. She also reached the higher-level goal—a meta-awareness of herself as an effective designer of instruction and curriculum.

> If you take a course, it kind of opens you up a little bit to something. This whole program [project] makes us actually stop, put down our thoughts, disciplines us to really stop and think about what we were doing and *why* we were doing it . . . I have begun to dissect the lessons more to the "reasons" I have used these and why they have been successful. I've learned new techniques in teaching. I feel more responsible for helping my students. (final interview)

CONSTRUCTIVE CONVERSATION: GOAL AND CONTEXT FOR ADULT GROWTH

The cases argue that both Merin and Diana did undergo a change in mindset and in their approach to teaching of writing, but the change was not easy or straightforward for either. They deepened their understanding and appreciation of the three big ideas about writing and conversation introduced at the beginning of the chapter: Writing is a process of social construction of meaning; certain kinds of conversation can facilitate that process; and teachers have critical, highly intentional roles to play in facilitating students' talking and thinking for writing. Both fundamentally shifted from a view of writing as a set of subskills to a view of writing as a process of building ideas through the interplay of individual and shared thinking through conversation and writing. Both teachers eventually abandoned their holiday writing projects, though Merin more painfully and with more conflict than Diana. Both teachers continued beyond the life of the project to engage students in challenging writing activities around personally relevant themes and compelling problems and topics that students chose themselves.

In different ways, the two teachers came to understand that they had an important role to play in facilitating students' talking, thinking, and writing. Both experienced considerable role confusion as they turned over more of the control for the thinking and writing to their students, yet they worked on different aspects of their roles and structured different formats for conversations. Merin experimented with facilitating one-to-one conversations around students' writing because of her intense interest in assessing students' progress and because of her greater comfort with the active structuring role rather than with the background facilitator role. She loved talking with children about their writing but found it difficult to follow and identify their growth areas when they worked in groups. Adult–child conversations became a core part of her subsequent unit on *Groundhog's Horse*, along with a considerable number of paired conversations among students.

In contrast, Diana actively experimented with her role in facilitating small-group conversation. She herself had had a powerful experience with changing her mind as a result of talking with other teachers about the difficult moral dilemma in the adult short story, and she wanted to create similar intellectual opportunities for her students. She used what she had learned from TAC workshops about interviewing students as a way to join the conversation and support individual students' participation in a small group. Diana evidenced an understanding of the connection between conversation and the purpose of the writing problem. She was able to engage students, through conversation, in the very thinking processes (weighing choices and consequences, imagining alternatives, considering the historical/social context) they needed for the kind of writing they were doing. "They were really thinking it [the problem] through carefully and that's why they ended up having something to say when they wrote." Both teachers took risks in trying new ways of interacting with students. The success both teachers experienced in their respective experiments gave each fresh confidence. After a certain critical point, neither looked back.

The five elements of the intervention—engaging in adult analogue experiences, building explicit thinking frames, tracking and designing for focal students, analyzing success, scaffolding teacher growth—all contributed to each teacher's growth in integrating constructive conversation with new approaches to writing instruction. One aspect of the intervention that was particularly critical for Merin and Diana in different ways was the ongoing opportunity to reflect on their progress through intensive interviews with project staff. Our purpose was to gather data about the teachers' change process, but we came to see that our periodic interviews were also valuable for the teachers. For Merin, they became occasions to acknowledge her conflict and discomfort with her new writing program and her own role. The tone of the interviews reinforced her freedom to backtrack and resist and provided necessary slack for engaging in the program at her own rate and in her own way. For Diana, the interviews were opportunities to engage in one-to-one conversations with another adult and to analyze the practices and beliefs that had been largely tacit and out of awareness for her. In extending this model beyond the life of the research project, it may be important to integrate the roles of interested observer and "critical friend," both to help teachers manage the conflict involved in fundamental conceptual change and to support them in bringing their practices and theories to a more intentional, explicit, and metacognitive level.

Finally, the teachers' different interests, teaching styles, approaches to other subject areas (particularly reading), and personal experiences in the workshops led them and the other teachers to explore different but complementary roles of conversation in writing. This phenomenon—that teachers participated in a common adult learning experience but were able to grow in varied ways—is a striking aspect of the TAC intervention. The program seems to have created "zones of proximal development" for individual teachers' growth. Vygotsky (1978) originally defined "zone of proximal development" as the region of activity that learners can navigate with assistance from a supportive context. Brown and colleagues (Brown et al., 1993; Brown & Campione, 1994) extend the notion of assistance to include people, materials, artifacts, even computer technology. Learning environments for adults, children, or both can be seeded with ideas that teachers and researchers value, on the theory that key ideas are not appropriated in the same ways or to the same degrees by all participants. Brown's group uses the term "mutual appropriation" (p. 237) from other research streams (e.g., Newman, Griffin, & Cole, 1989) to refer to the multidirectional flow and interpretation of ideas that take place. A collaborative teacher development program becomes a zone of proximal development for many participants if they can use the ideas that emerge in different ways and give and receive varied levels of support.

What is finally most striking about all of the teachers in the TAC project is their individual risk taking and experimentation, which enabled all the teachers and researchers to move forward. Their openness in ongoing workshop conversations throughout each cycle provided a context for distributing the new knowledge and expertise gained by individual teachers. Constructive conversation in our adult learning community allowed each of us, in our own way, to deepen our understanding of the role of conversation in the social construction of writing. Perhaps most importantly, the project demonstrated the effectiveness of constructive conversations as a tool for the social construction of new approaches to teaching and learning.

ACKNOWLEDGMENTS

This chapter draws on data from the Teacher as Composer project carried out between 1990 and 1994. We deeply appreciate the contributions of Dr. Sue Marquis Gordon, project director, and Carol Howard, research assistant, to the original work of the project. The research was supported by a grant from the Office of Special Education and Rehabilitative Services (OSERS), United States Department of Education, under the research initiative of "Research on General Education Teacher Planning and Adaptation for Students with Handicaps."

REFERENCES

Biddulph, F., & Osborne, R. (1984). *Making sense of our world: An interactive teaching approach.* Hamilton, New Zealand: University of Warkalo Press.

Brown, A. L., Ash, D., Rutherford, M., Nakagawa, K., Godon, A., & Campione, J. C. (1993). Distributed expertise in the classroom. In G. Salom (Ed.), *Distributed cognitions: Psychological and educational considerations* (pp. 188–228). New York: Cambridge University Press.

Brown, A. L., Bransford, J. D., Ferrara, R. A., & Campione, J. C. (1983). Learning, remembering and understanding. In J. H. Flaveli & E. M. Markman (Eds.), *Handbook of child psychology: Vol. 3. Cognitive development* (4th ed.; pp. 77–166). New York: Wiley.

Brown, A. L., & Campione, J. C. (1994). Guided discovery in a community of learners. In K. McGilly (Ed.), *Classroom lessons: Integrating cognitive theory and classroom practice* (pp. 229–270). Cambridge, MA: MIT Press/Bradford Books.

Bruffee, K. A. (1986). Social construction, language, and the authority of knowledge: A bibliographic essay. *College English, 48,* 773–790.

Bruner, J. (1978). Games, social exchange, and the acquisition of language. *Journal of Child Language, 5*(3), 391–401.

Cazden, C. B. (1973). Problems for education: Language as curriculum content and learning environment. *Daedalus, 102*(3), 135–148.

Englert, C. S., & Mariage, T. V. (1991). Shared understandings: Structure the writing experience through dialogue. *Journal of Learning Disabilities, 24*(6), 330–342.

Englert, C. S., & Palincsar, A. S. (1991). Reconsidering instructional research in literacy from a sociocultural perspective. *Learning, Disabilities, Research and Practice, 6,* 225–229.

Englert, C. S., Tarrant, K. L., Mariage, T. V., & Oxer, T. (1994). Lesson talk as the work of reading groups: The effectiveness of two interventions. *Journal of Learning Disabilities, 27*(3), 165–185.

Fleer, M. (1992). Identifying teacher–child interaction which scaffolds scientific thinking in young children. *Science Education, 76*(4), 373–397.

Gamoran, A., & Nystrand, M. (1992). Taking students seriously. In F. M. Newmann (Ed.), *Student engagement and achievement in American secondary schools* (pp. 40–61). New York: Teachers College Press.

Goldenberg, C., & Gallimore, R. (1991, April). *Teaching and learning in a new key: The instructional conversation.* Paper presented at the annual meeting of the American Educational Research Association, Chicago.

Harste, J. C. (1994). Literacy as curricular conversations about knowledge, inquiry, and morality. In R. B. Ruddell, M. R. Ruddell, & H. Singer (Eds.), *Theoretical models and processes of reading* (4th ed.; p. 1224). Newark, DE: International Reading Association.

Linn, M. (1987). The new thrust in science education research. Establishing a research base for science education: Challenges, trends, recommendations. In *Journal of Research in Science Teachings, 24*(5), 191–216.

Morocco, C. C., Dalton, B., & Tivnan, T. (1992). The impact of computer-supported writing instruction in fourth-grade students with and without disabilities. In H. Margolis (Ed.), *Reading and Writing Quarterly, Overcoming Learning Difficulties, 18*(1), 87–114.

Morocco, C. C., Riley, M. K., Gordon, S. M., & Howard, C. L. (1996). The elusive individual in teachers' planning. In Gary G. Brannigan (Ed.), *The enlightened educator: Research adventures in the school* (pp. 155–178). New York: McGraw-Hill.

Morocco, C. C., & Zorfass, J. (1996). Response: Unpackaging scaffolding: Supporting students with disabilities in literacy development. In M. C. Pugach & C. L. Warger (Eds.), *Curriculum trends, special education, and reform: Refocusing the conversation* (pp. 164–178). New York: Teachers College Press.

Newman, D., Griffin, P., & Cole, M. (1989). *The construction zone.* Cambridge, UK: Cambridge University Press.

Palincsar, A. S., & Brown, A. L. (1984). Reciprocal teaching of comprehension-fostering and comprehension monitoring activities. *Cognition and Instruction, 1,* 117–175.

Poplin, M. S. (1988). Holistic/constructionist principles of the teaching/learning process: Implications for the field of learning disabilities. In *Journal of Learning Disabilities, 21*, 401–416.

Riley, M. K. (1994a, November). *Assessment as assistance: An alternative to red marks all over the paper.* Paper presented at the annual convention of the Council for Exceptional Children, Denver.

Riley, M. K. (1994b, February). *Mirroring critical images: Developing self-assessment skills to promote continuing professional development.* Paper presented at the annual conference of the American Association of Colleges for Teacher Education, Chicago.

Riley, M. K., & Howard, C. (1994, April). *The power of analogue in teacher development experiences.* Paper presented at the annual meeting of the American Educational Research Association, New Orleans.

Riley, M. K., Morocco, C. C., Gordon, S. M., & Howard, C. L. (1993). Walking the talk: Putting constructivist thinking into practice in classrooms. *Educational Horizons, 71*(4), 187–196.

Rome-Flanders, T., & Ricard, M. (1992). Infant timing of vocalizations in two mother-infant games: A longitudinal study. *First Language, 12*, 285–297.

Saunders, W., Goldenberg, C., & Hamann, J. (1992). Instructional conversations beget instructional conversations. *Journal of Teaching and Teacher Education, 8*(2), 199–218.

Sternberg, R. J., & Martin, M. (1988). When teaching thinking does not work, what goes wrong? *Teachers College Record, 89*(4), 555–578.

Stubbs, M. (1976). *Language, schools, and classrooms.* London: Methuen.

Vygotsky, L. S. (1978). *Mind in society: The development of higher psychological processes* (M. Cole, V. John-Steiner, S. Scribner, & E. Souberman, Eds. and Trans.). Cambridge, MA: Harvard University Press.

Watt, M. L., & Watt, D. L. (1995). *Doing research, taking action, and changing practice with collaborative support.* Newton, MA: Education Development Center.

Wood, D., Bruner, J., & Ross, G. (1976). The role of tutoring in problem solving. *Journal of Child Psychology and Psychiatry, 17*, 89–100.

CHAPTER 6

From Expert to Novice

The Transformation from Teacher to Learner

Ada Beth Cutler and Faye Nisonoff Ruopp

The publication of the National Council of Teachers of Mathematics' (NCTM) *Curriculum and Evaluation Standards* in 1989 generated a widespread movement to reform mathematics teaching and learning in America's classrooms. Textbook publishers, curriculum writers, and mathematics supervisors have jumped on the standards' bandwagon with enthusiasm, publishing new materials and issuing new guidelines for the teaching of mathematics. Nonetheless, because the standards ask teachers to make significant (some would say radical) changes in what and how they teach, true reform of mathematics education will not be achieved without meaningful, ongoing, and intensive staff development for mathematics teachers.

This chapter describes one effort to provide such staff development for middle school mathematics teachers. Through biweekly seminars, classroom coaching, and opportunities to teach in after-school and summer school programs, this project attempted (1) to educate teachers about new materials, approaches, and pedagogical strategies and (2) to encourage and support teachers' use of them. For most of the teachers who participated in the project, incorporating these materials and strategies meant changing fundamental beliefs and classroom practices.

We begin with a description of our goals and philosophy, followed by a presentation of findings from a longitudinal, qualitative study that shows the ways in which the content and structure of the project enabled teacher participants to embark on the complex process of changing their beliefs and practices about mathematics teaching and learning. Through vignettes from classroom observations and examples of teacher reflections from open-ended interviews, we offer and analyze examples of conceptual and practical teacher change. These findings offer insights into the critically important role of staff development in fostering, nurturing, and enhancing conceptual and practical change among experienced mathematics teachers. They also speak to some of the subtle, but vitally important, factors that influence the environment of change—factors relating to the way teachers view themselves, their profession, their colleagues, and the process of reform.

PROJECT DESCRIPTION

The origins of the project rest on the central assumption that student success in mathematics depends on upgrading teachers' knowledge and skills. With funding from the National Science Foundation (NSF), Education Development Center (EDC) created and implemented a model staff development program entitled the Middle School Math Project (Improving the Mathematical Performance of Low-Achieving Middle Schools Students: A Teacher-Centered Model). Twice a month for 2 years, 32 middle school teachers from the Greater Boston Area attended half-day workshops at EDC that were designed to encourage professional sharing, risk taking, and reflection. The content of the workshops was guided by the NCTM *Curriculum and Evaluation Standards*, which we used to help teachers understand the variables that contribute to academic success. In addition, the framework and structure of the workshops were founded on some of our essential beliefs about teachers, teaching, and professional development:

Teachers are professionals. The design of workshops throughout the school year was predicated on the assumption that teachers, like other professionals, need time to become engaged in new ideas and approaches, grapple with problems, reflect on their own learning, and explore applications of what they are learning. Importantly, time for the workshops, which extended over 2 years, was allocated from teachers' regular workdays—a significant departure from most professional development programs for teachers. Typically, professional development programs consist of one-time workshops, frequently after school, with little follow-up support or technical assistance (Fullan, 1979, 1991; Pink, 1989). To ensure that there would be ample release time for teachers, we arranged for corporate co-sponsoring. Our partners—the Polaroid Corporation, Digital Equipment Corporation, NYNEX, GTE Labs—provided release time for employees to serve as substitutes for project teachers on workshop days.[1]

Treating teachers as professionals extended to the environment that project staff created for the teachers. At each workshop, EDC provided both breakfast and lunch, a rare treat for most teachers. Although this may sound trivial in the larger world of teacher development, teachers frequently commented that the catered meals made them feel valued and respected. In addition, although EDC did not pay teachers for their time, it did offer them college credit through a local state university.

After each seminar, project staff asked participants for written feedback on the seminar content and design. The project took seriously the notion that the focus of professional development programs should be on crucial problems of curriculum and instruction that are defined by the participants as areas of concern or interest (Fullan, 1979, 1991; Little, 1984; Loucks-Horsley et al., 1987). Teachers responded positively to being treated as professionals; they were presented with options, authority, and responsibility—the dimensions of empowerment (Lambert, 1987).

Teachers need opportunities to become active learners in a supportive, collegial environment. One of the project's primary goals was to establish a learning community, where teachers felt comfortable taking risks and reflecting on their experiences. At each seminar, teachers were engaged in doing mathematics together. Materials and activities were deliberately chosen to reinforce the project's view of students as active and capable learners. Just as teachers constructed their own knowledge of mathematics through doing, discussing, and reflecting upon the mathematics, project staff constantly drew the analogy to students behaving in similar ways in their classrooms. At the beginning of each seminar, workshop leaders instituted a sharing time, in which teachers would tell their stories of success and failure in grappling with their own personal changes. They used this learning community as a sounding board and source of support as they examined their teaching and experimented with new materials and strategies. Many teachers reported that such opportunities to share ideas were nonexistent in their own schools.

Teachers need first-hand experience with exemplary teaching strategies and materials. The NCTM *Curriculum and Evaluation Standards* put forth a vision for content and teaching standards. They ask teachers to teach in ways many have never seen before, with materials that are not always readily available. In our initial observations of participating teachers, we witnessed teacher-centered classrooms where information was delivered in the form of lecture, individual seatwork, and repetitive practice of newly learned skills. Project staff wanted teachers to shift their view of mathematics away from an emphasis on rote learning, computation, and symbol manipulation toward a vision of mathematics as problem solving, critical thinking, reasoning, and communicating. Staff chose problems for the workshop that reinforced these concepts (a description of one of these problems follows in the seminar portrait section) and gave teachers time to reflect on them at each seminar, whether in small groups, in their journals, or as a large group.

Whenever possible in seminar presentations, facilitators modeled teaching that reflected a new vision of what a mathematics classroom could be. They posed open-ended questions to teachers about the mathematics at hand; they encouraged discourse among participants by having them consider the conjectures of their colleagues; facilitators frequently had teachers work in groups so that they would get a sense of the power of bouncing ideas off one another; they posed problems that would encourage teachers' own construction of the mathematical principles to be learned. After each experience in doing mathematics together, facilitators asked questions such as: "What did you learn from this activity? What is the mathematics being taught? How is it different from the traditional way of teaching this concept?" Facilitators took advantage of any opportunity to create situations in which teachers were active learners.

Teachers need support in their classrooms when experimenting with a newly learned practice. The project's model of professional development recognized that teachers need opportunities to practice new skills with feedback if they are to expand their repertoires. Taking the risk of trying something new is not easy. Therefore, the project developed a coaching model that provided long-term support. During the second half of the school year, as teachers were trying new approaches and materials in their classrooms, project staff visited each teacher's classroom at least twice to provide feedback and coaching. During individual pre-observation conferences, teachers informed staff of their needs, which ranged from demonstration classes by project staff to learn a new piece of content or pedagogy, to refining a lesson with cooperative learning. The goal was to tailor the visits to the individual needs of a wide range of teachers. In addition, summer school classes organized by the project provided a laboratory for the teachers to try out new materials and strategies, as well as to work with colleagues from the project in a team-teaching arrangement.

Teacher development is highly individual. Teacher participants were selected on the basis of their willingness to look closely at their practice in order to consider change. The project accepted teachers who represented a wide spectrum of practice. Project staff knew that teachers would each take away something different from their experiences, and the goal was to help them expand their individual "comfort zones" (Lovitt & Clarke, 1988). For some teachers, working with a manipulative to uncover a new understanding of a concept represented a stretch in their thinking. Others were more concerned with the process of learning and how the tools of mathematics are used in a broader conceptualization of certain mathematical habits of mind. It was important, then, to choose activities and problems with a range of entry points, so that individuals could determine the relevance for themselves. Project staff understood each participant had a unique learning curve in the continuum of mathematical and pedagogical development; and we learned that this curve was neither smooth nor predictable. The profiles that follow of two participants provide a vivid illustration of the individualized and "bumpy" nature of development.

All teachers can learn and change. As often as possible, facilitators conveyed the expectation that participants would each be able to change their current practice in some way. The project expected them to achieve great things, just as it encouraged them to have high expectations of their own students in mathematics. The project accepted the basic premise articulated by

Lynn Steen, past president of the Mathematics Association of America, that we "must come to understand that achievement in mathematics is possible for all students, not only for those with a special talent" (Steen, 1987).

At the same time, project staff made special efforts to provide participants with caring, emotional support, and respect as they struggled to embrace reform and change their thinking. Through these interactions, facilitators came to understand the delicate balance between urging teachers to venture outside their comfort zone and respecting their need to maintain a sense of control and competency. We run the risk of alienating teachers if, in guiding them toward reform, we lead them to feel overwhelmingly unsettled and frustrated in their work. Project staff were mindful of how necessary it was to reassure teachers that changing beliefs means leaving their comfort zones and grappling with some uncomfortable shifts in thinking and feeling. Because of the staff's own experiences in the classroom, they understood how necessary it was to provide an atmosphere that buoyed teachers' spirits, introduced humor when appropriate, and provided a release for some of those feelings of frustration and doubt.

SEMINAR CONTENTS

Throughout the first year of the project, teachers examined a number of pre-algebra and algebra topics that were appropriate for the middle school level and that correlated closely with the *Curriculum and Evaluation Standards.* Teachers discussed national perspectives on mathematics curriculum for the 1990s, with attention to issues of equity and achievement. Project staff helped teachers select manipulatives and computer software appropriate for meeting different educational objectives. The project explored strategies for integrating calculators and a full range of computer applications into their teaching of particular topics.

Research was an important component of the seminars. Facilitators guided teachers to important articles on such issues as the effects of tracking, low teacher expectations, and lack of access to higher-level mathematics topics. The project provided articles on each of these topics, including the most current research, and staff held extended discussions on the research and its relevance to the teachers' own classrooms. Facilitators found that teachers did not have time to read during their days at school, and so provided this time during some of the seminars. (Interestingly, many resisted reading as well as writing initially.) Staff also encouraged teachers to conduct their own research on factors that influenced low mathematics achievement in their districts. In addition, some of the seminars focused on strategies that have succeeded in improving the motivation and achievement of poor performers. Teachers explored ways to accommodate different learning styles, ways to emphasize the utility of mathematics, the use of manipulatives, cooperative learning, and models that integrate challenging tasks into remediation.

Later in the project, teachers examined assessment strategies to observe and document student learning. In order to facilitate their judgments about interventions that make a difference in their classes, teachers created and explored specific methods of assessment of student growth and development: open-ended questions, portfolio assessments, and performance assessments.

SEMINAR PORTRAIT

Since the seminars were central to the teachers' experiences, we provide in this section a detailed description of one of the first-year seminars. Our intent is to illustrate the strategies, interactions, and pedagogy typical of the seminars as a whole, as well as the conceptual framework on which the design was based. The italicized text provides a commentary from the program staff on the rationales for including certain key elements in the seminar.

> It was a Thursday morning at 8:30 in the conference room at EDC. After chatting informally over coffee and a light breakfast, teachers were seated in eight groups of four at tables around the room.
>
> *Modeling our knowledge of diverse learners and their needs, we grouped the teachers heterogeneously so that those with stronger math backgrounds could facilitate the learning of those with weaker knowledge.*
>
> We began by asking if anyone had anything to share. On this day, at first no one responded, but we waited patiently.
>
> *This question was a routine one by now for the participants. We tried to create an atmosphere of trust and support by showing patience and constant reinforcement for teachers' willingness to share their thoughts and experiences. As a result, as the weeks went by, even in the large group of 32 teachers, more and more teachers shared their failures, triumphs, puzzlements, and new insights. We resisted the temptation to tell them what they wanted to know or to interpret their experimentation with new strategies and materials. Instead, we modeled the teacher's role by supporting and aiding construction of their own knowledge. We asked probing questions of our own to extend teachers' thinking and understanding, which elicited confirming stories or insights from other teachers.*
>
> When silence prevailed for a few more moments, we injected a touch of humor in an attempt to break the ice. "No one has anything to

share? Did school get canceled last week?" Everyone laughed, and just as we began to talk about the work of the day, a teacher said, "Wait! I have something to share—a great idea I had last week." He proceeded to describe how he used an equation balance beam to demonstrate addition and subtraction with integers. We asked him to bring it in the following week, "so we can play with it." Another teacher interjected, "He just jogged my mind." She told of trying to teach ratio and proportion with Cuisenaire rods and how some students couldn't "see" what she was trying to demonstrate.

The teacher said, "Rote they understand, but concepts they can't seem to get. I'm really struggling." We then encouraged the other teachers to think about examples for this topic and to bring them in the next time.

Teachers often confused work with manipulatives with "getting the concept." We knew that for some teachers, work with manipulatives was a first step in understanding different representations of mathematical concepts—such as representing fractional relationships with different-sized rods. However, we also understood that many teachers use manipulatives as just another algorithmic approach. For example, through practice students may learn that the blue rod plus the red rod equals the green rod, but that doesn't mean they are developing any understanding of addition of fractions.

Before we introduced the first activity, we asked what the issues and problems are for kids in making and forming graphs. The teachers readily contributed many issues, including the idea of uniform scale, the concept of independent and dependent variables, making projections from graphs, and understanding discrete versus continuous data.

In asking this question, we were gathering information to assess how teachers were accustomed to teaching about graphing, and what they thought was important about graphing. Many of the responses indicated that student knowledge of setting up values on the axes was of great importance, which was what we had expected. We hoped that the seminar would change their focus away from the "grammar" (Shell Centre for Mathematical Education, 1985) to the larger idea of graphs as a representation of mathematical concepts.

We then introduced an activity on qualitative graphing by reminding them of an earlier comment by one of the teachers—that often it is helpful to relate graphs to problem solving by connecting them to real events. We demonstrated by dropping a set of keys to the floor and putting up four graphs and asking which one represented the motion of the falling keys. (See Figure 6.1.) A discussion ensued, with the teachers disagreeing about the correct answer. A few of the teachers argued good naturedly about their opinions. We said, "This illustrates that reasoning from graphs isn't easy. We need to start out slowly with kids." Teachers then discussed among themselves in their groups and subsequently with the whole group which of the four graphs was correct.

The graphs each had the axes labeled "time" and "distance." None of the graphs had numbers on them, a distinguishing feature of qualitative graphs. The different shapes of the curves in the graphs forced teachers to think about concepts such as acceleration, constant velocity, and even the effects of gravity. (The speed of the falling keys increases as they get nearer to the ground. Or, put another way, the keys cover more and more distance over time, as shown in graph #3 in Figure 6.1.) We allowed all

Figure 6.1. Graphs of Keys Falling

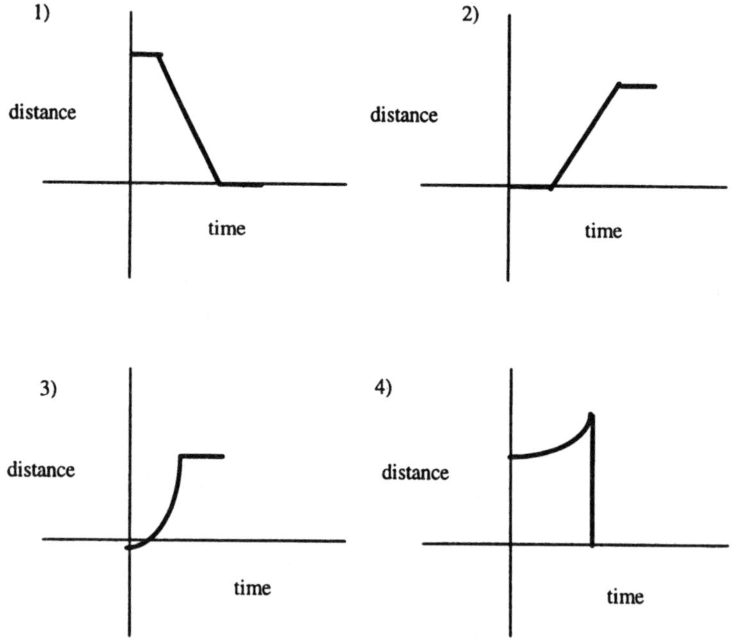

opinions to be heard without evaluating them, because we wanted the teachers to be free to think about the mathematics without having to worry about being corrected as right or wrong. We modeled accepting and encouraging multiple conjectures, so that the discourse took the pattern of teacher-to-teacher, rather than project staff-to-teacher. In fact, many of the teachers' conjectures were incorrect, yet participants felt comfortable in stating their positions because we had created an atmosphere of trust.

At various intervals, the teachers offered ideas for using these activities with students, what might and might not work, what might be too hard, and how to change them if that were the case.

After a break, we explained that graphs have predictive as well as descriptive attributes. The notion of slope is always a difficult one for students, and examining a mathematical model (a graph) based on a physical experience may make the concept more relevant. We explained that they would be going outside to collect some data they would then have to plot on a speed graph. The entire group went outside, and in pairs they walked and then jogged a measured distance while timing each other. Once again, good-natured kidding and joking were part of the activity.

This activity, Speed Graphs, is from the Mathematics Curriculum and Teaching Program (MCTP) (Lovitt & Clarke, 1988), a collection of mathematics activities from Australia that portray powerful mathematical ideas in thoughtful, interesting contexts, many of which include visual imagery, physical activity, and mathematical models. This particular activity gives personal relevance to the meaning of the general linear equation $y = mx$ by creating a model based on different walking and running speeds. (See Figure 6.2.) We used it because we felt it would have great appeal to middle school students because of its active and motivating nature, and because it illustrated the concept of slope realistically.

After returning to the seminar room, the teachers drew graphs of these two situations. We led a challenging discussion about slope and its meaning in this specific graph, and then referred them back to the keys problem they had worked on before. We continued to pose open-ended questions, pushing the teachers to stretch their math knowledge and their conceptions of slope. "Was the speed constant? What if the graph went like this, what would it mean? What could we extrapolate from this?"

One teacher noticed the significance of a parabola, and we discussed this with her and gave her some new insights. Teachers were

Figure 6.2.

In the Speed Graphs activity from MCTP (Lovitt & Clarke, 1988, pp. 567–571), students are asked to make a linear graph of walking and jogging speeds based on data they've collected themselves. The activity gives students a physical sense and model for linear (or straight line) graphs, which fit the equation $y = mx$. They find that in order to produce a linear graph, they need to maintain a constant speed. After gathering their own data and graphing the results for distance covered over 10 seconds, students create a mathematical model of their walk and jog speeds by extrapolating to times up to 30 seconds. The model provides students with a representation of slope and the equation $y = mx$, as shown in this example from MCTP:

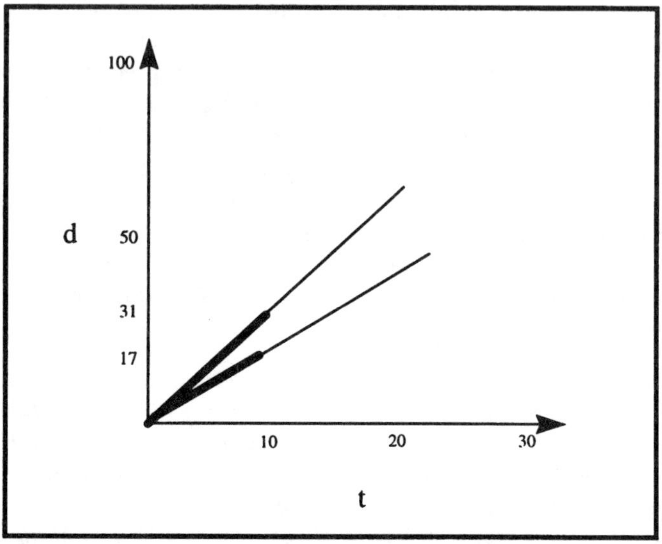

The slope and hence the equation of each linear graph can be found. In this case, walk d = 1.7t; jog d = 3.1t

open about their confusion, and when teachers said, "I don't understand," we would help them analyze what they didn't understand and guide them to better understanding.

This particular teacher wanted to explore the meaning of a parabolic curve. She was one of the most mathematically competent teachers in the group and was always looking for extensions in her work. Since her questions went well beyond the scope of the workshop, one of us took her aside and worked with her on the questions she had. Again, we wanted to support teachers taking an activity into a realm which interested them.

We pointed out that we had not yet given any formulas or even mentioned the word "slope" in the discussion, and we asked if they would do the same with students. "Remember, there are visual images of what slope is that students can understand before giving them formulas. Is it clear here that slope is being portrayed as a rate of change?" We then showed a video clip on polynomials that dealt with slope, further reinforcing the ideas and concepts we had demonstrated before.

Teachers often jump to the mathematical definition before students have an intuitive, conceptual idea of the mathematics. Often teachers had a difficult time "forgetting" what they know; that is, they tried to construct a forgotten algorithm before they gave themselves an opportunity to really think about the situation.

At the end of the seminar, teachers filled out written evaluations and took the next half-hour to talk informally over lunch about topics of personal interest.

As was the custom, all the materials and activities used during the seminar were distributed for the teachers to take home and hopefully use with their students. The materials used allowed for different levels of understanding, and we did not exhibit a need for all the teachers to be on the same level.

THE EFFECTS OF THE SEMINARS

The seminar series was clearly the centerpiece of the project and as such it served as the showplace for the values, skills, habits, and knowledge the project was trying to promote. As part of the longitudinal evaluation of the project, we interviewed the teacher participants at regular intervals. In addition, Ada Beth Cutler and Barbara Neufeld of Education Matters, Inc., conducted an independent evaluation study of the project. The study included regular interviews with the staff and teacher participants; classroom and seminar observations; periodic questionnaires for teachers, students, and industry participants; and document analysis. Teachers' reactions to the seminars and their reflections on what they learned there gave us important insights into what the teachers valued as learners and how what they learned became part of their own thinking and practice.

Teachers' Overall Reactions to the Seminars

In intensive interviews at the end of each year of the project, the teachers were asked for their general reactions to the seminars, what they liked best and least, and what suggestions they had for improvement. Overall reactions to the seminar series were overwhelmingly positive from a wide range of teachers—teachers from urban and suburban schools, teachers who were already implementing the NCTM standards in their classrooms and teachers for whom the standards represented radical departures from their curriculum and pedagogy, teachers who were initially eager to try new things and teachers who were timid and apprehensive about change. All found meaning, motivation, and materials in the project's seminar series.

When we analyzed teachers' statements about what they learned and valued in the seminars, we heard echoes of the project's philosophical underpinnings that we outlined earlier in this chapter. The importance of being treated as a professional, the value of being part of a community of learners, the eye-opening exposure to new visions of teaching and materials, the place of positive expectations for all students, and the benefits of nurturing and supporting teachers all came through loud and clear.

Being Treated as a Professional. Teacher participants appreciated the fact that this project "treated [them] as professionals" and allowed them to process and share their learning with colleagues in a meaningful way.

> I really gained a lot from the seminars, professionally. I think what did it was the fact that I was allowed to do this during school time, not after school. I was treated as a professional. I would go to a seminar and listen to everything that was discussed, the new idea, what people had to say, and then in the ride back to school I would process it and take out of it what was worthwhile for me and then I would use it.

Building a Community of Learners. The teachers' statements about what they liked best about the seminars revealed how important collegiality and an atmosphere of trust and professionalism are in the learning process of experienced teachers. Over and over we heard how much they valued having an accessible cadre of professional colleagues with whom to share ideas, experiences, expertise, and knowledge. It is an element missing in the lives of almost all teachers, and the participants in this project reveled in its existence within the seminars. Clearly there is more to teacher learning than content and pedagogy. If we are advocating more interactive learning for students, we must also offer opportunities for teachers to benefit from collegial learning and sharing.

The traditional source of knowledge and ideas for teachers is experts or outside consultants. In the course of the seminars, these teachers worked in groups and learned how to learn from each other. In addition, project staff modeled and structured professional sharing of ideas and dilemmas as part of the seminars. It appears that these efforts have had a major effect on the teachers' sense of appropriate sources of knowledge, ideas, and help. The majority of the teachers said they needed to spend more time observing, brainstorming, and planning with their colleagues (often specific colleagues from the project) in order to learn what they needed to know to teach better. From this, we learned just how far the teachers had progressed toward norms of collegiality and experimentation. As one teacher said:

> I can learn so much from sharing with the other teachers. In summer school [a component of the project], [one of the other teachers] had more background and experience with manipulatives than we did. So she would bring them in, and show us how to use them, and then help us use them. I think, as you learn about these things, you want to see how somebody else approached it and what they used, and now I've got things I've tried that other teachers can learn from. In fact, I'm bringing in a game to tomorrow's seminar that all my classes have loved, to share. It's like, "Here's my idea; we can learn from each other."

These notions are radical ones for teachers. Not only is this experienced teacher explaining how much she learned from another, younger teacher, she is, perhaps more importantly, explaining that she now sees herself as a source of valuable ideas and help for other teachers. The culture of teaching holds equality of teachers as a strong norm, but rather than equality coupled with collegiality, it usually means equality in isolation, with each teacher functioning as an independent, solo practitioner. In fact, in most schools teachers are reluctant to share ideas and triumphs for fear of being seen as a braggart or show-off. Conversely, they are just as reluctant to admit to failures or perplexing dilemmas lest colleagues perceive them as incompetent. At least within the context of this project, those norms have been broken. The following comment from a teacher participant supports this assertion:

> The sharing was so important for me. I got wonderful ideas from other teachers, but even more I got courage, I became a little braver, when I heard other teachers say, "I tried this and it didn't go so well the first time, but I changed X or Y the second time, and it was better." Teachers are so isolated—you never get to hear what's really happening in other classrooms. . . . In this [project] I found out what professional sharing is for the first time in my life and I've been teaching for 20 years.

Nurturing and Risk Taking. Providing an atmosphere that encouraged teachers to learn from and share with their colleagues wasn't the only important affective component to the seminar series. Risk taking is not a common norm in most schools, and project staff believe teachers need to feel supported and nurtured in order to establish that norm in their own classrooms. The following comments told us that teachers appreciated this affective aspect of the seminars:

> You know I was apprehensive at first, I'm apprehensive about changing and it's difficult for me to change. But [project staff] are so supportive. It really helps if someone helps you along. I'm trying things and I'm really looking forward to making more changes in the fall.

> [Project staff] really made us feel like equals, not that they're superior. They gave us so much freedom and let us express our frustrations and our successes. They never made us feel like we were being evaluated, just encouraged and respected. I loved that.

More Comfort with New Materials and Strategies. When we asked the teachers what they had learned in the seminars, almost everyone focused on new materials and strategies for teaching math. For the majority of the teachers, the model activities involving effective use of hands-on materials and cooperative learning were the most useful and exciting elements of the seminars. All of the teachers had heard or read testimonials to the value of manipulatives and cooperative learning, but very few had had the opportunity to experiment with activities that were designed to maximize the effect of these materials or strategies. Significantly, the teachers came to see manipulatives and cooperative learning as means rather than ends. For example, facilitators discussed both the power and limitations of manipulatives: In some activities manipulatives provide a concrete representation that leads students toward understanding of key concepts, while in other activities manipulatives serve merely as a substitute for algorithms or may even add a layer of confusion that obscures key concepts.

For many of the teachers, learning about and experiencing effective uses of manipulatives and cooperative learning opened their eyes to new ideas about who can learn and how learning takes place. The following quotes are illustrative of the teachers' comments:

> I'm a teacher of 25 years and I haven't ever used manipulatives before. To see how they could be used and then to come into the classroom and try them and see them received very well by the children, that's what I liked. The sharing of ideas I could take back to my classroom and see if they would work.

> I learned that there are other ways of teaching math than the way I've been doing it for 20 years. I realized that just because I can follow the rules, not everybody can. Just because you know an algorithm doesn't mean you understand math. It has opened my eyes and told me kids need pictures and concrete materials if they are going to understand this.

Positive Expectations—Everyone Can Learn. At the beginning of the project, most of the teacher participants believed that only some students could learn algebra in a meaningful way. This belief probably stemmed from their own experiences trying to teach algebra to all students in the same, rather abstract fashion. In the seminars, they learned of more concrete, accessible ways to present algebra that enable all kinds of learners to experience success. One of the teachers spoke for many of her colleagues when she told us:

> Algebra for everyone? "No way" I thought when I first heard this. In the seminars I learned that instead of the old way, the lecture way, kids can learn from each other. I learned that they can learn, that some kids need to have manipulatives and the hands-on in order to understand. I brought this back to my classroom, and I saw with my own eyes that it works.

Our interview data clearly reveal that many of the teachers believed their participation in the project profoundly affected their thinking about teaching and learning mathematics. In addition, observation data indicate that there were important changes in the teachers' classroom practices as well. In the following section, we present portraits of two teachers who underwent important transformations in their approaches to content and pedagogy, their use of materials, and the nature of their relationships with students. Although these two teachers were at different places in their willingness to take risks and relinquish control, these portraits highlight the kinds of evolution in beliefs and practices that all participants experienced.

Portraits of Change

In addition to extensive interviews, our evaluation study used classroom observations to assess program effects. The observations confirmed what we already knew about the teacher participants—they were a highly diverse group in a number of ways. Most had been teaching for more than 15 years, but a few had been teaching for less than 5 years. Some of the teachers had a strong academic background in math, others very little. At the beginning of the project, many of the teachers took an almost entirely procedural, algorithmic approach to teaching and learning math, while only a few used a conceptual approach that incorporated hands-on learning. Some teachers concentrated on frontal teaching of rote mathematical skills, but a few were already using cooperative learning groups and a problem-solving approach.

Regardless of where they were at the beginning of the project, after 2 years all the teachers showed evidence of some change in practice. These changes included using group work or cooperative learning, introducing hands-on materials for selected lessons, trying out new and different curricular materials, or a combination of these innovations. For a few of the teachers, these innovations were merely refinements of already adopted practices, but for others, these innovations were radical departures from the practices we observed at the beginning of the project. We saw relatively expert use of new methods and materials. However, we also saw teachers try to duplicate lessons they had experienced in the seminars, as though the demonstration lessons were scripts to be followed rather than examples of possible strategies.

It is important to note that these teachers were almost all veterans of 10 or more years in the classroom. After so many years in the classroom, experienced teachers are usually confident and comfortable when they teach. However one might categorize or evaluate their teaching practices, participants were, for the most part, "experts" at what they did. For such teachers, trying to teach in new ways, with new classroom configurations and/or new materials, necessitates leaving one's well-rehearsed "expert" status behind. One becomes a novice in many ways, experimenting without a memorized script, without a clear sense of what will happen or what could go wrong. At the end of 1 year in the project, we saw previously confident teachers become nervous and tentative, sometimes making careless mathematical errors and sometimes consulting their notes or papers for their next words. Often they were harsh in their self-evaluations after the lessons we observed, reflecting their discomfort with being novices in the classroom. Many of the teachers told us how important project staff's positive coaching encouragement was for them—how it pushed them to experiment and helped them achieve a sense of perspective on what they were trying to do.

There was real and noticeable change in the teaching practices of the project's participants. This finding is both heartening and daunting at the same time. It is unrealistic to assume that teachers can quickly become fully competent and comfortable with new teaching methods and materials. Sometimes, for example, teachers made an effort to introduce a concept with concrete models, but they didn't allow enough time for the discovery process or they neglected to help students make the leap from concrete models to abstract representations. On the basis of these observations, we acknowledge that as teachers move from rote, rules-bound teaching to a more conceptually based framework, initially their students may not learn very well or even as well as they did when their teachers felt confident and expert.

We point out these daunting issues not to denigrate the process of teacher change, but rather to emphasize its complexity and delicacy. In the following pages, we offer vignettes of two teachers at the beginning and at the end of the project. The vignettes are based on interviews and classroom observations that project staff and evaluators carried out throughout the project. Pseudonyms are used, and school names and locations are omitted in order to maintain confidentiality.

While these are portraits of actual individuals, not composites, they are representative of groups of teachers within the project. We hope that these mini-portraits will provide a picture of not only the range of teachers in the project but also, more importantly, the implications of that range for expected learning, growth, and change as a result of participation in such a project. As we will show, for some teachers learning was a matter of small increments of change, while for others learning meant a reconceptualization of mathematics and/or pedagogy.

Jane Regan

Jane teaches seventh- and eighth-grade math in a socioeconomically mixed suburban school. Most of the students are white, but there is a growing Hispanic population in the school. Jane has been teaching seventh- and eighth-grade math for almost 20 years and finds algebra her favorite course to teach. She admitted she has not changed her teaching methods very much during those years. She explained why she chose to become involved in the EDC project:

> Because I thought, after teaching almost 20 years, that I needed something different. There were some teachers' meetings and things about standards and that, maybe I should know a little bit more about it. And I wasn't getting it from just staying in the classroom. So when this seminar came along, I thought it was a great idea. And I thought this is something that I need to do . . . and to have somebody there to show me things.

When Jane was interviewed, she had already attended the first two seminars and was enthusiastic about them and the project in general. Her comments reflect the initial stages of a teacher who needed the support of being "shown how to do" something before trying out a new practice. Although this was not the project's ultimate goal in working with teachers, we nevertheless realized that for Jane, in particular, this first stage was essential in expanding her own comfort zone.

While Jane's enthusiasm for the project was evident in her responses to interview questions, so was her anxiety about implementing new teaching practices.

> I want to try this, you know, and see how it works in my classroom. And I have to remember that I have large classes, and I'm little bit apprehensive. Is this going to work? Are we going to have scissors all over the place, or rulers all over the place? You know, you have 25 students in a classroom trying to cut and paste and whatever. It's great when you have a small group of people. But that's not always reality.

Jane later admitted that she didn't have any experience with using hands-on materials but that she believed they might offer a "better way to teach." Her apprehensions about "whether these things are going to work" in her own classroom were shared by many of her colleagues in the project. Even when teachers have a sincere desire to change those practices, a great deal of anxiety is usually present.

During our interviews with teacher participants, we presented them with a series of hypothetical classroom vignettes. Jane's initial responses to the vignettes showed a ready understanding of, and a concentration on, algorithmic procedures, but also a real desire to learn how to teach these topics conceptually. For example, we presented Jane with this vignette about division with fractions:

> Imagine you are teaching your students division with fractions. One of your students raises his hand and says, "I'm very confused. This doesn't make sense. The answers I'm getting are greater than the numbers I started with! What am I doing wrong?" And he shows you one of the examples that he has done: $3\frac{1}{2} \div \frac{1}{4} = 14$
>
> What do you think is going on here? How would you respond to this student? What if that didn't help him? Is there something else you could do?

She responded to the vignette by saying she would tell the student, "You know, reciprocals. We set up division of fractions by using reciprocals. And it's hard to visualize the fact that it should come out larger than what you're dividing." She went on to explain she hoped the seminars would teach her better ways of visualizing this for her students.

A second vignette focused on exponents. When asked how she would respond to a student's assertion that X^2 is always greater than X, Jane said,

"Well, my first response is that 0 is one [exception]: 0-squared is equal to 0, and 0 equals 0. So that would be my response, that that's not true for every number." Once again, no conceptual framework was offered, and her pedagogical strategy was to tell the student "that that's not true for every number."

An observation of one of Jane's eighth-grade pre-algebra classes confirmed the interview findings that Jane's approach to teaching math was algorithmically based, with a concentration on traditional frontal teaching with students using only pencils, papers, and books. During the observation, Jane taught a lesson on multiplication of integers. She explained before the class that she wanted students to "figure out for themselves" the correct rules for these operations by finding patterns in a multiplication chart she gave them. Jane's class was set up with desks in straight rows. On this particular day there were 19 of the 25 students in the class present.

Standing at the front of the room, Jane asked for oral answers to fill in the multiplication chart she had handed out. "What's 3 × 3? What's 3 × 2? What's 3 × 1?" She called on students who had hands raised, and correct answers were offered. As she proceeded, she asked, "Does anyone see a pattern here?" One student volunteered, "They're decreasing by 3." Jane quickly responded, "So you just write in the next spot –3, then –6, then –9." Once the chart was completed, Jane asked if anyone had any rules yet. No one responded, and Jane quickly handed out two worksheets on multiplication of integers. Each worksheet had 42 problems, as well as rules for the operations written on the top. While the students worked through the 84 problems, Jane remained at her desk at the front of the room. No students talked to each other at any time during the class, and all appeared to be working. After 15 minutes, Jane said, "Let's see what conclusions you drew, but first let's quickly see what answers you got." She read through the answers very quickly and then turned to the board and wrote: RULES FOR MULTIPLICATION OF INTEGERS. She said, "You can use your own words, or the words on the pages for these rules. What's the rule for the first page?" A boy volunteered, "A positive times a positive equals a positive." Jane wrote this on the board and then asked for the rules for the second page. A girl volunteered, "A positive times a negative equals a negative and a negative times a positive equals a negative." Jane asked the class if it mattered whether the numbers involved were small or large, and a few students answered chorally, "No." She solicited one more rule ("A negative times a negative equals a positive") and then said, "Now you know the rules of multiplication of integers. These sheets were easy; now open to page 65 for harder examples." She went over a few examples orally, pointing out what happens when the problem has three numbers. At the end of the class, she instructed the class, "Your homework is problems 9 through 20. Do all your work, *no* calculators, and concentrate on the signs, OK?"

While the students had discovered patterns on the chart, Jane did not ask them to make any connection between the patterns and the rules. Since the rules were written on the top of the worksheets, and Jane had pointed this out to them, it was impossible to know if any of the students had figured out the rules for themselves. Jane's answers to hypothetical situations presented in the interviews and her classroom interactions with students indicated an approach to teaching as telling—an approach vastly different from the one advocated by the project. Nonetheless, Jane had explained that she wanted students to figure out the rules for themselves, again indicating at least a desire to adopt a more investigative, student-centered approach.

When we asked after the class if she ever groups students in class for work, she said she sometimes pairs them to go over test answers, but the size of this class (25) makes it difficult to use groups. In the interview Jane had expressed worries about discipline and control when using concrete materials. Given that, it was interesting to note that Jane's students were extremely quiet during her class, never speaking to each other or speaking out without being called on by Jane. It seemed clear that her conception of a well-disciplined class would have to change in order for her to introduce these new pedagogical strategies with any degree of comfort.

Jane Regan—Two Years Later. In the spring of the second year of the project, we visited Jane's class of seventh-graders while she taught a lesson on probability. Jane explained in a pre-observation interview that she would be using strategies and approaches that had been modeled in the project seminar series. Jane's enthusiasm for using concrete materials, cooperative learning, and student investigations was palpable:

> I can't believe how much more fun I'm having and the kids are having. After all those years of teaching the same way, I now know there are other ways to get across what I want them to learn. I know I'm not great at it yet, and sometimes I get discouraged, but I'm not afraid to have the kids doing things and using manipulatives. Remember how I told you I couldn't imagine giving them things they could throw? . . . Remember how I had to have [a staff member] teach a lesson with my kids before I would try cooperative learning?

Jane is describing here her need to have a pedagogical approach demonstrated using her own students; we realized that for some teachers, it was not enough to have a vision of someone else's classroom. They needed first-hand experience in order to believe that a technique might be possible with their own kids.

Early in the lesson, Jane asked questions about the meaning and occurrence of probability in real life. Contrary to her rather stiff demeanor when we first observed her teaching, Jane made genuine attempts to inject humor into her lesson. Mimicking a humorous device for introducing the notion of probability that project staff had used in a seminar, she asked her students what the probability was of Mr. Brooks (a teacher down the hall) coming in and asking her to go to a dance. Many students chuckled and most agreed the probability would be 0. About 15 minutes later, Mr. Brooks appeared and said, "Ms. Regan, could you possibly go to the dance with me tomorrow night?" The classroom erupted with laughter and comments, with students shouting, "Oh my God, was that planned?" and "Do you believe that happened?"

During the lesson, Jane had students working in small groups with bags of M&M's to derive the probability of drawing different-colored M&M's. The students were actively engaged in the task at hand, and Jane circulated to see how they were doing. She stopped periodically to comment on their efforts and to offer encouragement. With each group, there were opportunities to ask thoughtful questions, but Jane seemed to be following a lesson plan rather than seizing the opportunities for deeper learning. Later in the lesson, Jane forgot to tally all of the group's results for the M&M experiment, thus missing an opportunity to extend students' understanding of probability through a discussion of the variability of results and, more generally, the difference between theoretical and experimental probability.

Despite those missed opportunities, the differences between this lesson and the first lesson we observed in Jane's class were profound. There was very little frontal teaching, the content was relevant and tied to real-life situations, students talked to Jane and to each other about their work, students had concrete materials to use for learning concepts, and there was an air of excitement and engagement in the room. And though the lesson was nearly identical to one Jane had experienced as a learner in the project's seminar series, there was still much to cheer about in her presentation of the content, her comfort with the material and the students, and her willingness to let students construct their own understandings of probability through experimentation.

Lynn Selman

Lynn has been teaching math at the middle school level for 11 years. Prior to that she was a substitute teacher and a math tutor for 10 years. Her suburban school system serves a socioeconomically mixed group of primarily white students. Lynn explained that she always wanted to be a teacher and chose math because "math always gave me instant success. And I still feel that way, although I realize that are sometime many answers to problems." When asked if that idea represented a change in her thinking about math, she replied, "Well, I think it's a development. I don't think it's a radical change, but I've progressed to it."

Lynn's decision to join the project was rather spontaneous. She explained that her district math coordinator had passed out a flyer that piqued her interest and that "before you know it, we found ourselves walking up and saying, 'we'd like to fill out an application for it.' So it really happened rather quickly."

Lynn expressed her best hopes for participation in the project in this way:

> Well, I think it's sort of an evolution kind of thing with me. I try every year to stretch a little bit more in my occupation and what I'm doing. And this year, because I'm involved in this [project], and it's almost like an immersion, it isn't just a brief workshop, it's something running through the whole year, I hope to stretch a whole lot.

Lynn's responses to the interview vignettes also reveal a changing approach to and understanding of mathematics. Lynn prefaced her initial response to the question about division with fractions with the statement, "if we were teaching it in the standard way." When questioned about what she meant by "the standard way," she said,

> If you opened a general math text book, you'd see a problem like this and there'd be pages upon pages upon pages of just skills. No pictures, or very few. They'd show you how to do the first one and then ask you to do 50,000 more. Hopefully, we can get away from that kind of thing—maybe by using more manipulatives with the kids. If the kids can own it, they can understand it, and it'll make sense to them.

She proceeded to explain that she was planning to order new materials and that even "Hershey candy bars" might be good manipulatives to introduce these concepts. She admitted she hadn't yet "taught it" this way and would need "time to work on it on my own first to see how it would work."

The second vignette about exponents (is X^2 always larger than X?) brought a quick response indicating ready understanding of the content. Lynn said she would use a vertical number line and plug in different values, bringing the student down the line to 0 and then talking about what happened and why, "making sure the youngster does understand what the exponent means."

Lynn explained that she had been taking a graduate course about the NCTM standards that includes an emphasis on using technology and cooperative learning strategies in math classes. She said this course has affected how she teaches and how she thinks about her teaching. An observation of one of Lynn's eighth-grade pre-algebra courses revealed these effects.

Lynn told us before the class began that she would be working on evaluating algebraic expressions and "plugging in variables." The 17 students in the class were seated in straight rows facing the chalkboard. Lynn began the class by asking students how long it had taken them to do the homework. (Most said 15 to 20 minutes.) She called students by row to the board to put up homework problems. When each student explained his or her answer, Lynn asked the class, "Did anyone get anything different?" When students volunteered other ways of evaluating the expressions, she responded, "Good, there are different ways to do this." Lynn urged students to use math vocabulary, such as *product* instead of *answer*, and complimented students when they did use correct terms. Students freely asked questions, such as "Doesn't *and* mean *plus*?" (Lynn explained, not in algebra) and "Can't you write P6 instead of 6P?" (Lynn responded that the number always goes first for multiplication).

After collecting the homework, Lynn began to work on a worksheet from the textbook on the overhead projector. The worksheet had a series of 21 expressions to evaluate and a "decoder" with number values and corresponding letters on the bottom. The written instructions said to cross out letters in the decoder that matched each of the answers to the problems, and that the remaining letters left in the decoder would spell out the answer to a problem at the top of the page. Lynn tried to elicit from the class some system for doing the worksheet, but when students didn't respond immediately to her questions, she answered them herself. "What does 'cf' (the first expression to evaluate on the worksheet) mean we have to do?" When no one volunteered, she answered herself, "Multiply." How did we use the substitution principle?" Again, no volunteers, and she replied, "We substituted values." After going through the worksheet in this fashion, Lynn switched gears and assigned problems in the book to be done in groups. "Go to the group you worked with yesterday," she instructed, and they did so, moving their desks and chairs very quietly and quickly. No instructions or reminders were given for good group work.

While the students worked in groups of three (there were six groups), Lynn circulated and asked, "How are you working together? Are you doing your own work and then comparing?" (Heads nod "yes.") "Then I want you to work together, discuss how to do each problem, take turns reading the problems and asking for what to do." One group she never got to was clearly not on-task, discussing sports and friends, and another had one person announcing answers to the rest of the group.

Lynn interrupted the group work frequently so she could address the whole class with hints, insights, and questions. These interruptions were indicative of a common phenomenon; most teachers are uncomfortable at first when they no longer control the flow of information and knowledge for the entire class. This issue of control of knowledge is a significant hurdle for teachers to overcome as they try to change their classrooms from teacher-centered to student-centered environments.

After the class, Lynn said she was disappointed at how the class had approached the worksheet on the overhead. "I was disappointed they couldn't come up with the ideas themselves. But I think that will come." She went on to explain that she likes to use group work: "I have found it to be very fruitful. The kids are motivated. I hear comments like, math is fun, oh, is the lesson over already?" She admitted the groups weren't always on-task, that they "drifted" at times, but said she was pleased generally with the way groups work in her classes.

Clearly, Lynn had begun to make changes in both her approach to mathematics and her pedagogical strategies. Nonetheless, it was also clear that she needed guidance and concrete suggestions on how to use these approaches and strategies more successfully. It appeared that this project represented a way to continue an evolutionary process that Lynn had already begun. Lynn and the teachers like her in the project were ripe for the kind of hands-on struggling with curricular ideas, materials, and strategies that was offered in the seminars.

Lynn Selman—Two Years Later. By the end of the project, Lynn's classroom environment and her teaching had changed radically. Instead of the rows of slanted desks we saw on our first visit, Lynn now had tables for groups of students in her room. She told us how she had practically "begged, borrowed, and stolen" to get these tables, and she told us how thrilled she was to get rid of her old desks. Her room was filled with student math projects, constructions, and charts. She went on to explain other changes:

> Sometimes I can't believe how far I have come from where I was a few years ago. I started by trying a few new lessons and cooperative learning. Now I hardly ever use the book in my general math classes. I'm always looking for new ideas, new materials. My kids do projects and I try to keep the work they do relevant to their lives. They learn so much better this way.

It became clear in our interviews and observations with Lynn that she had gone far beyond merely replicating lessons she had seen in the project seminars. Instead, she had internalized certain values about teaching and learning math: It had to be relevant, students should be active learners, it should be concrete whenever possible, and the "almighty book" was no longer the curriculum. This did not mean all of Lynn's lessons were expert. In fact, during the lesson we observed in the winter of the second year of the project, Lynn became stumped when she tried to present a concrete model for multiplying integers. Nonetheless, she wasn't embarrassed that we had seen her "failure," explaining to us that she was willing to fail once in a while as she attempted to broaden and deepen her teaching skills.

In the spring, we observed Lynn teaching a lesson on qualitative graphing. She showed graphs from *USA Today* and asked her students to explain what a graph is and what it can tell us. Later in the lesson, she gave out graphs to each table of students and asked them to construct a story based on the graph. All of the groups stayed on-task and everyone seemed to understand their roles and the problem. Lynn asked probing questions as she visited each group. "What is it about the graph that tells you that happened?" "Does anyone disagree with that part of the story? Why do you disagree?" At each table, Lynn pushed the students to offer evidence for their conjectures and to expand their stories.

Clearly, Lynn had become adept at explaining the task at hand and organizing materials so the groups could function smoothly. We observed Lynn circulating among the groups asking questions and offering encouragement. She no longer interrupted their work to address the whole class, and she seemed comfortable with the fact that different groups attained different insights and attempted different strategies for completing their work. Although Lynn's classroom was not yet one in which more knowledge was discovered than told, she had made real progress toward a student-centered classroom.

The two teachers in these vignettes made valiant and important efforts to change their practices to fit the new conceptions and beliefs about teaching and learning math that they were learning in the project. Their efforts were highly representative of what we observed in other teachers' classrooms. Both of these teachers said they were committed to making long-term changes in their teaching; what we saw was not a one-time show designed to impress evaluators.

FURTHER REFLECTIONS: ON BUILDING A CULTURE OF CHANGE

In the second year of the project, we began to see increasing signs of long-term change in several of the participants. While most of the teachers had introduced some materials or strategies from the seminars during their first year in the project, during the second year they were able to incorporate more into their everyday teaching, they became more comfortable and adept at what they tried, and they came to view themselves as "changed" because of their participation in the project. These are all developmental markers in the process of change.

One of the key challenges facing designers of any staff development program is to figure out ways to extend the process of change beyond the life of the program. Two years may be a long time period for a staff development program, but it's a short time period in the process of changing long-held practices and beliefs. For that reason, the goals of the project went beyond the reform of instructional techniques to lay the groundwork for more deep-seated changes in the culture of teaching. From the structure of the seminars to the tone used to address participants, project staff attempted to present teachers with a model of a different way to view their schedules, their colleagues, the teaching environment, and their profession.

Schedules and Use of Time. From teachers' comments and our own observations, the value of an extended period of time for learning and reflection *during the school day* had an extraordinary effect on teachers' development. When they arrived at the seminars in the morning, they were refreshed and ready to learn. The prevalence of staff development models that occur after school on a "one-shot" basis, models that have traditionally failed, points to the need for adopting more programs that free up teachers from their classes. We did note, however, that many teachers felt ambivalent about leaving their students, especially on a regular basis for an entire morning. That anxiety seemed to lessen with each new seminar, as teachers weighed the magnitude of their increasing professional growth against the time lost in class.

Collegiality. Over the 2-year period teachers formed strong relationships, as they supported each other in learning new material and pedagogical methods. The time allotted for sharing personal experiences at the beginning of each seminar provided meaningful mutual support that only teachers can give to one another. Initially, the sharing time was dominating by venting frustrations, but it gradually grew into a powerful conversation among concerned colleagues. Teachers felt as though they were not able to get this support, especially the pats on the back for trying something new, in their own school systems. The seminar time provided a missing link in their professional growth.

Risk-Taking Environment. The project established a comfort level to support risk taking, allowing participants to fail when necessary, supporting their efforts, and giving positive feedback whenever appropriate for their achievements. The coaching component of the project provided an additional avenue for teachers to take risks, in that project staff were seen as a support in helping teachers try out new ideas in their classrooms. Interestingly, the word "upbeat" was often used to describe the seminars. We consciously wanted our teachers to view their experiences as pleasant, yet demanding; fun, yet hard work. They were highly responsive to the atmosphere we created, and some teachers drew an analogy of the effect of environment on their students' learning as well.

Professionalism. Teachers left the project feeling as though they were treated as professionals. They were given choices for the direction of their work in the seminars; project staff asked for their input concerning seminar content; they were treated to lunch at each seminar (we were initially surprised at the degree to which they appreciated the small contribution of a catered lunch!); and they were given a budget for purchasing their choice of materials. These factors all contributed to their sense that they were valued as teaching professionals.

These changes in beliefs and practice notwithstanding, all the teachers in the project had some distance to go before reaching the level of teaching described in the NCTM standards. Specifically, they needed to become more proficient in facilitating student-centered discourse to allow the generation of mathematical ideas; creating classroom communities that place a high value on problem solving and conjecturing; and connecting mathematics to students' experiences. We hope and believe that the program succeeded in laying the groundwork for teachers' continued growth and improvement, but our experience tells us that those kinds of changes are much more likely to occur when teachers have access to continued, long-term support and mentoring in three key areas.

First, we believe it takes a much more intensive, ongoing coaching component to help teachers achieve the level of change called for in the standards and the current reform movement. Most teachers need regular feedback and help in order to become expert practitioners of new pedagogical strategies. While many of the teachers' beliefs about teaching and learning mathematics did change, it is likely that a more fundamental epistemological shift would be needed for teachers to make the complex change from traditional to student-centered teaching. Since it appears that conceptual and practical change occur in tandem, one would hope that a stronger focus on classroom coaching would also affect conceptual change.

Second, teachers need to feel part of the larger teaching community in their schools as they pursue changes in their teaching. Although our teachers came in pairs from their districts, they often commented on their feelings of isolation from their fellow mathematics teachers. In fact, at the end of the 2 years our teachers believed they had grown so much more than their school colleagues that they found it difficult to go back to the same departmental routines. These results point to the need for building communication and influence skills among teacher participants, as well as including math supervisors and curriculum leaders in staff development efforts. Teachers do not always feel comfortable in gathering support for change, and the inertia of past experiences often stifles their efforts.

Third, teachers need support over the long term in their pursuit of change toward investigative, student-centered teaching. Many teachers expressed a desire to continue with the project beyond the 2-year duration; they feared "falling back" into routines established over decades of isolation in their classrooms. The concept of on-the-job training, while prevalent in industry, should be considered in the teaching profession as well. Teachers need time to reflect on their teaching and to share experiences with their colleagues as part of their daily routines.

Effecting these kinds of systemic changes in the culture of teaching will require continued evolution in our approach to staff development. We need to create new models for programs that are long-term, broad-based, and well-integrated into the broader school reform movement.

NOTE

1. EDC has for several years been recruiting corporate sponsors in the Boston area to release teachers to participate in professional development projects. In the EDC model, used for mathematics staff development in the Middle School Math Project and the Teachers, Time, and Transformation Project, classroom teachers leave their students for professional development activities while industry volunteers replace them on a regular basis throughout the year. In the past 4 years, these projects have provided 7,264 hours of professional development time for 76 mathematics teachers in elementary, middle, and high schools. The corporate sponsors are from Polaroid, Digital Equipment, NYNEX, and GTE Labs. (For a further description of this model, see Cutler & Ruopp, 1993; EDC, 1994).

REFERENCES

Cutler, A. B., & Ruopp, F. N. (1993). Buying time for teachers' professional development. *Educational Leadership, 50*(6), 34–37.

Education Development Center (EDC). (1994). *Industry volunteers in the classroom: Freeing teachers' time for professional development.* Newton, MA: Author.

Fullan, M. (1979). *School-focused in-service education in Canada.* Report prepared for the Centre for Educational Research and Innovation (OECD), Paris.

Fullan, M. (1991). *The meaning of educational change.* New York: Teachers College Press.

Lambert, L. (1987). *The end of staff development.* San Rafael, CA: Marin County Office of Education.

Little, J. W. (1984). Seductive images and organizational realities in professional development. *Teachers College Record, 86*(1), 84–102.

Loucks-Horsley, S., Harding, C., Arbuckle, M., Murray, L., Dubea, C., & Williams, M. (1987). *Continuing to learn: A guidebook for teacher development.* Andover, MA: Regional Laboratory for Educational Improvement of the Northeast and Islands and National Staff Development Council.

Lovitt, C., & Clarke, D. (1988). *The mathematics curriculum and teaching program.* Melbourne, Australia: The Curriculum Corporation.

National Council of Teachers of Mathematics. (1989). *Curriculum and evaluation standards for school mathematics.* Reston, VA: Author.

Pink, W. T. (1989, April). *Effective staff development for urban school improvement.* Paper presented at the annual meeting of the American Educational Research Association, San Francisco.

Shell Centre for Mathematical Education. (1985). *The language of functions and graphs.* Manchester, UK: Joint Matriculation Board.

Steen, L. A. (1987, July 17). Mathematics education: A predictor of scientific competitiveness. *Science*, pp. 251–253, 302.

CHAPTER 7

Principals as Colleagues in the Reshaping of Science Teaching and Learning

CAROLEE S. MATSUMOTO

Now, my principal wants me to try a program that doesn't even have a textbook. How does he expect me to teach any science facts without some information for the kids to read? We tried all that hands-on stuff back when I first started teaching. We couldn't understand the science ourselves, let alone figure out how to manage all that stuff. I know the students enjoyed playing around with the materials, but I kept thinking, "Is this all that happens? Are they learning anything? Am I supposed to be doing anything?" My principal used to sigh a lot when he would come in my classroom. He just couldn't stand the noise and mess and used to make hints that I should have a neater room. No wonder we went right back to textbooks!

I have to admit I was suspicious when my principal said she wanted to support us as we tried to make changes in our science teaching. I thought, I bet she just wants to check on if we are doing a good job. Then, I started hearing that my principal had really followed through and helped a couple of teachers in their classrooms. I heard she assembled materials, worked with students as they were experimenting, and even taught a class! My curiosity got the better of me, so I signed up to have her help me a few weeks ago. (She reserves Wednesday mornings to help teachers with their science teaching.) Things have worked well. My principal wants me to invite one of the other fourth-grade teachers in to see what my class is doing. She is going to teach that teacher's class while she is observing my class.

—Quotes from two teachers participating in the Principals as Leaders in Science program

Against a backdrop of national, state, and local initiatives, the spotlight continues to shine center stage on teachers, the primary actors in science education reform. Current reform efforts place primary focus on motivating, coaching, and supporting teachers in their efforts to make changes in their classrooms and to extend those changes to engage entire schools.

If teachers are the lead players on the reform stage, principals should be thought of as the best supporting actors. As the two opening quotes indicate, the relationship between principals and teachers is a key factor in a teacher's openness to change, risk, and experimentation. Through our work in the Principals As Leaders in Science (PALS) Center at Educational Development Center (EDC), we find evidence that science reform efforts are more likely to be successful when principals work as colleagues to support teachers who are attempting to make changes in their classrooms and to share leadership roles and responsibilities for schoolwide reform. In fact, we believe that the formation of truly collaborative and collegial relationships between teachers and principals is essential if the science reform movement of the 1990s is to overcome the obstacles that have defeated past reform efforts. It is only through such relationships that schools can address the interwoven challenges of reforming resources, training, and curricula in ways that lead to a hands-on, inquiry-driven approach to science education for all students.

In recognition of the central role teachers occupy in the reform movement, most professional development initiatives—and much of the literature—focus on changing teacher practice and attitudes (see, e.g., Fullan, 1993; Fullan & Steigelbaum, 1991). Despite my own predisposition toward programs aimed at teachers, my work over the last 10 years has convinced me that professional development of principals can serve as the lever to more widespread and immediate changes to science teaching. Even if teachers are able and willing to make changes, principals have the power to facilitate or hinder their individual change efforts. Principals are also in a unique position to provide the leadership and resources to facilitate schoolwide change.

While reform literature pays homage to the centrality of principals in supporting teacher change, we still lack a body of knowledge that helps science education reformers fully understand the knowledge and skills principals must possess to effect significant improvement in science teaching. These questions helped motivate my personal interest in developing a model that would train and support principals as they attempt to change science teaching in their schools. The invitation for EDC to become the New England PALS Center offered the challenge to develop these ideas into training for elementary school principal–teacher teams, to teach them to work as colleagues building their own knowledge and skills and leading schoolwide changes in science teaching. The core of the PALS program was a series of workshops for principal–teacher teams in which they jointly engaged in three essential activities: ***hands-***

on science learning, *long-range planning*, and *colleagueship* with fellow teachers and principals from other schools as well as with their own team partner. The development of the EDC PALS Center and the stories of our principal–teacher teams provide some promising practices to draw on as we work to improve science teaching and learning.

LESSONS LEARNED FROM PAST REFORM EFFORTS

The origins of the PALS program nationwide are firmly rooted in the history of science education reform. In fact, many of the underlying assumptions that informed the development of the program grew out of the failures of past science reform efforts. The most serious and most common of the failures was the lack of a broad and integrated vision for reform. While some of the past reform efforts produced useful models for improving parts of the system, none of the initiatives addressed how the system *as a whole* functioned—or failed to function. As we have seen time and again, large-scale reform efforts are much more likely to succeed when they take a systemic approach to the interwoven elements that determine whether or not real change will occur. Among the most critical of these elements are:

1. A content-rich *curriculum* that is accessible to all students and teachers
2. *Training* that facilitates teacher and principal learning about content and pedagogy
3. Financial *resources* to purchase quality materials and to support teachers
4. A schedule and a system that afford teachers the *time* and the opportunity for training, action research, and colleagueship

Beyond those essential four elements, I would add a fifth: *school culture*. In order to change the dynamics in individual classrooms, you must also change the dynamics of the entire school, particularly the relationships among teachers and between teachers and administrators. As Ames and Miller (1994) write:

> Creating a healthy climate for children begins by supporting healthy relationships among adults. . . . Such relationships are important for several reasons. First, they provide a safe environment for honest, open communication and risk taking. Second, they facilitate shared decision making, in which individuals not only have a voice but real choice. They lay the foundation for a true learning community, one in which teachers are willing to serve as peer coaches, collaborators, and critical friends. And they model the kind of cooperative learning and mutual respect that teachers expect of their students. (p. 181)

In the PALS program, we sought to use these relationships as a springboard for the kinds of systemic changes Ames and Miller describe. By fostering and guiding effective collaborations among teachers and principals, we provided the teacher—principal teams with tools for reforming their school's approach to curriculum, training, resources, and time.

More than anything else, it was the absence of effective collaboration and systemic thinking that doomed the well-intentioned science education reform efforts of the past 40 or 50 years. Perhaps the most notable of these efforts was the so-called Golden Age of science curriculum development in the 1960s and 1970s (Hurd, 1978; Kyle, 1984).[1] Fueled by the launch of *Sputnik I* in 1957 and fears about Soviet superiority, as well as concerns about American students' poor performance on international science achievement tests, the federal government began a massive effort to allay the public's perception that there was a crisis in science education in the United States. The period between 1955 and 1974 marked an unprecedented federal attempt to improve science education. Through the National Science Foundation (NSF), which was established in 1950, the federal government began massive efforts to improve the quality of science education, particularly in the area of curriculum development. The NSF assembled teams of leading scientists, mathematicians, and scholars to develop curriculum materials (Jackson, 1983).

In many respects, the curricula developed during the Golden Age provided strong models for hands-on, inquiry-based science teaching. Studies comparing the curricula with more traditional, textbook-oriented materials have indicated that the Golden Age curricula were more effective in helping students develop positive attitudes toward science, higher-level intellectual processes, analytic skills, and creativity (Bredderman, 1983; Hofwolt, 1984; Kyle, 1984; Shymansky, Kyle, & Alport, 1983).

The serious shortcomings of the Golden Age curricula provide equally important lessons for contemporary science education reformers. The Golden Age curricula improvement effort focused primarily on students who were academically gifted and likely to become scientists (Graham & Fultz, 1986). Curricula materials were organized according to the traditional science disciplines and included laboratory activities to help students develop higher cognitive skills and verify and apply science concepts. At the high school level, curricula were designed in physics, chemistry, and biology and offered to the few students capable of the rigor. Although science educators and scientists have long argued that everyone needs to be scientifically literate to understand, live, and work effectively in a society that is increasingly scientific and technological, our history of science education is characterized by programs that have cultivated a "scientific elite" (Graham & Fultz, 1986). This has resulted in estimates that as much as 90% of our adult population is scientifically illiterate

(Federal Coordinating Council for Science, Engineering, and Technology [FCCSET], 1991; Yaeger, 1981).

Not surprisingly, the Golden Age curricula also failed to address the issue of scientific literacy among science teachers. The developers of the 1960s and 1970s curricula believed their materials would be powerful enough to overcome the inadequate preparation of teachers (Hawkins, 1983). The materials gave little attention to the factors that motivate and help teachers change the ways they teach science (Watson, 1963). Because the curricula were too advanced for teachers without science backgrounds and because the materials did not provide sufficient guidance on how to implement the hands-on, inquiry-based teaching approach, teachers reverted to their own strategies, which were limited to their level of expertise and knowledge (Tobin & Fraser, 1989). Teachers' sense of isolation was exacerbated by the fact that the reform movement made no attempt to address the systemic issues that produce a profound effect on what happens inside the classroom—including the political, institutional, and community realities that work against the educational change process. After initial training institutes and workshops, most teachers found themselves trying to implement dramatic changes largely on their own, with little or no support from the administration, the community, or outside experts.

As we look specifically at the role principals played in the reforms of the 1960s and 1970s, it is clear that the initiatives failed to engage principals and, in return, principals failed to embrace the reforms. On the whole, principals understood neither the philosophy nor the value of the curricula and its hands-on, inquiry-based approach. As a result, they provided minimal in-school leadership for change and failed to create, or even support, significant opportunities for teacher development. And when critics began calling for the abandonment of the new curricula in favor of a back-to-basics movement, few principals fought to save the reforms (Kyle, 1984). By the late 1970s, the Golden Age curricula had been largely replaced with textbook learning (Marcuccio, 1983).

THE ORIGINS OF PALS

The lessons of the Golden Age were not lost on the reformers of the 1980s and early 1990s. In the past two decades, the NSF and several leading educational associations have launched dozens of initiatives that provide models for integrated, systemic approaches to changing both school culture and classroom practice (several are described in other chapters of this book). In 1989, the NSF and the National Science Teachers Association provided funds to Ken Mechling and Donna Oliver to build a national network of PALS Centers to train school principal–teacher teams to improve elementary science. They developed the design of the 12 PALS Centers from their many years of work with principals and teachers in Pennsylvania. (The work of the PALS Centers has been informed and supported by collaborations with many public and private organizations, including the National Association of Elementary School Principals, the National Science Supervisors Association, the Council of State Science Supervisors, and the Council for Elementary Science International.)

From 1988 to 1991, the 12 regional Centers that made up the PALS network provided training for principal–teacher teams at unprecedented levels. More than 50 Regional Science Leadership Conferences (RSLCs) were held throughout the United States, with close to 2,000 principals–teachers participating—about 70% more than anticipated in the original program proposal. In addition, the PALS Centers held more than 200 Local Science Leadership Conferences throughout the United States, with more than 5,500 principals, teachers, parents, school board members, and children participating.

The PALS Center based at EDC modified the original PALS design by placing specific emphasis on two issues that held a special place in EDC's history—curriculum development and systemic science reform. Drawing on EDC's decades of experience and expertise in curriculum development, we provided sessions aimed at helping principal–teacher teams learn how to select good science curricula and how to modify and expand them, if necessary. We also spoke, from a wealth of EDC experience, about the critical need to look beyond curriculum and teacher training in order to achieve true science reform in schools and school districts. The EDC PALS Center provided opportunities for the principal–teacher teams to learn systemic reform models developed in EDC projects, as well as to engage in collaborative strategic planning and problem solving aimed at effecting schoolwide science improvement, assessing and changing district policies, selecting and implementing curricula, improving assessment and evaluation practices, strengthening professional development programs, and increasing parental involvement. This chapter describes the structure of the PALS training as practiced at the EDC PALS center.

At the heart of the EDC/PALS work is the belief that science teaching can be reformed schoolwide when a collaborative relationship exists between a principal and a teacher who attempts making changes in his or her teaching and who is willing to take a leadership role in the school. Specifically, the PALS trainings had three key goals:

1. To provide teachers and principals with first-hand experiences with, and insights into, *hands-on science learning*
2. To engage principals and teachers in a collaborative process of *long-range planning* to reform science teaching in the school
3. To foster *colleagueship* between teachers and principals and to build a network of teacher–principal teams

PALS training was designed around an interweaving of these goals, with activities structured and sequenced to provide direct links among the tasks of learning, planning, and colleagueship. For example, after having experienced learning through hands-on, inquiry-based materials, teachers and principals were better prepared to plan for changes in curriculum, training, and resource allocation. And after working side-by-side as learners and planners, teachers and principals were laying the groundwork for strong, collegial relationships.

HANDS-ON SCIENCE LEARNING

> It all started last year when I asked my principal if there was any money in her budget to buy an aquarium. The next thing I knew, she was asking me if I would be willing to try a new science unit that uses aquariums to study environments. I thought, . . . if it will get me an aquarium, OK. When the curriculum unit arrived, I flipped through it and saw some interesting activities to try with my students. To make a long story short, the children loved the activities. After the aquariums, the children wanted to know what we would do next for science. My principal already had the answer in three more units from that science program. That was last year. This year, I find I don't have to spend so much time getting everything ready. So, I can look for books the students can read or figure out how they can use the computer to write up their observations.

Hands-on, inquiry-based teaching requires a significant pedagogical shift for most teachers and principals—as it does for most students. For that reason, the PALS training provided many opportunities for the principal–teacher teams to experience learning just as students would. As part of the training, each participant was given a box of curriculum materials and activities called A Science Survival Kit. At the EDC PALS center, most of the materials and activities were drawn from the EDC-developed Insights curriculum.

In addition to providing participants with a set of Insights activities and materials they could take back to their schools for in-service trainings, the Survival Kits introduced principals and teachers to a pedagogical process for teaching science. The Insights activities are built around a five-stage model of student science learning:

- In the first stage, teachers probe students' prior knowledge and experiences to identify their present level of understanding, motivate them, and pose problems or challenges. Students share their ideas (and misconceptions), make connections to their lives, raise questions, make predictions, and set goals.

- In the second stage, students solve problems and meet challenges by manipulating materials and phenomena, making observations and collecting, comparing, analyzing, organizing, and interpreting data.
- In the third stage, teachers encourage students to make meaning of their hands-on experiences. Students share their observations and data, evaluate and synthesize, and construct and communicate their new conceptual understandings and explanations.
- In the fourth stage, teachers ask students to evaluate and apply what they have learned to other subject areas, the community, or their homes. Students integrate and transfer their ideas, create and invent ways of expressing what they know or can do, and ask new questions.
- Throughout all stages and at the conclusion of activities that develop a concept, teachers assess students' understanding. Teachers use a variety of assessment strategies, including asking students to use materials to demonstrate they understand a concept or have learned a skill; engaging students in discussion, writing, drawing, or diagramming; challenging students to solve problems or to design a project that demonstrates their learning; and asking students to assess themselves. On a daily basis, and over time, teachers use the results of the assessments to make decisions about whether or not to repeat or modify activities, or to proceed to the next learning experience for one, some, or all the students.

Figure 7.1 contains an excerpt of one of the Insights activities used in the PALS training. In this activity from the "Circuits and Pathways" unit, students are given a battery, a bulb, and a piece of wire and are asked to experiment to find as many ways as possible to light the bulb. The activity provides a strong model of the kind of open-ended, hands-on science explorations we hoped the PALS teams would bring back to their schools and their students. Activities such as this one give teachers a first-hand sense of the rich learning that can come out of well-designed explorations that encourage students to experiment, exchange ideas, and struggle to build understanding.

The overall structure of the PALS trainings was designed to use the hands-on activity sessions as springboards to wider discussions of research, pedagogy, and policy. Participants engaged in the activities at three points throughout the 2-½–day training, each time in different groups and each time with a different set of framing questions. For the first session, teachers and participants were asked to approach the activities as learners, to put themselves in the role of their students. These initial sessions were videotaped and replayed to help

Figure 7.1.

Lighting the Bulb
Teaching Sequence

Getting Started

Students are challenged to light the bulb in several different ways.

Explain to the class that each student will experiment with one battery, one bulb, and a piece of wire. The challenge is to find as many ways as possible to light the bulb.

Explain that students will be working on their own within their groups, and that they should use their fellow group members as resources.

Instruct students to make drawings of their attempts, both those configurations which work and those which do not work. Knowing which configurations do not light the bulb is as important as knowing which ones do.

On the board, draw a battery, a bulb, and a wire to demonstrate that simple drawings are sufficient. Accuracy in observation, not perfect artwork, is what's important here.

Exploring and Discovering

Students explore all the ways they can use their materials to light the bulb.

Divide the class into its groups and let one member of each group pick up its materials box of bulbs, batteries, and wire.

Allow time for students to explore.

As you circulate from group to group, do the following:

- Ask students to identify the critical contact points on the battery and bulb that must be connected to make a complete circuit.
- Urge students to help one another find as many variations as they can.
- Monitor students' progress as they work. Encourage systematic problem-solving strategies.
- Resist the temptation to rescue students who are struggling.
- Make sure students draw all their attempts.

Source: EDC, 1991

participants reflect on how it felt to be a hands-on learner. What processes did they use? What misconceptions did they need to work through? In the second session, participants were asked to take turns playing the role of the teacher. Afterwards, they came together in job-alike groups to share their reactions and to problem-solve around the obstacles they saw from a teacher's perspective. Then the group went on to discuss specific questions about reform challenges, delving into such topics as curriculum, teacher motivation, and professional development. The third hands-on session featured performance assessment activities. This session led into the culminating work of the training, in which teachers and principals developed action plans for reforming their school's science program.

As part of the follow-up discussions, trainers provided participants with a range of information and questions designed to place the activities in a larger context and to move participants from the learning phase to the planning phase. For example, participants were given information about what research and exemplary practice define as good hands-on, inquiry-based science teaching and learning and shown other examples of effective activities. Discussion questions focused on such issues as:

- Assessing and building on children's ideas and explanations (including misconceptions and naive theories)
- Teaching strategies to help children learn science, including cooperative learning, inquiry, and thinking and process skills.
- Criteria for selecting a good science curriculum
- Integrating mathematics and science with other disciplines

Beyond providing participants with first-hand experiences with effective teaching and learning strategies, the hands-on activity sessions were also designed to encourage support for risk taking and experimentation in the classroom. The only way to truly understand and appreciate the pedagogical change that comes with rich, inquiry-based science activities is to engage in them as a learner. And engaging in these activities as part of a cooperative group helped to underscore the nonlinear and highly individual nature of this kind of learning. Many participants found that activities that might appear to be engaging, fun, and perhaps even simplistic on paper can lead to surprisingly deep examinations of content when you actually delve into them in a group setting. As they reconnected with the role of learner through these hands-on sessions, participants began to broaden and rethink their conception of the role of teacher. Instead of focusing on the teacher as knowledge dispenser, they saw the value of the teacher as facilitator, coach, and co-learner. For many teachers, this is an exciting and empowering realization, as this quote from a PALS participant indicates:

> I feel like a kid again. In our science workshops, all of the teachers and our principal are actually doing every student learning experience. I can see why kids enjoy science when they get to work with the materials. I took the [electric circuit] materials home and asked my husband to light the bulb with only the wire and battery. He struggled as much as I did. Now, I can understand why it is important to give kids time to experiment in the classroom and to work with others. Everyone in our school is trying to change our science. With in-service, lots of help from the principal, and all the teachers sharing and helping each other, I am changing my science teaching, and I am learning science . . . finally.

This reconception of the teacher's role is perhaps the most critical transition both teachers and principals need to make as we move to a new model of science education. If we want students to engage in inquiry learning, to be creative, to have critical thinking, problem-solving, and decision-making skills, and to be risk takers, we must allow teachers to develop and display those same characteristics. Teachers who do practice these characteristics—teachers whom I refer to as self-initiating, innovative teachers—often face a variety of disincentives. Many are discouraged by their peers or principals who are fearful of science, intolerant of the additional work, untrained in the strategies necessary in implementing the approach, or resentful of competition from teachers engaged in ambitious change. Since these self-initiating teachers tend to be isolated, their potential to serve as leaders, models, coaches, or resources for other teachers is lost. A principal who has a genuine understanding of hands-on, inquiry-based learning can go a long way toward removing these disincentives and creating a more nurturing environment for innovative teachers.

THE IMPORTANCE OF COLLABORATIVE, LONG-RANGE PLANNING

As successful as the hands-on sessions and the Science Survival Kits were in changing attitudes and behaviors, we knew that, by themselves, they weren't enough to set in motion the kinds of schoolwide reforms we were seeking. One of the key features that set the PALS program apart from many other professional development initiatives was its emphasis on collaborative planning. Just as most teachers need the support of a principal to make real changes in the classroom, principals need the support of teachers to make real changes in the school. In the PALS training, we set out to teach teachers and principals how to plan in partnership and how to use their cumulative knowledge to develop reform efforts that are both visionary and practical.

The strong link between teacher change and school change is well documented in recent reform literature. According to many researchers, teachers are most likely to make changes in their teaching when they are involved in collegial and collaborative decision-making, planning, implementation, and evaluation meetings and activities (Fullan, 1993; Fullan & Steigelbaum, 1991; Rosenholtz, 1989; Talbert & McLaughlin, 1994; Wasley, 1991). In their summary of characteristics that typify successful staff development programs, Loucks-Horsley and colleagues (1987, p. 8) underscore the importance of placing teacher change within the larger context of school change:

- Collegiality and collaboration
- Experimentation and risk taking
- Incorporation of available knowledge bases
- Appropriate participant involvement in goal setting, implementation, evaluation, and decision making
- Time to work on staff development and assimilate new learnings
- Leadership and sustained administrative support
- Appropriate incentives and rewards
- Designs built on principles of adult learning and the change process
- Integration of individual goals with school and district goals
- Formal placement of the program within the philosophy and organizational structure of the school and district

We designed the PALS training in such a way as to lay the groundwork for school change, by giving teachers and principals an immediate experience with collaborative, long-range planning—as well as by providing some specific planning tools and strategies. In alternating hands-on learning with planning sessions, we hoped to capitalize on the excitement created by the activities and lead participants to begin to generalize their experiences and to think about what kinds of changes would need to be made in the school environment to improve science teaching. The planning agenda for the PALS training included the following topics and stages:

- School teams plan strategies for the acquisition, maintenance, and refurbishing of *instructional materials.*
- School teams learn about *science education improvement efforts* in their own and other states, including NSF Statewide Systemic Initiatives (SSI) and other NSF projects; and other state, regional, and national initiatives, such as the Mathematics and Science Alliances.
- Teams review and discuss the *implications of policies* that direct their programs, including *national and state standards and frameworks,*

assessment and accountability systems, and instructional materials adoption processes.
- Teams generate *criteria for a good science program* in their own schools.
- School teams write an ***action plan*** with strategies to assess their current program and to develop a science program in their school.
- School teams design a ***support system*** for each other, including professional development plans, peer coaching and mentoring, the development of a safe environment for experimentation with new teaching strategies and instructional materials, and the formation of a district leadership team.
- School teams develop strategic plans for their district leadership team to implement a *systemwide science reform plan*.
- School teams generate a plan to *collaborate with people and organizations* in their own community and in the larger state and national community of businesses and institutions.

The training was designed to build participants' planning skills by providing them with a range of information and planning prompts. The various worksheets walked participants through a process in which they (1) assessed the current state of their science program; (2) prioritized elements of the program that needed improvement; (3) articulated specific objectives; and (4) developed an action plan, complete with a schedule, a budget, and evaluation mechanisms. Figure 7.2 shows an excerpt from an action plan as completed by a participant in the training.

The PALS training used a formal planning process designed to provide the principal–teacher teams with an action plan, resources, motivation, and support to make schoolwide science improvement. The process began with a self-assessment. Prior to their participation in the PALS training, principals completed the Principal's Checklist that led them to begin their assessment of "weaknesses" in the school science program. The initial lists of weaknesses were confirmed and expanded as the teams engaged in hands-on science learning and as the principals and teachers began a dialogue about the strengths and weaknesses of their school science program. Opportunities provided during the PALS training for analysis of science learning from students', teachers', and principals' perspectives helped to clarify and elaborate the areas for improvement.

To guide the development of their action plans, the teams used a planning worksheet that helped them identify target areas for improvement, gather ideas, and begin preliminary planning strategies. We facilitated and encouraged the exchange of ideas, resources, and models through team and cross-team sessions, as well as job-alike sessions. The teams were coached to include

Figure 7.2. Action Plan

1. **Brief description of your school.** My school, a Boston Public School, has a student population of approximately 330 students in grades K through 5 (48% black, 22% white, and 30% other). The majority of the teachers have been at the school over 10 years. Since the arrival of a new principal in September 1988, the faculty has been involved in planning and implementing several new schoolwide initiatives, i.e., whole-language activities, the use of math manipulative materials, and a science fair.
2. **Your title and responsibilities.** I am a graduate student in the School Leadership Program at Wheelock College and am completing my practicum as an intern. I attended the PALS 2-day conference as the principal's designee.
3. **From the Principal's Checklist, list several science program weaknesses:**
   A9—The annual budget does not specify funds to finance the science program.
   A12—The budget does not cover staff development for science—consultants for local in-service programs, staff travel to conferences, and teacher attendance at conventions.
   E16—A substantial part of the children's class time is not spent on activities beyond reading and listening.
   F1—Science materials are not sufficiently available so that all science students can work with them.

4a. **From your list of weaknesses, identify one or more priorities for improving the science program in your school:** To develop with the faculty a long-range plan to be implemented in FY92 and then to secure funds to purchase more science materials and trade books and to provide in-service training to best utilize these new supplies.

4b. **Please check one of the following which identifies the area of your top priority for improvement:**

___curriculum selection	___curriculum improvement/maintenance
_✓_staff development (long-range priority)↑	_✓_other, please describe <u>to involve the faculty in developing a long range science plan</u>

5. **Specific objectives to be accomplished:** Long range = to increase the amount of hands-on science experienced by students. Short range (FY91) = (1) to write a long-range plan and secure funding, and (2) to present a school-based inservice to integrate science and math.
6. **Proposed plan of action (including time line):**

Form Science Planning Committee	Sept. 1990
Science Committee meetings with faculty	Sept. through May 1991
Take inventory of science texts/materials	October 1990
Organize science supply closets	October 1990
Planning for in-service meeting	December 1990
In-service meeting with consultant	January 1991
Grade-level meetings with consultant	Jan. through April 1991
Complete long-range plan/submit grants for funding	May 1991

7. **Budget required:** $1,000

the following in their action plans: teacher training workshops (for which the PALS Center provided monetary stipends); a structure for curriculum review and development; and strategies for effecting systemic changes in their district to support their schoolwide improvement plans.

The action plans ranged from short-range, low-investment projects to create materials or train staff, to long-range, ambitious restructuring efforts. The action plan quoted below, written by a science teacher and a principal, is an example of one of the more ambitious plans:

> ***Statement of Problem***
>
> Teacher: D-13 has no systematic ongoing science curriculum K–12. One exists for 7–12, dated 1974. We have an opportunity to embed progressive, hands-on, inquiry science education in the curriculum to be written [by teachers].
>
> Principal: The school and the district lack a clear, coordinated K–12 science curriculum.
>
> ***Worksheet Objective***
>
> Teacher: (1) Write a systematic, ongoing science curriculum K–12. (2) Embed in this curriculum . . . hands-on, inquiry-based science education K–12, with balance of process and content.
>
> Principal: To write a philosophy consistent with a hands-on science process. To write a clear, coordinated, future-oriented K–12 science curriculum.
>
> ***Proposed Plan of Action***
>
> Teacher: Summer 1992: Prepare curriculum committee to write philosophy of goals. (1) Share readings from PALS. (2) Research potential speakers/facilitators. (3) Schedule summer meeting times for committee group work and decision making. (4) Rough-out agenda for these meetings, set the game plan for moving the group along Spring 1992 and Summer 1993: Prepare curriculum committee to write objectives; write objectives
> 1993–94: Pilot specific units
> 1994–95: Adopt successful units districtwide
> 1995–96: Assess and Evaluate science curriculum and programs

Principal: Continue the work of the science curriculum committee. This summer, a philosophy will be written; next school year (1992–93), some hands-on units will be tried on a pilot basis, while a curriculum-writing committee—with teacher representation from each grade level—pulls together a written curriculum for the district. The final, working copy of the curriculum will be adopted in spring of 1993. In-service for teachers to be included.

Budget

Teacher: $5,000.
Principal: $5,000; $10,000 ideally to hire a support person.

In addition to the need for new curriculum materials, the most common recurring themes in the action reports were the lack of time and resources necessary to implement reform. In our years of work with principal–teacher teams, we saw and helped to develop a number of creative solutions to the time and money problems. Some PALS participants sought grants to fund the hiring of support staff, purchase materials, or even extend the school day. Others figured out various ways to free up teachers for planning, training, and mentoring. Among these ideas: encouraging teachers to sign up for the weekly time slot on the principal's schedule "reserved" for helping a teacher with science in the classroom; actually teaching the hands-on, inquiry-based learning experiences themselves; organizing a cadre of parent/ community volunteers and/or student science aides to co-teach, serve as classroom aides, or manage materials collection, distribution, and clean-up; training local business volunteers to provide regularly scheduled, expert substitutes (see Chapter 6, this volume, for a fuller explanation of this model); hiring a long-term substitute or an additional teacher from funds freed by teachers willing to have classes with a few more students.

BUILDING A COLLABORATIVE SCHOOL CULTURE

It isn't scary to try something new at my school. We all know our principal is really concerned about making sure all students learn . . . like us. Everyone is always trying something new, and our principal supports us and encourages. When I want to try something new, my principal's style is to get into the classroom to help me figure out what needs to be done and how he can help make it happen. Sometimes, he wants to see if a new idea will work, and he will ask one of us to try it for him. At faculty and grade-level meetings, we are expected to and

> just naturally want to share what we are learning with all of the other teachers.

The importance of a collaborative school culture to authentic reform is a key theme in the recent literature of school reform. Several commentators have proposed that a sense of partnership is a necessary component of the school environment if change is to be successfully initiated and sustained. Such environments have been described variously as "communities" (Sergiovanni, 1994), "learning organizations" (Fullan, 1993), "cooperative work environments" (Astuto, Clark, & Read, 1994), and "learning communities" (Senge, 1990). Both Sergiovanni (1994) and Fullan (1993) make the case that the learning community is critical to education reform because change is extremely complex; is subject to political shifts and priorities; requires as-yet-undeveloped solutions; and involves flexibility, shared purpose, resources, and the support of many individuals.

Like much of the reform literature of the early 1990s, the current emphasis on school culture and supportive environments grows out of the lessons we've learned from the failures of past reform efforts. By placing so much of the burden of initiating change on the shoulders of individual teachers, past reform efforts charged innovative teachers with an undoable task and placed them in untenable positions. Not only did these teachers lack the training, time, and resources they needed to make significant changes, but they were frequently targets of ridicule by other teachers who resented the reforms they were championing. Even under the best of circumstances, teaching can be a very isolating endeavor; for the reform-minded teacher in a traditional school setting, that isolation can be compounded by ostracism. Although innovative teachers are motivated by what they are attempting and are able to overcome obstacles for a time, these teachers are continually "at-risk" for potential alienation of their peers. As a result, innovative teachers feel pressure to camouflage their efforts or even retreat from contact with their colleagues. The situation worsens when principals and the overall school culture are not supportive of change. Such an environment undermines not only individual teacher's change initiatives but also other significant school improvement efforts, as well as threatens the norms of collegiality and perpetuates competition among teachers.

The PALS program set out to address these issues of teacher isolation and school culture directly by designing the training for teams of teachers and principals and laying the groundwork for successful collaborations. Simply the process of attending the trainings together and engaging in collaborative problem solving and planning deepened the collegial relationships between principals and teachers. Many teachers commented that it was the first time they had seen their principal as a colleague—and it was probably the first time many of the principals had seen themselves in that light. Beyond that, we set out to design the training in a way that would extend that sense of colleagueship beyond the training participants and into the schools they would return to. By placing the teachers and principals on a level playing field as cooperative learners, we hoped to reduce the sense of hierarchy that serves as a barrier to true collaboration. These hands-on sessions were also intended to place the principals in the shoes of the teachers, and to place both principals and teachers in the shoes of the students. By the same token, the follow-up discussions and planning activities helped to give teachers greater insights into the kinds of challenges principals face as they work to balance educational needs with competing demands for limited resources.

Clearly, the task of reinventing the culture and relationships of an individual school was beyond the reach of the PALS program, which was designed to begin the process of change rather than achieve any particular reform. We hoped that the relationship we fostered between one teacher and one principal would produce ripple effects throughout a school system, and that the program as whole would provide a model and a springboard for other systemic reforms. Our research into the results of the PALS program (see next section) indicates some progress. Clearly, however, we have much more work to do. We need to develop new initiatives that link the reform of content, curriculum, and assessment and the professional development of teachers with more widespread efforts to transform the school culture and relationships.

TRACKING THE IMPACT OF THE PALS PROGRAM

Evaluation Instruments

From the beginning of PALS, evaluation was a major component of the project. Many of the evaluation instruments were designed in conjunction with the independent PALS evaluation team: Among the instruments were the following:

- *PALS network regional conference participant evaluations.* This was an eight-item instrument designed to measure the participants' reactions to the regional conferences in terms of design and presentation. (See Figure 7.3.)
- *PALS network pre/post science leadership attitude measure.* Participants completed this questionnaire both before and after the regional conferences. Sample questions (using a 5–point Likert scale from Strongly Disagree to Strongly Agree) included:

  An effective elementary science program is unlikely without the committed support of the school principal.

Figure 7.3. Principals for the Advancement of Leadership in Science Network (PALS Network) Conference Evaluation

Program Presenter(s) ____________________

Location ____________________ Date ____________________

For each of the statements below, please indicate your agreement with the statement by circling SA if you Strongly Agree, A if you Agree, N if you feel Neutral, D if you Disagree, or SD if you Strongly Disagree. Thank you.

1. The PALS Conference was well presented.	SA	A	N	D	SD
2. The presenter(s) seemed well prepared to do the program.	SA	A	N	D	SD
3. The presentation will help me in my role as a supervisor or curriculum/instructional leader in science.	SA	A	N	D	SD
4. I can use many of these ideas to improve science in my own school(s).	SA	A	N	D	SD
5. The Science Survival Kit will be useful to me in my efforts to improve science education.	SA	A	N	D	SD
6. Overall, the presentation was effective and useful.	SA	A	N	D	SD

7. How can the PALS Network provide service to elementary principals and supervisors in the future?

8. COMMENTS. In the space below, please make any additional comments you wish to make concerning the PALS Network program or the manner in which it was presented.

Hands-on science activities are essential components of an effective science curriculum.

I feel confident in leading a hands-on science lesson to demonstrate effective science teaching at the elementary level.

- *PALS network pre/post science leadership cognition measure.* This 20–item, multiple-choice instrument included such questions as:

  The use of an exploration activity at the beginning of a science lesson is an effective method of enhancing both:

  A. student attitude and academic performance
  B. student discipline and attitude
  C. student discipline and academic performance
  D. student behavior and academic performance

Student behaviors that are acceptable during hands-on science include:
A. increased noise, if the students are on-task
B. excitement, if the students are on-task
C. increased mobility, if the students are on-task
D. All of the above are acceptable.

- *PALS network pre/post science leadership activity questionnaire.* In the final year of the PALs regional conferences, participants were asked to complete this questionnaire before the conference and then 6 months later. Pre- and post-conference results were compared, and the results were also compared to questionnaires completed by a control group of principals not participating in the PALS conference. Sample questions included:

  There is a written science curriculum plan describing planned, coordinated and sequential experiences for:
  A. no grade levels
  B. 1–2 grade levels
  C. 3–4 grade levels
  D. 5–6 grade levels
  E. all grade levels

  The number of in-service programs specifically dedicated to science needs this year is:
  A. 0
  B. 1
  C. 2
  D. 3
  E. 4 or more.

- *PALS network science leadership questionnaire longitudinal study.* This instrument was designed to track levels of leadership activity by principals participating in the program 6 months, 1 year, or 2 years following attendance at the conference.
- *PALS network principal leadership case studies.* PALS evaluators interviewed 15 randomly selected participants, using a 50–item instrument, to gain further anecdotal evidence and background to tie with the statistical analyses.
- *PALS network site visits.* During the final year of the project, several of the PALS network sites were selected as evaluation visits. A member of the PALS headquarters staff visited each of these sites to formally interview the site director, to observe the facility, and to discuss with the director the overall project mechanics and outcomes.
- *PALS action plan progress reports.* Each PALS team was asked to provide the project with a progress report after they had returned to their schools and begun implementation of the action plan they had generated at the PALS training.

Evaluation Results

All the various research instruments were consistent in showing that the PALS program had a significant and positive effect on participants' attitudes, knowledge, and practices related to hands-on, inquiry-based science education. For example, conference evaluation scores indicated that the conferences were well-received and that the Science Survival Kits were very useful to the participants. The results of the attitude study indicated that participants as a group gained approximately 6 points on the 100–point scale, which was statistically significant well beyond the accepted .05 level. The cognition and leadership instruments showed similarly positive results.

Perhaps more revealing of the kind of impact that PALS had on individual participants are the anecdotal reports contained in the case studies and the action plan progress reports. The following excerpt from one case study from a principal is typical of the responses we received:

> Our greatest barrier is the teachers', parents', and administrators' fear of change. Programs like PALS can assist by showcasing schools that have made successful changes.
>
> Since the PALS conference, our students enjoy science. The teachers are using more hands-on experiences. Continuing science experiences are provided through interest centers, learning centers, plants, animals, and science bulletin boards in the classroom. A science lab has been built using community funds and a grant. Our staff is resisting change. Some teachers were slow to adopt hands-on experiences, fearing they wouldn't cover the material and parents would object. The major hurdle to ensuring good science teaching is that principals have to feel secure and confident to help teachers feel secure and confident to do what we know is best for the children. PALS and programs like it can emphasize that teachers and principals know what is best for children and encourage them to use that knowledge. . . .
>
> I show leadership in science by encouraging and supporting hands-on activities and noticing exciting activities. I offer opportunities for teachers to compete for grants. I participate in science activities in the classroom. I evaluate science lessons, noticing the excitement evident in the teachers and students. Learning is demonstrated by the teachers and students. I have led one science in-service for my staff.
>
> Overall, I rate our science program as fair. Its strengths are dedicated, well-qualified teachers; ample time scheduled for science; and the availability of textbooks. We need more student involvement in activity-based science. We need more supplies and a more efficient method of storing and sharing them. I have not yet been able to write

> grants for science equipment or money for field trips and guest speakers. In the future, programs could provide more activities for teachers that are motivating and exciting. I would like to improve the students' and teachers' understanding the science is part of everything that we experience—not something that we read about in a textbook.

Action plan progress reports, which participants filled out and sent in in the school year following the workshop, were consistent with the case study findings. In a typical progress report, participants reported success in introducing hands-on, inquiry-based activities to the entire school staff through sessions modeled on the PALS training. Here are excerpts from two progress reports completed by principals:

> We now have a common experience that raised issues of science to continue discussion within our preestablished teacher study groups. Teachers will report on the specific changes that they attempt as a result of this workshop. The state assessment test with open-ended questions for all students is providing some impetus for increased concern in examining outcomes in science, math, reading, and social studies.

> Enthusiasm is high and everyone is very involved in the teaching of science. Quite frequently science is integrated very effectively. At our annual Welcome Evening, parents were effusive in their praise re how much science is clearly taking place. I definitely feel that we have the cooperation and support of teachers, parents, children, and central administration.

CONCLUSION

The clearest theme that comes out of all of the research data—the case studies and progress reports in particular—was the change in curriculum materials and the move toward more hands-on activities. That is to be expected, in that the Science Survival Kits and the hands-on activity sessions provided participants with tangible, easily implemented reforms. Still, the data also contains strong evidence that the PALS program achieved some of its more subtle and more systemic goals. Unlike the Golden Age science reforms that limited their vision and their reach to curricular and classroom practice changes, the PALS program set out to place those curricular changes directly in the context of systemic school reform. While the systemic changes take longer to implement and are much more difficult to assess, our evaluation of the PALS program suggests that the trainings did produce positive effects on participants' attitudes, knowledge, and relationships, as well as on practice and behavior. Of course, the impact of the PALS program was limited by its duration; the scope of the intervention, which was primarily centered on relatively short, intensive trainings; and the number of participants it reached. Additionally, further longitudinal studies would need to be conducted to assess the permanence of the changes our evaluation instruments revealed. Those limitations notwithstanding, it is clear that the PALS program provides a model of the next wave of needed reforms, which should focus on further integration of hands-on, inquiry-based activities; long-range planning; and strong collaborative relationships among teachers and principals.[2]

ACKNOWLEDGMENTS

This chapter was made possible by the incredible support and expertise of: Dan Tobin, who could distill a clear message from my systemic thinking; Millie Solomon, who provided encouragement and support; Donna Oliver and Ken Mechling, who conceived of the PALS Network; and Mary Budd Rowe, who first inspired my work with principals and whose legacy of helping science teachers will be supported by this work.

NOTES

1. EDC played an important role in the development of the Golden Age curricula. EDC was founded in 1958 when a group of scientists at the Massachusetts Institute of Technology joined forces with teachers and technical specialists to develop PSSC Physics, a high school physics curriculum that became widely used throughout the United States. Lessons learned from EDC's extensive study of PSSC Physics and the Elementary School Science curriculum informed the development of the mathematics and science curricula the organization has developed over the last several decades.
2. Since this chapter was written, EDC has launched several new science projects that focus on systemwide reform of science education. Many of these projects are carried out under the newly formed Center for Science Education. The Center's approach is described in NSF (1997).

REFERENCES

Ames, N. L., & Miller, E. (1994). *Changing middle schools: How to make schools work for young adolescents.* San Francisco: Jossey-Bass.

Astuto, T., Clark, D., & Read, A. (1994). *Roots of reform: Challenging the assumptions that control education reform.* Bloomington, IN: Phi Delta Kappa International.

Bredderman, T. (1983). Effects of activity-based elementary science on student outcomes: A quantitative synthesis. *Review of Educational Research, 53*(4), 499–518.

Education Development Center (EDC). (1991). *Insights: A hands-on curriculum.* Newton, MA: Author. ("Insights" curriculum now available from Kendall-Hunt, Cambridge, MA).

Federal Coordinating Council for Science, Engineering, and Technology. (1991). *By the year 2000: First in the world.* Washington, DC: Committee on Education and Human Resources.

Fullan, M. G. (1993). Why teachers must become change agents. *Educational Leadership, 50*(6), 12–17.

Fullan, M. G. & Steigelbaum, S. (1991). *The new meaning of educational change.* New York: Teachers College Press.

Graham, P. A., & Fultz, M. (1986). Curriculum-proof teachers in science education. In A. Champagne & L. E. Hornig (Eds.), *Science teaching: The report of the 1985 National Forum for School Science.* Washington, DC: American Association for the Advancement of Science.

Hawkins, D. (1983). Nature closely observed. *Daedalus, 112,* 65–90.

Hofwolt, C. (1984). Instructional strategies in the science classroom. In D. Holdzkom & P. Lutz (Eds.), *Research within reach: Science education* (pp. 43–57). Washington, DC: National Science Foundation.

Hurd, P. D. (1978). The golden age of biological education, 1960–1975. In W. Mayer (Ed.), *Biology teachers' handbook* (pp. 28–96). New York: Wiley.

Jackson, P. W. (1983). The reform of science education: A cautionary tale. *Daedalus, 112*(2), 143–166.

Kyle, W., Jr. (1984). Curriculum development project of the 1960s. In D. Holdzkom & P. Lutz (Eds.), *Research within reach: Science education* (pp. 3–24). Washington, DC: National Science Teachers Association.

Loucks-Horsley, S., Harding, C., Arbuckle, M., Murray, L., Dubea, C., & Williams, M. (1987). *Continuing to learn: A guidebook for teacher development.* Andover, MA: Regional Laboratory for Educational Improvement of the Northeast and Islands and National Staff Development Council.

Marcuccio, P. (1983). Responding to economic sputnik. *Phi Delta Kappan, 64*(9), 618–620.

National Science Foundation. (1997). *Foundations: A monograph for professionals in science, mathematics, and technology education.* Arlington, VA: Author.

Rosenholtz, S. J. (1989). Workplace conditions that affect teacher quality and commitment: Implications for teacher induction programs. *Elementary School Journal, 89*(4), 421–439.

Senge, P. (1990). *The fifth discipline: The art and practice of the learning organization.* New York: Doubleday.

Sergiovanni, T. (1994). *Building community in schools.* San Francisco, CA: Jossey-Bass.

Shymansky, J., & Aldridge, B. (1982). The teacher crisis in secondary school science and mathematics. *Educational Leadership, 40*(2), 61–71.

Shymansky, J., Kyle, W., Jr., & Alport, J. (1983). The effects of new science curricula on student performance. *Journal of Research in Science Teaching*, *20*, 387–404.

Talbert, J. E. & McLaughlin, M. W. (1994). Teacher professionalism in local school contexts. *American Journal of Education*, *102*(2), 123–153.

Tobin, K., & Fraser, B. J. (1989). Case studies of exemplary science and mathematics teaching. *School Science and Mathematics*, *89*(4), 320–334.

Yaeger, R. (1981, September). Science education. *ASCD curriculum update.* Alexandria, VA: Association for Supervision and Curriculum Development.

Wasley, P. (1991). *Teachers who lead: The rhetoric of reform and the realities of practice.* New York: Teachers College Press.

Watson, F. G. (1963). Research on teaching science. In N. L. Gage (Ed.), *Handbook of research on teaching* (pp. 1031–1059). Chicago: Rand McNally.

CHAPTER 8

Teacher Inquiry Groups: Collaborative Explorations of Changing Practice

James K. Hammerman

In the literature of reform, one of the ways we describe the challenge facing teachers is in terms of creating a "culture of inquiry" among students in a classroom. In the Mathematics for Tomorrow (MFT) project of Education Development Center's (EDC) Center for the Development of Teaching, we are working to create another kind of culture of inquiry—a culture of inquiry among teaching colleagues engaged in a professional development program. We are experimenting with new group structures that bring elementary and middle-grade teachers together to form ongoing discourse communities, which we refer to as "inquiry groups." Inquiry group teachers meet regularly to critically examine their own and each others' mathematical and pedagogical knowledge, beliefs, and practice as they work to make changes therein.

Inquiry groups spring from an important set of propositions about the process of teacher change:

1. Change in the spirit of the vision of the reform documents (National Council of Teachers of Mathematics [NCTM], 1989; 1991) requires substantial shifts in teachers' understanding, knowledge and beliefs, and the playing out of those in a complex, situated practice (Ball, 1995; Lampert, 1985; Nussbaum, 1990). It is not merely a set of "technical fixes" that can be learned relatively quickly.
2. Because of this depth and complexity, it is clear that change will take substantial time (Goldsmith & Davenport, 1995). It is an ongoing process with no clear endpoint. We envision teachers continuing to grapple with the dilemmas inherent in reform visions over the course of many years as they work out the implications for practice. For many teachers, ongoing dialogue with others struggling with similar issues can aid in exploring these implications.

3. Creating such a support structure for change requires new relationships among teachers—and long-term structures to support those relationships—as teachers continue to explore important issues over months and years (Little & McLaughlin, 1993).

We are developing the inquiry groups to provide a structure in which teachers can experiment with, and build, these supportive relationships—what Lord (1994) calls "communities for critical colleagueship." We hope to create an environment in which teachers can help one another challenge and develop their mathematical and pedagogical knowledge and beliefs, along with their teaching practices, *as* they continue to teach. Our evolving conception of inquiry groups is informed by other kinds of group structures teacher educators have created to guide and support teachers involved in examining and changing their practice. Some have developed specific methods for promoting such examination (Carini, 1975, 1979; Schifter, Russell, & Bastable, Chapter 2, this volume; Shulman, 1992; Watt & Watt, 1991). Others have begun to describe some of the characteristics of the work done in teacher groups (Cochran-Smith & Lytle, 1992; Freeman, 1991; Keiny, 1994). Lord (1994), for example, talks about the need for reciprocity in risk taking in the context of a resource-rich professional community. Kallick (1989) describes an "interpretive community" as one that takes time to think and reflect together on the variety of understandings that its members bring to an issue. Still others have described some of the effects of teachers meeting together in groups—how they can create shifts in the power structure of schools and schooling by helping teachers find, voice, and legitimate what they know (Cochran-Smith, 1991; Lytle & Cochran-Smith, 1992; McDonald, 1986).

This chapter begins to examine what it means for teachers to be critical colleagues by providing profiles of some emerging MFT inquiry groups. We look at examples of the groups' explorations of mathematics and pedagogy, and consider how these may be affecting teachers' knowledge, beliefs, and classroom practice. We then address issues arising from the change process itself. Our focus throughout is on how the community being formed supports teachers' learning in these realms, as well as how these different explorations build on one another to create a community of supportive but critical discourse. Clearly, this is a dynamic process.

THE CONTEXT

MFT is a systemically embedded teacher development and research project involving 25 K–8 teachers in school-based teams from three Greater Boston Area districts. The districts present a range of demographic characteristics:

Arlington is a small, suburban, white, working-class community; Brookline is a medium-sized, linguistically diverse, urban-suburban, middle- to upper-middle-class community; and Cambridge is a medium-large, economically and racially mixed, urban community.

For teachers, the program consists of two summer institutes, biweekly inquiry group meetings after school in schools during 2 academic years, and four classroom consultations and four day-long workshops each academic year. Teachers are asked to regularly reflect on their practice in writing and, starting in 1994, were provided the opportunity to consult with each other in classrooms. Teachers receive an annual stipend for their participation in the project, and districts contribute funds to cover release time for workshop days and peer consultations and for teachers to buy classroom materials.

In a second phase of the project, we will work with a different group of 36 to 40 teachers from the same districts plus Boston for another 2 years. Some currently participating teachers will work with staff in phase 2 to facilitate inquiry groups, and then will continue facilitating groups independent of staff when the project shifts to district-based funding under the auspices of the Educational Collaborative of Greater Boston (EdCo). Under EdCo, summer institutes and inquiry groups will be made available to its 23 member districts, using MFT-trained teacher facilitators as teacher leaders in new groups.

THE CONTENT OF THE INQUIRY GROUPS

The inquiry groups serve to ground the more general work we do in summer sessions and all-day workshops in the particulars of classroom practice. In inquiry groups, we focus on investigations of mathematics and pedagogy, with occasional discussions of issues of school culture and requirements, the role of parents and other community members, and the tensions between new ideas from the project and others that are prevalent in schools. In each of the sections below, we describe how inquiry group interactions support teachers' own learning about content, as well as about what it means to be part of a professional development community.

Mathematics

Doing Mathematics. Many teachers recognize the need to broaden and deepen their own mathematical understanding so that they can make pedagogical decisions grounded in a clear conception of what's important about subject matter (Schifter & Fosnot, 1993). In inquiry groups, teachers explore mathematics together in order to better understand not only mathematics but also what it means to *make* mathematics. By sharing the variety of ideas and hypotheses they develop about a specific topic, and by challenging one another to clarify and elaborate on their ideas, teachers develop a real, working, mathematical community. There, they struggle together to understand mathematics as meaningful and inventable, rather than as a disparate collection of facts and procedures passed down, too often, from long-dead authorities. Like students in Ball's (1993) third-grade classroom, teachers in MFT inquiry groups learn mathematics from one another as they make conjectures, clarify, support, and revise their ideas.

For example, because teachers wanted students to learn traditional mathematical algorithms, we spent several sessions in the spring of the first year exploring multiplication algorithms. This began with our own attempts to model multiplication with manipulatives and to record our work. It became clear from discussions about this sometimes difficult process that, in general, the algorithms we created required finding ways to break problems into smaller pieces, somehow to multiply each piece, and then to put the pieces back together correctly.

As part of our exploration of multiplication, we also examined a number of algorithms from different cultures throughout history. These included Egyptian and "Russian peasant" multiplication, which both involve keeping track of successive doubling and halving; Lattice/Gelosia multiplication, which involves keeping track of place value through use of a grid; and several variations on modern methods. Teachers learned the techniques involved in these methods, but they spent most of their time trying to understand *why* they work. As they pushed themselves to talk through the reasoning behind each of these methods and the conceptual difficulties they had in understanding them, teachers came to some important insights about place value and number operations. Some noticed the connection between Egyptian multiplication and base-2 representations of number. Others were grappling with the structural strengths and conceptual difficulties associated with a system, such as our base-10 system, that uses powers of a base to represent number. Still others were pondering the connections between different physical representations of number operations—arrays versus discrete groups, for example—and the symbolic representations of those processes.

Clearly, we didn't come to full resolution about these deep issues. Nonetheless, by raising the issues in the context of the group, teachers helped one another struggle with important mathematical ideas. They came to see themselves as people who could work together to make sense of mathematics and, perhaps, to see that mathematics is something about which communities can make sense. For some, this had an important impact on their own attitudes about math and, therefore, on their teaching (see below).

Yet questions still remain about what is needed to make these mathematical discussions fruitful. As the teacher educator facilitating these explorations and discussions, I brought to the group knowledge about both mathematics content—which mathematical ideas are important and potentially generative—and mathematics as a discipline—what it means to work "mathematically," to look for patterns, make conjectures, and try to find reasoned arguments that will prove or disprove these conjectures.[1] I used this knowledge to make more or less subtle judgments in selecting the materials and problems I brought to the group, as well as in the focus and challenges I provided in the course of group discussions. How much knowledge of mathematics—both its content and ways of working—is needed in a teacher group to keep the focus true to "mathematics"? How can teachers in the group develop the knowledge, skills, and attitudes to be self-sufficient in such a group when the support of a teacher educator is no longer available? How explicit do I need to be about my "moves" —the reasoned choices I make as facilitator of the group—to create a culture of mathematical investigation in a group if I hope that it will become institutionalized and maintained in the long term?

Attitudes About Math. Teachers have varied emotional reactions to the experience of participating in a group to do math and to come to really understand it. For some, math has always been interesting and exciting, and this work only adds zeal to their previous energy:

> Math is powerful!! It has felt that way to me in my own math experiences and I have seen a similar effect on my students. My experiences teaching math this year have been entirely different from any other year.
>
> In trying to tease out just what has made the difference for me, a few things come to mind. The most important of these is my own inspiration about math. I have made discoveries and connections, and experienced the high of understanding math in new ways. This "math buzz" infected my whole classroom at times. The heightened awareness I brought to math allowed me to take risks and push kids into bigger ideas and projects than I'd attempted previously. I heard kids professing math to be their favorite subject, and they seemed to anticipate math with excitement. This was news!! (S. Kranz, portfolio reflections)

For other teachers, excitement about math is a newfound thing. For example, several teachers were both surprised and delighted to find themselves continuing mathematical explorations from the inquiry group in their free time. This excitement is especially important for the large number of elementary teachers who come to the program feeling "math-phobic"—that is, confused by or afraid of math. For these teachers, the experience of making sense of mathematics in a community can be truly liberating. In a journal entry in the middle of the year, one teacher wrote:

> Here's some math news you'll like. At one of my parent conferences my student's father was telling me how he'd been teaching his daughter about base 2. He and the daughter then began enthusiastically teaching me. We messed around doing math problems for a half hour. That would not have happened a year ago, I don't think. I would have said, "Base 2. Hmmm. Interesting. Henrietta's doing great in reading . . ." (M. King, portfolio reflections)

But not all teachers find this new way of viewing math exciting. For them, math is the last vestige of a clear-cut subject—there was always a single right answer, and getting that answer was all that mattered. If math, too, requires interpretation, arguing for a position, and justifying the reasonableness of an answer, then no field can be simple and clear-cut in a teacher's day. When knowing math meant memorizing facts and procedures, it was easier for teachers to check their own knowledge. If it requires continuously making sense of phenomena, then some teachers feel much less competent and confident. This reduced confidence can undermine a teacher's ability to teach.

How, then, can the group validate and acknowledge this range of emotional reactions—confusion, frustration, excitement, competence, fear—as an important concomitant of the process of learning something new (Goldsmith & Davenport, 1995; Weissglass, 1994)? How can it support teachers to become more comfortable *being* confused, and dealing with the inherent ambiguities of this new view of mathematics teaching, while they work ideas out? Can groups develop images of *uncertainty* that enable teachers to maintain a sense of control (McDonald, 1992)?

On the other hand, how do teachers' own experiences making mathematics in a community of their peers relate to the kinds of communities they create for their students in the classroom? Clearly having a viable image of such a community may make it possible, but this is not a simple translation. There is much to be studied here.

Pedagogy

Teachers use the group not only to explore new ideas and develop new attitudes about mathematics but also to address explicitly pedagogical issues—that is, questions about how students *learn* mathematics and how to help them grapple with important mathematical ideas. Some of these ideas come directly out of teachers' reflections on their own mathematical learning. In these reflections, teachers ponder the relationship between doing and understanding, and the role of a teacher in facilitating learning.

> [In past years,] did my kids really understand what I was teaching them, or were they simply repeating steps I had taught them? The children left my room with some basic math skills, but I'm not sure exactly what they left under-

> standing. I never gave much thought to their understanding. I always assumed that if they could perform the process, that they must understand what they were doing. I was quick to forget that, for myself, performance did not equate understanding. . . .
>
> A lot has changed for me and my students since I joined the program. They now have a teacher who is open to much more exploration, more questioning, and to mathematical integration within all subject areas. (S. Cyr, portfolio reflections)

In addition, teachers use the group to sort through pedagogical issues that arise from their classroom practice. For example, late in the first year of inquiry group meetings, one teacher came to the group asking for help designing an activity that would get the children "having a heated debate about the issues." The group began by probing into what she meant by "the issues." Through some discussion it became clear that "the issues" she wanted them to debate involved understanding the equivalence of multiple ways of representing a number within a place-value framework—for example, seeing that 241 could be represented with 2 hundreds blocks, 4 tens blocks, and 1 unit block; *or* with 1 hundred block, 12 tens blocks, and 21 unit blocks; *or* in several other configurations. This teacher wanted students to grapple with how these representations were the same and how they were different—and, consequently, with the nature of the rules in a place-value system and when they can be intentionally broken—so that students could talk about when different representations are useful in performing calculations.

Based on their deep probe into the concepts that the teacher felt were important for students to grapple with, the group was able to generate several possibilities of what the teacher might do next. One of these possibilities was picked to develop further, and together the group then designed a classroom activity through which the children would explore these issues. The group used their analysis of the mathematics data they had about prior students' understanding of these ideas, a process that was open to diverse approaches and hypotheses, and the need to clarify ideas in the group to develop a specific plan that met the teacher's initial goals. Interestingly, the teacher later reported that the activity hadn't engendered the heated debate she wanted, because the students found the equivalence of these representations much more obvious than she had expected. In this case, while the activity "flopped" in that it didn't meet her goals, it gave the teacher information about her students' understanding that was quite useful. In addition, the process of working together to deeply analyze an idea and to develop and discuss various hypotheses about how to teach it was important for *teachers'* learning about mathematics and pedagogy.

Another example may further illustrate the kind of discourse that we're hoping to promote. In pondering how to integrate a new curriculum into their ongoing practice, teachers were struggling with issues of pedagogical coherence. The curriculum was built on a spiral model, so that ideas addressed one day might not be addressed the next day but were certain to resurface a few weeks later. Teachers were uneasy about this model. They wanted to use some of the more in-depth, long-term investigations of particular issues they had developed in the past because they thought those gave children a chance to think deeply about an idea over time. Yet persisting with a particular topic would mean cutting pieces from what they considered (and were told was) a very carefully crafted curriculum. Some asked, "How much can I take out [of the new curriculum] and still have it make sense?"

Others thought they might build coherence by helping students make connections *across* topics in the curriculum. Having the teacher "make the connections *for*" students didn't fit the teachers' view of learning, which required learners themselves to make connections among ideas. Yet just "leaving room" for connections sounded quite laissez-faire—teachers were clear that random juxtaposition of ideas without a context in which to build connections was not enough. The question then turned on what it means to "leave students room to make connections," on how teachers can structure the environment to facilitate that, and on how they would know that these connections were being made. These are subtle questions, grounded in practice but touching on deep philosophy.

As teachers work together to analyze and understand each others' practice, our goal is that they begin to see themselves as a community of professionals examining issues of teaching in order to improve it. Yet because such a vision is new to teachers, what this means and how it gets enacted in the group are potentially problematic. We're finding, for example, that it takes a fair amount of preparatory discussion to shape a question to bring to the group so that it embodies a good balance between specific detail and theoretical issues. What goes into this shaping process? What can we learn from others exploring case-based teacher education about the process of drawing theory out of specific classroom instances (Barnett, 1991; Shulman, 1992). And how can teachers learn to support one another to delve deeply into the mathematical and pedagogical issues at hand; to engage *with* each other about substantive issues in teaching, bringing in data and stories (Carter, 1993) to support or refute points made by others, posing questions that challenge assumptions but are seen, nonetheless, as supportive rather than evaluative?

THE PROCESS OF CHANGE

In inquiry groups, teachers begin to work together to examine complex issues of teaching embedded in very particular situations. This kind of professional discourse is new and takes time to develop. It also feels very different to teachers from the evaluative reports of classroom activity and idea swapping that are more typical of teacher talk (Lortie, 1975). The discussion about curriculum coherence described above served to focus, but not answer, the questions raised. Shifting views of mathematics open up possibilities but do not resolve them. How comfortable do teachers feel with this lack of closure? How does their level of comfort change over time, and what causes this change? In this section we briefly explore how teachers individually and in the context of the inquiry group grapple with their changing ideas and practice.

As we move into the second year of work with a single group of teachers, we're finding that conversation has changed. These changes enable the group discussion to probe more deeply into mathematical and pedagogical issues. We think these changes may have several causes: (1) Many teachers have gained confidence in themselves as mathematical thinkers, along with new knowledge about mathematics, learning, and teaching. (2) Teachers can do different things in their classrooms—and thus bring different things to the group—because they're starting the second year with a new group of children and can invent a classroom culture and norms from the beginning of the year. (3) Teachers know the staff, the expectations of the project, and the other members of the inquiry group and feel more comfortable sharing aspects of their teaching that are potentially problematic. (4) Finally, for some teachers, the first year of MFT served to throw their thinking about mathematics and teaching into substantial disequilibrium, and much of the year was spent struggling to put the pieces back together. In the second year, teachers are starting on more solid ground.

Several teachers commented on these changes and this struggle to put things back together in their portfolio writings from the end of the first year of work together.

> While reading [this portfolio] please keep in mind that I am "a teacher (not a work) in progress." This portfolio has forced—yes, forced—me to reflect upon the inklings and nagging thoughts that have begun to assault me since the start of this journey. I am confident that one day I will reflect upon this early time and see its stage as necessary for change. Right now I feel piecemeal. I think, I experiment, and I read patiently. I feel hodgepodge. I haven't made any all encompassing discoveries about how I view my teaching of mathematics. I have blurbs: "meaningful; teach for understanding; the why's not just the how's; use manipulatives; provide time for experimentation and discovery; discuss in groups of different sizes; cooperative learning groups; and write about mathematics." I have points, not philosophy. I hope to pull myself together and translate this mayhem into teaching that most prepares and excites my students to the world of mathematics—a world, which since high school, has excited and challenged me. I love math. I want my kids to feel and know that love for themselves. (C. Wilson-Callender, portfolio reflections)

Wilson-Callender was trying to find a coherent practice in the "hodgepodge" of ideas she was encountering. She was trying to balance cognitive and affective goals; philosophical and practical concerns. Cournoyer, too, acknowledged her changing goals and the challenge of putting them into practice.

> When I think about how what I am learning will impact my teaching style, I become somewhat frightened. I guess that's because I see great changes in store. I've never seen myself as a teacher with math strengths, but I've always been able to get to the answer procedurally and I'm good at memorizing. So, I fared well in my own math attempts and felt helping students to succeed in the same fashion would, in itself be successful. Wow, how my thinking has changed!
>
> I know too well now that math is more than numbers and procedures and memorization. . . . I need to assist students with developing a thinking process that enables them to raise questions and discover answers without relying on memorized procedures or rote learning.
>
> In order to provide my students with all that I wish, I myself need to relearn, to question, to take activities I've been providing steps further. It's apparent to me what I want to do, the real question lies in "how." (A. Cournoyer, portfolio reflections).

In the inquiry groups, we are trying to support one another in grappling with this question: *How* can teachers teach, given their new assumptions about mathematics, learning, and teaching? What structures and cultures in the classroom will support students' robust constructions of important mathematical ideas? In many ways we also need to apply our thinking about this question reflexively to our own learning in the group. How can we create structures and cultures of support in inquiry groups that build on our sense of the complexity of the subject matter and of learning as an active, constructive, and social process? Clearly, this is more than the familiar "sharing good ideas and activities." We've just begun to develop ways to investigate particular examples of teaching practice brought in by teachers as a vehicle for learning about essential issues in teaching.

Such inquiry into practice requires new norms for interaction. Examples of these norms might include a deep respect for teachers as learners and for the effort required to learn dramatically new ways of looking at and being in the world; a focus on judging ideas rather than individuals; a focus on intellectual rather than technical content; a respect for novel and diverse ideas; and clear expectations that we will grapple with new ideas even if these are difficult. How important are these and other norms? How do they get communicated, established, and developed?

Finally, as the project begins to pay explicit attention to the development of teacher leaders who will act as ongoing facilitators of inquiry groups under the EdCo part of the program, we wonder about issues of cultural conflict and expansion. What resources—in the form of knowledge and skills—will teaching facilitators, or other group members, need to continue our inquiry group experiment after funding for staff support is gone? How many people who are familiar with the "culture" of the group are needed to maintain that culture? We know that perpetuating the culture of inquiry of the group depends in part on pressures that the groups experience from outside. We don't know enough yet about how inquiry groups, and the teachers who participate in them, are seen by their non-MFT colleagues. These will be important issues to consider as we imagine the inquiry group structure for professional development expanding throughout schools and districts. How, for example, will the norms and structures of inquiry groups support or clash with those in the broader school community?

CONCLUSION

In this chapter, we have begun to describe the interrelationship between teachers' collaborative learning of mathematics and pedagogy in inquiry groups and the creation of a community for professional development there. Our description of some of the mathematical and pedagogical explorations that take place in inquiry groups, as well as their meaning and importance to teachers in their own growth and development, has raised a variety of questions about the workings of the group and the process of teacher change. We have much work in store for us as we continue to develop our understanding of the nature of the inquiry group and its role in facilitating teacher learning via investigations of issues grounded in classroom practice.

AFTERWORD

The Mathematics for Tomorrow project has continued into its second phase since this chapter was initially written. Inquiry groups still focus on careful and collaborative examination of mathematics, student thinking, and pedagogy through the vehicle of actual classroom examples. They all provide opportunities for teachers to talk about what's going on in their classrooms and to explore their assumptions about what they see and what is possible. Yet the different groups have also evolved cultures and ways of working that feel quite distinct—one group does more writing about what they see in classrooms, focusing especially on student thinking; another is more philosophical in tone and is experimenting with reading articles and papers to inform their analysis;

some groups are quieter and more cautious, others are more lively and energetic. These cultures reflect the specific interests, styles, and learning needs of the teacher and teacher educator members of the group.

In addition, we are finding that teacher leadership of these groups raises extremely complex and difficult issues. Teachers taking on these roles find themselves grappling with the need for new and deeper knowledge about mathematics and pedagogy, new issues around what it means to teach adults, and shifting relationships with their peers as they are seen simultaneously as "expert" and "colleague." This learning is complicated and takes both a deep trust and a lot of time. We are continuing to learn about how to support teachers as they take on these new roles. At the same time, some of the groups are working to develop a more shared form of leadership in which all members will take on both the specific responsibilities of running the sessions and the more ephemeral task of carrying the culture and pushing each others' thinking. Again, this work is in the early stages, but it holds out much promise.

ACKNOWLEDGMENTS

I would like to thank my colleagues Ellen Davidson, Barbara Scott Nelson, Amy Morse, Lynn Goldsmith, Annette Sassi, and Tom Bassarear for their comments and insights in the work described in this chapter. I would also like to thank the teachers who participated with me in MFT inquiry groups for bringing their practice to the group to be discussed and analyzed. This paper is based on work supported by the National Science Foundation (NSF) under grant no. ESI-9254479. Any opinions, findings, and conclusions or recommendations expressed in this paper are those of the author and do not necessarily reflect the views of the NSF.

NOTE

1. Throughout this chapter I use the plural voice to talk about findings. Here I switch to the singular "I" to describe my own role as teacher educator in the group itself.

REFERENCES

Ball, D. L. (1993). With an eye on the mathematical horizon: Dilemmas of teaching elementary school mathematics. *Elementary School Journal*, *93*(4), 373–397.

Ball, D. L. (1995). Developing mathematics reform: What don't we know about teacher learning—but would make good working hypothoses? *NCRTL Craft Paper* (pp. 94–95). East Lansing, MI: National Center for Research on Teacher Learning.

Barnett, C. (1991). Building a case-based curriculum to enhance the pedagogical content knowledge of mathematics teachers. *Journal of Teacher Education, 42*(4), 263–272.

Carini, P. F. (1975). *Observation and description: An alternative methodology for the investigation of human phenomena.* Grand Forks: North Dakota Study Group on Evaluation, University of North Dakota.

Carini, P. F. (1979). *The art of seeing and the visibility of the person.* Grand Forks: North Dakota Study Group on Evaluation, University of North Dakota.

Carter, K. (1993). The place of story in the study of teaching and teacher education. *Educational Researcher, 22*(1), 5–12, 18.

Cochran-Smith, M. (1991). Learning to teach against the grain. *Harvard Educational Review, 61*(3), 279–310.

Cochran-Smith, M., & Lytle, S. L. (1992). Communities for teacher research: Fringe or forefront? *American Journal of Education, 100*, 298–324.

Freeman, D. (1991). "To make the tacit explicit": Teacher education, emerging discourse, and conceptions of teaching. *Teaching and Teacher Education, 7*(5/6), 439–452.

Goldsmith, L. T., & Davenport, L. R. (1995). Affective issues in developing mathematics teaching practice. In B. S. Nelson (Ed.), *Inquiry and the development of teaching: Issues in the transformation of mathematics teaching* (pp. 27–36). Newton, MA: Center for the Development of Teaching, Education Development Center.

Kallick, B. (1989). *Changing schools into communities for thinking.* Grand Forks: North Dakota Study Group on Evaluation, University of North Dakota.

Keiny, S. (1994). Constructivism and teachers' professional development. *Teaching and Teacher Education, 10*(2), 152–167.

Lampert, M. (1985). How do teachers manage to teach? Perspectives on problems in practice. *Harvard Educational Review, 55*(2), 178–194.

Little, J. W., & McLaughlin, M. W. (Eds.). (1993). *Teachers' work: Individuals, colleagues, and contexts.* New York: Teachers College Press.

Lord, B. (1994). Teachers' professional development: Critical colleagueship and the role of professional communities. In N. Cobb (Ed.), *The future of education: Perspectives on national standards in America* (pp. 175–204). New York: College Entrance Examination Board.

Lortie, D. C. (1975). *Schoolteacher: A sociological study.* Chicago: University of Chicago Press.

Lytle, S. L., & Cochran-Smith, M. (1992). Teacher research as a way of knowing. *Harvard Educational Review, 62*(4), 447–474.

McDonald, J. P. (1986). Raising the teacher's voice and the ironic role of theory. *Harvard Educational Review, 56*(4), 355–378.

McDonald, J. P. (1992). *Teaching: Making sense of an uncertain craft.* New York: Teachers College Press.

National Council of Teachers of Mathematics. (1989). *Curriculum and evaluation standards for school mathematics.* Reston, VA: Author.

National Council of Teachers of Mathematics. (1991). *Professional standards for teaching mathematics.* Reston, VA: Author.

Nussbaum, M. C. (1990). The discernment of perception: An Aristotelian conception of private and public rationality. *Love's knowledge: Essays on philosophy and literature* (pp. 54–105). Oxford, UK: Oxford University Press.

Schifter, D., & Fosnot, C. T. (1993). *Reinventing mathematics education: Stories of teachers meeting the challenge of reform.* New York: Teachers College Press.

Shulman, L. S. (1992). Toward a pedagogy of cases. In J. H. Shulman (Ed.), *Case methods in teacher education* (pp. 1–30). New York: Teachers College Press.

Watt, M. L., & Watt, D. L. (1991). *Teacher research, action research: The logo action research collaborative*: Newton, MA: Center for Learning Teaching & Technology, Education Development Center.

Weissglass, J. (1994). Changing mathematics teaching means changing ourselves: Implications for professional development. In D. Aichele & A. Coxford (Eds.), *Professional development for teachers of mathematics* (NCTM Yearbook) (pp. 67–78). Reston, VA: National Council of Teachers of Mathematics.

CHAPTER 9

Professional Development Through Interdisciplinary Curriculum Design

Judith M. Zorfass

As soon as the bell rang, Carlo headed to social studies, where his seventh-grade class was to interview a cardiologist from the local hospital. His interview questions, prepared in advance and tucked into his journal, were carefully crafted. Working in a small cooperative group in science class, Carlo and three classmates had generated a set of questions last week after using a computer simulation on the human circulatory system. Later, to sharpen their speaking skills, they had role-played the interview in their language arts class.

The interview with the cardiologist was part of an interdisciplinary unit on the human body that Carlo was undertaking with his whole class. Students were pursuing their own individual research questions related to the general topic. Carlo brought his own special passion to his particular topic: Since his father's recent cardiac arrest, Carlo had become increasingly interested in understanding how the heart works. When his teachers noticed entries on the subject in his journal, they responded to his writing with a set of probing questions. Thus, with his teachers' encouragement, Carlo had begun to formulate the specific research question he would investigate for the human body unit.

By the time the interview with the cardiologist was over, Carlo was convinced that he wanted to focus on how the human heart mends the damage of a heart attack. Beyond his personal stake in the research question, Carlo was motivated by a desire to contribute to the whole-class endeavor. "I know I can get some terrific information," his teacher reported his saying. "This will help our class."

INTRODUCTION

This vignette is based on case material from a middle school in Lawrence, New York, but the kind of research Carlo is conducting and the interdisciplinary team of teachers guiding his research are part of a nationally growing movement of middle school reform. Such interdisciplinary teams—in this case made up of science, language arts, social studies, and mathematics teachers—are working to redress some of the major shortcomings of traditional junior high school instruction. Historically, junior high schools have failed dismally to meet the developmental needs of young adolescents (California State Department of Education, 1987; Carnegie Council on Adolescent Development, 1989; Cuban, 1992; Johnson & Markle, 1986; Merenbloom, 1988). Dramatic changes take place in students spanning the ages of 10 to 14 (Hill, 1980; Lipsitz, 1983). Physical changes occur more rapidly than at any other stage except infancy. With the advent of the formal operational stage of thinking, young adolescents are capable of thinking in more abstract and complex ways. Socially, students develop an expanded sense of self and begin to explore new roles and relationships with peers and adults.

In emulating the high school model, traditional junior high schools typically offered a fragmented learning environment at a time when young adolescents most need integrated and meaningful learning experiences. Fortunately, the middle school reform movement is encouraging organizational and curriculum changes designed to meet the diverse needs of young adolescents. Many schools are reorganizing to establish teams, with teachers from different disciplines sharing the same students. The creation of interdisciplinary teams makes possible another major recommendation of the middle school reform movement—that teachers provide a meaningful context for teaching and learning that connects, rather than separates, disciplines (George, Stevenson, Thomason, & Beane, 1992; Lounsbury, 1991).

Our own research indicates that thoughtful integration of disciplines provides a powerful learning opportunity for teachers as well as students. Over the past 6 years, in collaboration with hundreds of teachers working in more than 100 schools across the nation, we have developed, field-tested, and published a process for supporting interdisciplinary teams of teachers as they undertake the challenge of teaching in new ways. These new approaches go beyond interdisciplinary instruction to include other tenets of the middle school reform movement—such as cooperative learning and a constructivist learning environment. One of the unique aspects of our work is that we extended those pedagogical strategies to teachers: We ask teachers not only to foster interdisciplinary, constructivist, cooperative learning for their students, but also to engage in that kind of learning themselves. We organize teachers into groups of teams to create inquiry-based research units that allow students to build their own knowledge and research skills as they delve into subjects that are personally relevant to them.

Extensive work with diverse teams of teachers has enriched our understanding of the curriculum design process and our appreciation of it as a constructive process that promotes professional development. The purpose of this chapter is to describe the curriculum design process, drawing on case examples from the many schools we have worked with. We describe and reflect on the process we have designed, noting the opportunities it affords for teacher growth as well as the obstacles one should expect to encounter in undertaking this sort of endeavor.

HISTORY AND FOUNDING ASSUMPTIONS

Our work began in 1986 when we received 5 years of funding from the U.S. Department of Education, Office of Special Education Projects for a project entitled "The Middle School Technology Integration Project." The project's goal was to understand what it takes at the school and classroom levels to successfully integrate technology into the curriculum to benefit students with mild disabilities who are in regular education classes.

Findings at the end of the first phase of the study (1986–1989) broadened the focus of our project in two significant ways:

- While we began with a focus on students with mild disabilities, we realized early on that the traditional middle school curriculum wasn't only failing to engage students with mild disabilities; it was failing to engage middle school students in general. For example, our work across four diverse middle schools revealed that doing a research report was a common "rite of passage" during grades 6 through 8. Unfortunately, we found that this was often an unsatisfying experience for teachers and students (and the parents who lent a hand at the 11th hour).
- We also shifted our focus somewhat from technology to broader curriculum issues. Our research clearly indicated that the potential of technology could only be realized when it was integrated into a strong curriculum that met the needs of developing adolescents (Zorfass, Morocco, Tivnan, Russell, & Zuman, 1989). We found, repeatedly, that technology tools that could support and enhance research often collected dust on storeroom shelves. This "problem" became our "opportunity" to help teachers develop strong curricula that integrated technology to benefit diverse learners.

The I-Search Process

The book *The I-Search Paper,* by Ken Macrorie (1988), provided the foundation for conceptualizing the "I-Search Unit." In an I-Search Unit, a class carries out a long-term investigation (approximately 6 to 8 weeks) on a socially relevant theme (such as ecology or justice) that intrigues young adolescents. Within this context, each student investigates a personally meaningful question. Learning occurs in a social context, with students working together in cooperative groups. Using multiple sources of information, learners go through several cycles of learning as they pursue answers to research questions. The unit culminates in a final product—a written paper and an exhibition (Blumenfeld et al., 1991).

The desired outcomes of an I-Search Unit are consistent with the goals of most current standards-based reform efforts. Students should construct knowledge and deep understandings across disciplines (Perkins & Blithe, 1994), acquire inquiry-based skills and processes (posing a research question, developing a plan, integrating information), and develop pyschosocial skills (e.g., working with peers, persevering in a task). A growing body of evidence suggests that inquiry-based learning can foster thinking and learning in students with diverse learning needs (Englert & Palincsar, 1991; Morocco, Dalton, Tivnan, & Rawson, 1992; Poplin, 1988) and that students develop concepts and gradually internalize important problem-solving processing by working cooperatively with others (Johnson & Markle, 1986; Morocco et al., 1992; Slavin, 1983, 1990). Additionally, research indicates that, creative experiences (student-centered, student-directed, and student-developed activities that allow students to express themselves creatively), a multimaterial approach, and interdisciplinary team teaching are among the elements that contribute to a successful middle school experience (Wiles & Bondi, 1986).

A central tenet of the I-Search approach is that the students take an active role in posing and answering research questions that are relevant and meaningful. The units are designed by teachers with their own students, communities, and local standards in mind. Within the general topic framed by the teachers, students are given the freedom and opportunity to choose their own research questions and investigate themes that are both personally relevant and valued by the local community and larger society (Beane, 1990; Jacobs, 1989). Carrying out an inquiry unit can last from 6 to 12 weeks, during which time students work both independently and in cooperative groups. They participate actively in a variety of learning experiences and construct their understanding of their subject over time by integrating data from a rich variety of sources (Alexander & George, 1993; Beane, 1992). The work students carry out is authentic and meaningful because it is relevant to their personal lives and to real-world issues and problems (Brown, Collins, & Duguid, 1989). Moreover, it is carried out in a way that mirrors how professionals do their work (Sizer, 1992). As one student noted, "So it's like my dad's work. He's a chemist. He has to think of stuff to make, research it, make it, think of new ways to make it better, and then write a report about it."

In our adaptation of the I-Search model, we developed a framework for a four-phase, I-Search Unit:

- *Phase 1.* Teachers immerse students in the overarching theme of the unit (e.g., water conservation) in order to elicit prior knowledge, build background knowledge, model ways of gathering information through a variety of resources, and encourage each student to pose a personally meaningful question to investigate.
- *Phase 2.* Teachers guide students to develop a search plan. The search strategies, technology, materials, and resources students incorporate into these plans are modeled after the types of methods and materials teachers use in phase 1. Teachers help students to determine not only which materials and resources they will use, but also the sequence in which they will use them.
- *Phase 3.* Students work individually and in cooperative groups to gather, integrate, and analyze information from a wide variety of sources.
- *Phase 4.* Students prepare I-Search papers and exhibitions to express what they have learned. The format of the report/project mirrors the search process: My Questions, My Search Plan, What I Have Learned, What This Means to Me, and References.

Teachers integrate technology and media into this inquiry-based curriculum in real and meaningful ways that can benefit all students, those with and without disabilities. The technology and media components allow students to:

- Have access to rich sources of data—text, video, sound, graphics—to gather information related to the theme/concepts of the unit
- Have access to tools that allow them to interact with, manipulate, and analyze information
- Convey to others what they have learned, not only via text, but also through graphics, video, and sound, integrated within multimedia compositions

MAKE IT HAPPEN!

In the second stage of the Middle School Technology Integration Project (1989–1991), we developed and field-tested a curriculum and professional development package called "Make It Happen!: Integrating Inquiry and Technology in the Middle School Curriculum" (Zorfass, Morocco, Tivnan, Persky, & Remz, 1991). The package consists of a teacher's guide to the I-Search, a videotape, and a manual for school-based facilitators of the I-Search process. The goal of Make It Happen! is to help interdisciplinary teams of teachers, including regular and special education teachers, collaborate to design, implement, and evaluate one or more I-Search Units. Make It Happen! guides a facilitator through the process of working intensively with both teachers and school-based administrators. It also recommends establishing a site-based management team whereby the teachers and building administrators can jointly make decisions and solve problems, along with the special education director, curriculum coordinators, and media and technology specialists.

From 1989 to 1991 we field-tested Make It Happen! in four middle schools in New York, New Hampshire, and Massachusetts. Since its publication in 1991, Education Development Center (EDC) has been called upon to provide training and technical assistance to schools across the country implementing the approach. We also had a major opportunity to implement Make It Happen! through EDC's Middle Grades Improvement Project (MGIP), a large school-restructuring project in Indiana funded by the Lilly Endowment. This systemic school reform project aimed to change the ways in which middle schools are organized, provide services, are linked to the community, and design and implement curriculum (Ames & Miller, 1994).

CONSTRUCTIVISM

Just as the I-Search Units are based on a constructivist approach to student learning, the Make It Happen! materials are based on a constructivist approach to curriculum development and professional development. We believe that one of the keys to the success of Make It Happen! in guiding teachers to change their practice is that the program makes teachers active players not only in implementing new materials but also in authoring those materials through an inquiry-based process. The program allows teachers to construct and apply their own knowledge of content, pedagogy, and the needs and abilities of their specific students.

Current constructivist learning theories view learners, including adult learners, as being actively involved in constructing their understanding of the world. Constructivist theory contrasts with the view that learners are passive receivers of knowledge and that their understanding develops from the sequential acquisition of skills and bits of information (Eylon & Linn, 1988; Linn, 1987; Poplin, 1988; Resnick, 1983; Smith, 1989). From the perspective of the constructivist set of beliefs, knowledge does not exist independent of a knower, but instead is brought into being through a transaction between the learner and the environment. Learning is not reacting passively, but building constructively, actively, and passionately (Lester & Onore, 1985). The main principles of the constructivist view, woven into our curriculum design process, are that learning is anchored, socially mediated, recursive, facilitated, and reflective. We hoped that teachers would come to understand the importance of these principles for designing appropriate classroom experiences for their students, but we also recognized that our own efforts to promote shifts in teachers' beliefs and practices would have to be grounded in the same principles. Thus we strove to create a process that had these characteristics, believing that teachers must experience their own learning this way if we expected them to provide similar sorts of learning experiences for their students.

Anchored

"Anchored" means that learners engage in meaningful activities that are "situated" and "authentic," that is, that connect to real work and promote real problem solving (Bransford, Sherwood, & Hasselbring, 1988; Brown et al., 1989; Dewey, 1933). In the Make It Happen! case, the authentic task is creating an inquiry-based unit that effectively meets the needs of students with and without learning difficulties. To keep the focus clear, teachers are encouraged to ask themselves repeatedly: What are the strengths and weaknesses of individual students? What do we want students to be learning and doing and how does this translate into desired outcomes? What kind of teaching and learning will allow students to achieve these outcomes? How will we be able to assess whether students are achieving these outcomes? How can we best work together to make sure we are succeeding in these goals? These questions "anchor" the curriculum design process, ensuring the relevance of the teachers' pursuits.

Socially Mediated

Single individuals rarely possess all the knowledge that is critical to designing a "juicy" inquiry-based, interdisciplinary unit. For example, teachers would need knowledge of several disciplines, instructional strategies, assessment strategies, and materials and resources that involve a variety of technology applications. Working together to design the unit, teachers have continuous contacts with one another, enabling them to "distribute" their own particular knowledge to all of the key participants (Kinnaman, 1990). Through the listening, sharing, and negotiating that takes place, teachers gradually internalize important problem-solving processes (Slavin, 1990; Tateyama-Sciezek, 1990; Vygotsky, 1978).

Recursive

Thinking and learning are recursive, nonlinear processes. In Make It Happen!, there is a recommended step-by-step process for teachers to follow and modify as they see fit (which we describe below). However, the process unfolds in such a way that teachers keep revisiting key issues, such as student outcomes, core concepts related to the unit's theme, and ways to coordinate instruction. Over the course of the design process, they keep refining their ideas and plans as they gather and apply new information.

Facilitated

In our curriculum design process, teachers have access to facilitation in two important ways. First, the interdisciplinary team works with someone designated to serve as a facilitator (e.g., a team leader, assistant principal, curriculum coordinator, or media or technology specialist). The facilitator makes sure that all teacher-learners are contributing, gathers resources and materials, documents the team's thinking, and encourages reflection. Second, the facilitator and team have access to procedures, tools, and resources contained in the Make It Happen! materials themselves.

Reflective

When learners reflect, they examine their beliefs in the light of their practices and vice versa (Bullough, 1989; Clift, Houston, & Pugach, 1990; Schön, 1983). Opportunities to reflect, individually and as a group, are consciously built into the Make It Happen! curriculum design process. For example, teachers are encouraged to reflect on students' needs, the theme and activities of the unit, and their working relationships. After teachers design and implement the unit, there is specific time set aside for a "retreat." During the retreat they review what has occurred, reflect on their professional growth, and determine how their new knowledge can be used to improve future instruction.

Such reflection seems critical to the process of teacher change and mirrors the mindfulness we hope teachers will call for in their students. Teachers have said that by being actively involved in reflecting on their experiences, they take ownership of the learning process and thus are better able to understand the desired learning process for students.

CURRICULUM DEVELOPMENT AS PROFESSIONAL DEVELOPMENT

Through our development, testing, and implementation of Make It Happen!, we came to see what a powerful tool the curriculum design process can be for the professional development of teachers. The process meets three professional goals for teachers:

- To develop and use a repertoire of skills, knowledge, and strategies to design curriculum units
- To develop a set of strategies that enhance collaboration among team members, administrators, and students
- To develop a feeling of efficacy—a positive feeling about themselves as professionals who competently meet all students' needs

The complexity and immediacy of the curriculum design process proved to be particularly effective in helping teachers build their teaching and collaborative skills, and thus their feelings of professionalism and competence. The Make It Happen! approach to curriculum design asks a lot of teachers (as illustrated by the program description and case studies presented below) and, in turn, provides them with particularly rich opportunities for growth, risk taking, and reflection. In coming together with colleagues from other disciplines to craft a tangible product that they all will use, teachers are called upon to articulate—and often defend—their approach to pedagogy and content. They negotiate every aspect of the unit's development, from the choice of general research topic to the interweaving of particular disciplines, to the division of labor, to the assessment of student work. All the teachers also place themselves in the position of learners, conducting their own research prior to guiding student projects. As they forge a path that they know their students will soon follow, teachers continually evaluate the effectiveness of the curriculum they are designing: How will this play out in my classroom? Are the activities feasible, given the time and resources we have available? Are they accessible to all students? Have we provided students with enough guidance while still leaving them room to pursue their own questions?

All of these questions and negotiations can be daunting for teachers, particularly those who are used to working independently and teaching a fixed curriculum. Most of the interdisciplinary teams struggle repeatedly with issues of control and philosophy. Our experience has shown us that these struggles can provide tremendous opportunities for professional development, provided teams can air and resolve their differences rather than letting them become unspoken barriers to collaboration. For this reason, the Make It Happen! materials place a good deal of emphasis on the role of the facilitator in keeping team members working productively.

The Role of the Facilitator

We recommend that each team work with a facilitator—someone whose main role is to ensure that the process of curriculum design remains productive and on track. As the name implies, this person facilitates the group's interaction by clarifying issues, posing questions, summarizing key points, making sure each member has an opportunity to participate in the discussion, gathering needed information, and documenting the team's emerging thinking. The facilitator, giving sustained help over time, also serves as a liaison between the team and administrators, bringing issues to the table, arranging meetings, and implementing group decisions with appropriate next steps.

In some cases, such as those described below, project staff from EDC served as facilitators or co-facilitators with school-based staff. We have also held training-of-trainers institutes to build ability. A facilitator can be anyone in the school who meets the following criteria: demonstrated ability to be and interest in being a change agent; some power and influence in the school to make change happen; and a flexible schedule. We have seen assistant principals, team leaders, school- or district-level curriculum coordinators, media specialists, technology coordinators, special education teachers, and master teachers take on the role of facilitator.

As we describe the steps in the curriculum design process below, we show how a good facilitator is key to success. In some ways, the facilitator resembles a juggler, managing complexity for the group. Keeping "all the balls in the air," the facilitator keeps discussion and planning going simultaneously on multiple levels. If a ball drops, the facilitator reintegrates the topic (e.g., student needs or overarching concepts) into the conversation. Occasionally, just as a juggler flings one ball higher into the air than the others, a facilitator needs to know when some important topic needs to be scrutinized in a more thoughtful way.

The facilitator plays a critical role in resolving emerging conflict among team members. The Make It Happen! curriculum design process is an intense and intensely collaborative one for teachers. Conflict and resentments can often arise when team members fear that others will not carry through with promised tasks, keep the unit on a steady course, be committed to the team effort, give the students consistent messages about the unit, or "work as hard as others." Successful facilitators do not shy away from conflict, but rather help teams work through these critical issues. When one facilitator perceived that she was heading for "troubled waters," she reminded the group of her slogan, "Problems are our friends. If we don't recognize them, we can't begin to find solutions." The next time another potential conflict arose, a team member helped reduce growing tension by saying, "Well, here's another new friend for us."

Steps in the Curriculum Design Process

The term "step" is loosely applied in this section to designate the key components of the process. Although these components, or steps, are listed in sequence, the process is in no way "lock-step" in approach. A tremendous amount of fluidity is critical so that teachers can move forward and backward as needed to construct a meaningful unit.

We recommend setting aside 4 or 5 consecutive days for a curriculum design workshop. Working intensively, the team carries out these steps (several of which are discussed in the section that follows.):

- Define and discuss inquiry-based learning.
- Select and refine unit theme.
- Identify and gather potential materials and resources.
- Identify overarching concepts related to unit content.
- Select and refine student outcomes and related standards.
- Generate and refine instructional activities for the unit's four phases.
- Document plans by writing up activities and flow charts.
- Design building-block strategies to help teachers and students stay focused and organized.
- Review unit for cohesiveness and coordination across classrooms.
- Plan for introduction to students.
- Plan for continued collaboration.

Define and Discuss Inquiry-Based Learning. We recommend that facilitators begin by having teachers close their eyes and picture one student from their classes to anchor the conversation. Then, asking each teacher to describe the student's characteristics, the facilitator records these on chart paper or on an overhead transparency to help the team discuss their combined list in terms of cognitive, social/emotional, and physical characteristics. This activity, or alternative ones like it, is important for reminding the group that they are embarking on a student-centered approach to teaching and learning.

Next, facilitators help teachers develop a shared vision of inquiry-based learning, which becomes the basis for discussing their beliefs about teaching and learning. We recommend all or some of the following activities:

- Reading and discussing the case study of teachers carrying out a unit included in Make It Happen!
- Recalling and discussing experiences from their past that represented an authentic form of inquiry learning (e.g., buying a car, finding a vacation spot)
- Engaging in and discussing simulated inquiry-based experiences (such as the paper towel experiment described below)
- Viewing and discussing the Make It Happen! videos of different teams designing and carrying out I-Search Units
- Reading and discussing the set of "classroom close-ups" (a description of activities in all four phases of the I-Search Unit written about a fictitious unit)

These activities engage teachers as active participants and thus serve as a model of inquiry-based instruction.

Many teachers have commented on the power of engaging in a simulation and then debriefing about it immediately afterward. In the paper towel activity, for example, we give the team a few sheets of paper towels from three different brands. With only the following information—cost, thickness, and dimension of each sheet—they must decide which is the "best" brand. They do this by establishing criteria for "best" and then devising experiments to test each criterion. To test absorbency, softness, and strength (commonly identified criteria), teachers creatively develop a wide array of experiments. After teams share the results of their inquiry, the debriefing focuses on two key questions: What did it feel like to be a learner? What are the implications for teaching? In response to the first question, teachers say such things as: "I liked the fact that I was carrying out an investigation and I didn't know what the answer was before I started." "I learned from the others in my group." " I was fully engaged." The question about implications for teaching raises issues related to classroom management, standards, and assessment strategies. Often serious concerns surface with comments such as: "It must feel like chaos with the teams working simultaneously." "How can I be everywhere at once?" "How do students know how to work together?" The facilitator makes notes for the group to return to these issues for further discussion at appropriate times.

Following the hands-on activity, facilitators encourage the teams to think again of their students by asking teachers to relate the benefits of inquiry-based teaching and learning to the characteristics of the students they identified at the start. Teachers tend to say things such as: "Because kids need to move around so much, the active, hands-on learning makes a difference." Or "Working with peers to problem-solve is important to students of this age, when peer interaction and acceptance is so important." Or "Kids really get into topics that have social value."

Select and Refine the Unit's Theme. A team typically begins this task with some strong possibilities based on preliminary conversations among the teachers and/or administrators and curriculum coordinators. These conversations take into account discipline-specific standards related to content required by the district or school for particular subjects.

With some possible themes in mind, the team begins to apply criteria to narrow down the choices. Nevertheless, finding a focus is hard work and requires skillful facilitation. The following questions serve as helpful criteria for making their selection: Will the theme motivate young adolescents? Does it connect to social issues? Does it link to the personal concerns of young adolescents? Does it develop important and meaningful concepts? Does it lend itself to using a variety of materials and resources? Does it strengthen the link between content areas in real and important ways?

When teams evaluate possible themes, teachers find themselves becoming advocates for one or another theme. To encourage open discussion, the facilitator asks proponents of a particular theme to persuasively "speak on its behalf," by linking the theme's attributes to the criteria listed above. These conversations often illustrate good negotiation, an element of social mediation. For example, a school in Wayne Township, Indiana, generated the following partial list of potential unit themes:

- Health and Diet (changing nutrition/lifestyles, food production)
- Zoos
- Environmental Issues (pollution, ecology)
- Evolution of Fashion (production, economy, fashion shows)
- Role of Women (changing family structures, children, rites of passage)

The social studies teacher argued that in past years he found students fascinated by World War II, especially because so many of their relatives were veterans willing to talk about their military experiences. The language arts teacher asked, "Do male and female students equally share this fascination?" The social studies teacher admitted that perhaps boys were more enthusiastic. Recognizing the social studies teacher's investment in this topic, the language arts teacher began imagining how the role of women could be woven into a unit on World War II. "You know," she added, "women were in the military, replaced men in factories, and supported the war effort at home in a myriad of ways." As she spoke, the facilitator listed her ideas, diagramming connections among ideas for the whole group to see. These ideas stimulated others to add ways of integrating the two topics.

Reaching and maintaining consensus on a theme can be a difficult challenge for teams of teachers, who are often used to working independently. More than one team has committed to a theme early on, only to reject it later because they find it unworkable. For example, the New York team mentioned in the opening vignette about Carlo, first decided to do a unit on the Civil War. It soon became clear, however, that the unit wouldn't work, because the social studies teacher, a second-year teacher, expressed strong discomfort in deviating from the required curriculum. Listening to the team embroiled in a heated discussion, the co-facilitators (the author and the technology coordinator for the district) realized that a complete shift in thinking was needed. At this juncture, it was important for the facilitators to help the team construct a new unit, while making sure that they didn't feel as if they had wasted time or that the social studies teacher had let them down. Once they accepted the notion of making a dramatic shift, the team agreed on the theme of the human body, with the science teacher taking the lead. Team members said later that they had learned something important about engaging in a recursive process.

Although a team in one New Hampshire school knew they wanted the unit to be about their town, when they brainstormed a long list of directions in which the unit could go, the facilitator realized their ideas were too disparate. Again, the facilitator's role proved crucial. She helped the team "web" their ideas, by listing the name of their town in the center circle and all of their related ideas as spokes radiating from that circle. Reviewing all the ideas they had generated, she asked them to categorize their ideas. This step led the team to identify three topics—economy, architecture, and people's lifestyles—which became the organizing structure for the unit, named "Milford: Back to the Future."

Identify and Gather Potential Materials and Resources. There are two important reasons for teachers to gather materials and resources related to the theme of the unit. First, if teachers are going to teach without textbooks, they need to feel confident that there will be sufficient materials for students to use. We recommend that teachers, with the help of media specialists, spend time in the school, town, or district library and/or media center to identify possible materials/resources. The potential materials and resources might include technology applications (simulations, databases, timelines, spreadsheets, CD-ROM encyclopedias, graphics programs, etc.), reference materials, audiovisual media (e g., videotapes, filmstrips, audiotapes, slides, records), periodicals, books, speakers, and field trips.

In the New York school that implemented the unit on the human body, the team included the librarian/media specialist. Harriet, the K–12 computer coordinator, was the facilitator. With these professionals offering assistance, and with time set aside to browse in the media center, teachers gathered a number of simulations (e.g., *The Human Body Systems*), filmstrips, books of all reading levels, and pictures. They also contacted doctors, nurses, and the school health teacher, asking if they would volunteer to be interviewed by students.

When the team in New Hampshire began exploring their town library, they were disappointed to find few materials. Undaunted, each teacher set out to locate resources by conducting a minisearch on one "big idea." The mathematics teacher traced the development of the town's leading bank through reading newspaper articles and interviewing bankers. The language arts teacher traced his family's lineage, which was linked to the town's history. Finally, the special education teacher, studying architecture, produced a video essay that captured changes in homes over time. She ended her video by saying, "As I end this video, I am sitting on a rock in my own backyard. And I'm wondering how many other people who have come before me may have seen these big trees, may have heard these birds chirping. How many children grew up in this backyard, became grandparents, and passed away? It makes me wonder all the more, how important it is to learn about the people that came before us."

These teachers later used their individual searches as a way to introduce the unit to their students, talking not only about the content but also about what it felt like to search. As they introduced the unit to students, they described the "search" process like this: "It will be an opportunity for you to go out and use materials and search for information in ways you've never done before. Some of it will be outside of this school—you'll be taking field trips to the library, to the newspaper offices, to Town Hall, and interviewing all kinds of people."

The second reason for gathering materials and resources is so that teachers can "dig into" the content related to the theme of the unit. Often teachers get excited about a theme that cuts across disciplines but need to develop expertise about the content. In order to be valuable coaches to students, teachers need a firm grasp of the content. One team in Massachusetts wanted to focus their unit on, "How does the Atlantic Ocean affect life in Massachusetts?" They began having "fuzzy ideas" about the effect of the Atlantic Ocean the economy, environment, community life, and arts/recreation of Massachusetts. It wasn't until they went on a field trip, visited the public library, read books, and watched videotapes, however, that they could clarify what they really meant by these main ideas.

Identify Overarching Concepts. Overarching concepts are the key understandings or big ideas that teachers want their students to develop over the course of an I-Search Unit. These overarching concepts form the major conceptual goals of the unit. They become the framework, or context, for anchoring each student's individual search. In the early stages of the curriculum design process, it is essential to clearly articulate the unit's overarching concepts. They serve as "beacons of light," guiding teachers as they identify learning objectives and generate activities.

To introduce and build an understanding of the term "overarching concepts," facilitators often show teams the following sample included in Make It Happen!, developed for a unit called "Coming to America":

- What social, political, religious, and economic conditions within the United States and in other countries have brought people to the United States throughout history?
- What social, political, cultural, economic, and religious factors have had an impact on where and how people live in the United States once they have arrived?

- How have people who have come here from other countries changed the political, social, cultural, economic, and religious fabric of our society?

Teams, as well as facilitators, report that this step is the most challenging part of curriculum design. It requires articulating a knowledge base, understanding how specific disciplines organize knowledge, sharing perspectives and biases, and determining what knowledge is fundamental based on standards. Facilitators cannot rush this process. They must make sure teachers draw on the resources they have gathered; listen to one another; generate, weigh, and reject suggestions; and take the risk of revising their thinking as needed.

The transcript below is from a preliminary conversation held by the teachers in New York as they planned their unit on the human body.

Facilitator: What do 12-year-olds need to know about structure and function?

Science teacher: Our curriculum—it's hard. There's a lot of little things they need to understand. They have to know the digestive system. They need to know enzymes: the names of them, where they work, what they do, when they work, how they work. The circulatory system. The blood . . .

Facilitator: They need to know the specifics, but what do they need to know in general? What do we really want them to come away with 2 years from now. And what do we want to hook in from English and social studies into this big concept?

Science teacher: They need to come away with the fact that the human body has several systems in it.

Facilitator: OK. All right.

Science teacher: And these systems need to function properly in order for the human, or any living thing, to work properly.

Facilitator: (*writing*) "Function properly." OK, now I know when I go home and I talk to my children about functioning properly, they have a really different idea about functioning properly. Dave [to language arts teacher], you're well experienced with this age group—what do you think is going to connect them to the "function properly" concept?

Language arts teacher: Kids at this age, as we said before, are fascinated by things that go wrong. And I'm sure they're concerned that things are maybe going to go wrong with them, or they want to be reassured that things, if they do go wrong, can be fixed.

After much more discussion, they agreed on three overarching questions, which they presented to students as overarching concepts: (1) How does the structure of a body system relate to its function? (2) Describe the cause and effect of a malfunction in a body system. (3) How are advancements in genetics shaping the future of medicine? After the unit ended, teachers commented that, as expected, their early adolescent students had no trouble finding relevant topics to explore within the context of the overarching questions. Examples of students' questions included: How does a mother's body change when a baby is growing inside? How is the brain, only the size of your fist, able to control everything we think and do? What happens to a person who has AIDS? What is cancer? What is anorexia and how do you cure it?

One Indiana team focusing on Native Americans realized they were being "fuzzy" in their thinking about the content knowledge related to each broad, overarching concept. They began to identify specific content related to each concept. One persistent teacher kept asking, "Will students understand the way we arrayed the knowledge? Will they be able to find a meaningful I-Search question to explore within our framework?" What this teacher was inadvertently doing was posing criteria to determine if concepts would be clear instead of fuzzy to students. One teacher suggested that the team engage in some role playing, with each teacher playing the role of a student. Through their role playing, teachers uncovered weaknesses in the way they had linked ideas. It pushed them to go back and clarify even further what they meant by each concept, the related content, and the directions student exploration could take.

Select and Refine Student Learning Objectives. The objectives, or desired outcomes, for an I-Search Unit fall into three areas: constructing knowledge related to the unit's theme, developing and applying inquiry-based skills and processes, and developing lifelong learning habits. In this step, facilitators encourage teachers to talk about adolescents' cognitive, physical, and psychosocial development; revisit their thinking about the overarching concepts; and use a standards-based approach to identify what knowledge and skills students need to have.

For example, one team in Evansville, Indiana, was designing a unit on ecology. The unit was going to begin with an extended field trip to a reserve located on an island in the middle of the Ohio River. Although teachers had gone on this trip before with students, they had never used it as a kick-off activity for an interdisciplinary unit. The facilitator, Cynthia, pushed them to discuss the kinds of interpersonal skills students could develop by participating in environmental games, living in dorms, and taking responsibility for a task within a cooperative group. Cynthia asked teachers to specify the kind of information students would be exposed to, the vocabulary they would need, and the mathematics skills required to carry out essential tasks (e.g., calculating percentages). Teachers said that in the past, they had not "pulled the trip apart" in such a way that helped them identify a clear set of student outcomes.

Though disagreements are inevitable and priorities must be negotiated, there should be agreement with the main point—namely, that students will be developing inquiry-based skills: posing questions, developing a plan, persevering to gather information, integrating information in a meaningful way, and conveying to others what they have learned. The two teams currently participating in the research study on student impact have developed a set of indicators of student growth, corresponding to each phase of the I-Search Unit.

By identifying objectives, teachers find themselves face-to-face with two critical questions: "What instructional activities will help students meet these objectives? How will we know if students are accomplishing these objectives?" Their responses lead directly to the next step.

Generate and Refine Instructional Activities. Once teachers reach this point, they feel as if they are on familiar territory: Now they can think concretely about what will actually happen in their classrooms. In fact, facilitators report having to "hold teachers back" from designing activities earlier in the process until they are clear about the unit's overarching concepts and desired outcomes. We encourage facilitators to review the four phases of the curriculum development process and to proceed with brainstorming phase-by-phase.

The brainstorming for phase 1 is usually the most intense. In a unit on conflict resolution, teachers in Indianapolis generated activities that involved watching videos, visiting the courthouse, having a mock trial, following current events, and reading short stories that involved conflict. However, after the initial brainstorming, teachers recognized that they had "more activities than we need." To pare down the ideas, the facilitator asked them the following critical questions:

- Does the activity introduce, define, or elaborate one or more of the overarching concepts?
- Does it elicit prior knowledge and build knowledge?
- Does it allow for process time? (Note: The *Search Organizer* software developed for Make It Happen! helps students process information.)
- Does it model a method of gathering information by reading, watching, asking, or doing?
- Is it linked to one or more desired student outcomes?
- Are student assessments built into the activity?
- Will it intrigue students, provoking them to think about possible I-Search questions?

Facilitators need to listen for a "no" to one or more of the above questions. This response serves as the catalyst for evaluating the overarching concepts, the learning objectives, and the relationship of one phase of instruction to another. If necessary, the facilitator needs to guide teachers to reexamine and modify earlier thinking.

The facilitator also works to make sure that the curriculum plan is realistic and coordinated. The facilitator reminds teachers to apply a set of logistical criteria to the list of activities: How long will each of these activities take? What are the costs and benefits of spending time on this activity? Are the activities redundant? To help themselves be as concrete as possible, the facilitator introduces a week-by-week calendar. They work together to lay the activities out across days, anticipating how many days each activity will take. As each teacher involved in the team charts out his or her activities, a lot of negotiating takes place. Teachers realize the need to interlock activities so that students will be able to follow their inquiries across classrooms. The following conversation is typical:

Social studies teacher: Let's plan the field trip to see the war memorials in downtown Indianapolis for Tuesday and Wednesday.

Language arts teacher: If we do that, I should make sure we read the literature from the Chamber of Commerce on Monday to set the context.

Social studies teacher: At the same time you are doing that on Monday, I should be reviewing the map of Indianapolis, having students identify where the memorials are and planning out our walking route.

Art teacher: Before we go, I think I want to introduce students to types of memorials and materials used, so students will have something to be looking for.

Facilitator: Are we giving ourselves enough time to prepare for the trip, so it's as meaningful as possible for students? Let's be sure we know what we want students to be getting out of the trip so we can set the context and plan follow-up activities.

The design of phases 2, 3, and 4 is a bit more ambiguous than that of phase 1 (students develop individual search plans in phase 2, carry them out in phase 3, and draft their reports in phase 4). Because students' work is determined by their questions and plan, it's hard for teachers to predict exactly what will happen in later phases. However, the Make It Happen! materials do help teachers and facilitators develop strategies for guiding students in such critical processes as the integration of information in phase 3. As one teacher said, "It's not hard for kids to accumulate index cards bound into packs with rubber bands. What I worry about is how do they link ideas?" To respond to this concern, facilitators can help teachers brainstorm strategies and expand upon them by consulting the suggestions in the Make It Happen! facilitator's guide. These include having students color-code cards with related ideas; sort cards into smaller piles; participate in cooperative discussion groups; and use *Inspiration,* a software program designed to promote semantic webbing of ideas.

Document Plans. Documentation involves writing up activities and filling in flow charts that show the progression of the activities across classrooms over time. The activity write-ups include identifying the objectives, the procedures, the materials/resources, and the ways in which teachers will carry out ongoing assessment of student growth and progress. Teachers usually do this individually, volunteering to write up those activities that they will be responsible for leading.

The process of documentation encourages teachers to reflect again on their central goal of student learning and related issues of assessment. Teachers routinely ask themselves such questions as: What will students be doing? Why? What will I be looking for as indications they are constructing knowledge, developing skills and processes, and developing positive self-esteem? What assessment strategies will I use? How will students know if they are working productively? A good facilitator reminds teachers that the design process is recursive and that it is never too late to modify an activity—or even discard it if necessary.

Design Building-Block Strategies. The purpose of the building-block strategies is to help teachers and students stay focused and organized. This is especially critical when instruction aimed at meaning-making is taking place across classrooms. As teachers become invested in linking instruction in meaningful ways, they strive to find ways to make sure that students do not become lost in the process, that their needs do not fall between the cracks, and that they do not see the numerous learning activities as unrelated experiences.

During one team's planning, the teachers were very concerned that students' journals and portfolios might not travel with them as they changed classes. These teachers were sensitive to early adolescents, who are often disorganized and lose important items. The teachers worked out a simple system of collecting the materials at the end of each class and handing them over to the next teacher. As an added benefit, the brief contact during transfer enabled teachers to give each other a concise update of what had happened in class. Often this information helped the next teacher to make a slight, but needed, modification in teaching.

Review the Unit. Looking over all the documented plans, facilitators ask teachers to review the unit as a whole by asking themselves: Is the unit cohesive? Is it well coordinated across classrooms? Will students be able to construct meaning? Are our activities related to our outcomes? This step provides teachers with an opportunity to reflect on the whole and make necessary modifications.

Plan for Introduction to Students. It is important to set a context that will motivate students and clarify what they will be doing. Teachers in New Hampshire introduced their I-Search Unit by sharing their own prior mini-I-Searches. One teacher showed her videotape of historic homes with its narration about the age, architecture, and history of each. The language arts teacher displayed some old family portraits as he discussed his family's roots in the community through nostalgic and humorous stories about his ancestors. The third teacher used a feature article from the local newspaper about the recent 100th anniversary of their local bank to spark interest and discussion in the changes in the economy over the past century.

Some teachers have held assemblies that brought together all the teachers and students who would be part of the unit. In other schools, the team adjusted the class schedule for "kick-off day," creating a two- or three-period block of time in which to introduce the unit. In some cases, the team also wrote a letter to students and their parents explaining the goals, plans, and some particular logistics of the unit.

At the outset, teachers have distributed handouts of the four phases of the I-Search Unit, graphic webs of the theme and overarching concepts, portfolio organizers, and criteria for the I-Search papers and exhibitions. Later they have said that the more concrete the materials, the less students feel overwhelmed.

Plan for Continued Collaboration. The curriculum design workshop involves planning before the fact. Once the unit is underway, modifications, sometimes on a daily basis, are needed. Teachers have found that they need to talk daily, to share what happened in their classes, and to relate how individual students reacted. Ongoing assessment is a team endeavor, requiring continuous conversation. The facilitator needs to develop a plan with teachers so they can continue planning, meeting, sharing, and monitoring student work.

TEACHER CHANGE

After the interdisciplinary teams have implemented the curriculum units they designed, we recommend that the team plan a retreat. The purpose of the retreat is for teachers to reflect on their experience. Away from professional pressures, teachers can appreciate more fully all the levels of accomplishment of the team and the students, celebrate the completion of a new challenge, and think realistically about how they would like to grow and change in the future. The teachers are joined by the facilitator, and often administrators and other key players attend for all or part of the session. Materials in Make It Happen! guide facilitators to help teachers, both individually and in groups, identify a set of evaluation questions, gather materials, analyze information, and reflect on how they've met their learning goals for teachers as well as students. Some of the sample reflection questions included in the Make It Happen! facilitators guide are:

- How well did we meet the needs of all students?
- How well did we carry out our instructional application of the I-Search?
- How well did we grow professionally and collaborate as a team?

Teachers' analysis of their own change reveals several different kinds of shifts in beliefs and practices; growing tolerance for ambiguity; improved curriculum development skills; comfort with professional collaboration; greater willingness to try new forms of teaching; and new insights into students' abilities. We discuss each of these changes below.

Tolerance for Ambiguity and Comfort with a Recursive Process

Teachers are not usually given the luxury of time for in-depth thinking about teaching and learning in the daily swirl of activities. When given the chance to think and rethink key issues, they find themselves digging more deeply, letting go of first-round thinking, and developing ideas that seem clearer, surer, and more effective. Teachers say they appreciate it when facilitators explicitly say that changes in thinking are legitimate. They gradually come to see the work they are doing as a process, with a product (the curriculum unit) that is organic. As one team was working on its second interdisciplinary unit, one teacher said about some preliminary plans, "Let's stick with this for now, but we all know it will change as we really figure out what we're doing." This tolerance for ambiguity and comfort with an iterative process are fundamental because they enable teachers to continually and actively reconsider the unit's theme and concepts in light of the students' needs.

Better Curriculum Development Skills

During the course of curriculum design, the Make It Happen! materials and the facilitators stress the importance of having three or four overarching concepts guide the content of the unit. In one school in Massachusetts, teachers wanted to develop a unit that would help students differentiate between race and culture. Although they engaged in heated debate about what was at the core of this unit, they never clearly articulated the underlying concepts of the unit. During the retreat, they agreed that the unit always felt as if the "ground was shifting under their feet," an uncomfortable feeling for a team of experienced teachers. Because of the unit's lack of clarity, teachers reflected that students never quite "got what we were doing." This recognition of student confusion had become evident to teachers while the unit was in progress, because teachers engaged in ongoing monitoring and discussion. At the time, they used this information to make a major mid-course correction, to turn a fragmented unit into something that felt cohesive to the students. Even though this discussion brought forth painful memories at the retreat, teachers also said that they learned something important about interdisciplinary instruction that would be invaluable for their future endeavors. As one teacher said, "We took a risk and we learned something important that will help our future teaching." The curriculum design process depends on this kind of open evaluation by teachers, where their own experiences feed back into their growing knowledge of teaching and learning.

One major factor differentiates a "clear" from a "fuzzy" overarching concept. That is, the concept is an accurate superordinate heading for a body of knowledge that can be clearly elaborated. Teachers achieve clarity when they take the time to understand and organize the knowledge base related to the unit's theme. For example, a team in Indianapolis was designing a unit called "A River Runs Through It." They wanted students to investigate a major river in the world and compare it to the White River, which runs through their city. They pushed hard to clarify the important ways in which to describe and characterize rivers. This differentiation became the basis for defining their overarching concepts. Interestingly, the team approached the design of the river unit with 2 previous years of interdisciplinary curriculum design under their belts. They unanimously agreed that their current effort was the best ever. One teacher summed up the other's comments: "This is the first time we'll be heading into a unit really understanding the knowledge base; we'll be able to clearly tell students our expectations; and we'll be better able to help and guide students." These are exactly the reasons why teachers need to clarify concepts.

Another important element in curriculum development is recognizing that less can be more, an insight many of the teachers come to on their own through participation in the design process. For example, at the retreats teachers talked extensively about the need to pay careful attention to logistics. They recognized the futility of trying to cram in too many instructional activities. In reflecting back on the curriculum design process, teachers recognized that they "were afraid to let go" of some of the activities they had brainstormed. They talked about becoming invested in particular activities that they thought would be meaningful and/or motivating to students. But for some of these activities, they had not fully considered the costs and benefits during the design stage. Some activities had drained resources, taken too much time, and side-tracked students. Teachers consistently said, "Because we have learned that everything takes longer than expected, we need to plan to do less, not more."

Collegiality and Professional Collaboration

For many teachers, working closely with others in the context of a team is a new experience. Teachers are accustomed to working in isolation, comfortable in developing and executing their own plans. At the outset of the curriculum design process, some teachers voice concerns about developing joint plans, coordinating instruction across classrooms, covering "required" content, assessing students, and losing individual planning time.

Working with others to construct knowledge most certainly involves risk taking. When teachers share ideas about teaching and learning, brainstorm ideas about instruction, present dissenting opinions, and negotiate plans, they say they feel they are "opening themselves up" to close scrutiny by colleagues. Sometimes teachers feel vulnerable when they reveal deep-seated beliefs or generate new ideas. Teachers readily acknowledge that it takes them a while to trust their colleagues, build bonds, develop mutual respect, and accept diverse opinions. Besides the risk taking, collaborative curriculum design demands time and energy. It takes time to reach consensus, weigh viewpoints, write up plans and distribute them, and meet regularly for status reports and further planning.

In some cases, it takes time to build relationships and integrate new members into a team. In the New York school that carried out the unit on the human body, the special education resource room teacher joined the team in order to plan and implement the unit. This was a new experience for her as well as for the other teachers. The team designed their unit in the summer and planned to implement it in the winter, immediately after Christmas vacation. All through the fall, the team met regularly twice a week. During this time, they developed a habit of talking about how the special needs students were doing in relation to their strengths and needs. This led to discussions of how teachers could modify instruction to better meet student needs. By the time the interdisciplinary curriculum unit actually began, teachers had developed effective strategies for these students, had carried over these strategies to other students, and had developed a way of documenting student change. Just as they felt more comfortable about including students with disabilities in their classes, they also came to consider the special education teacher to be an important contributing member of the team.

Given that the curriculum design process involves risk and is demanding, do teachers feel that it is worth it? Do they feel that such an endeavor contributes to their professional development? The materials in Make It Happen! guide teachers to evaluate professional development in the context of team collaboration and communication. At retreats, as teachers talk about their responses to the checklist and use this as a catalyst to reflect further on their experiences, they repeatedly mention the esprit de corps they feel. They talk about feeling part of a community or family, feeling less isolated as a professional. The actual curriculum unit, a document that contains their plans, becomes a shared history that reflects their knowledge about students, concepts, learning objectives, and instructional activities.

For example, in one school in South Bend, Indiana, teachers at the retreat recounted how they walked through the school together (almost shoulder to shoulder), smiling. They wanted to convey nonverbally to others that they belonged together, that they were pleased with what they were accomplishing as a team, and that they wanted to serve as models to other teams in the school. A feeling of esprit de corps is important, not just because it feels good but also because it creates the conditions necessary for a real learning community—one in which teachers are willing to take risks and try out new behaviors and roles.

Willingness to Try New Forms of Teaching

Making the shift to inquiry-based learning often means that teachers have to leave behind familiar ways and try new approaches. For example, one teacher, who unhesitatingly called himself a traditionalist (never in the past straying from the textbook), designed an ecology project that took students into the community. His colleagues kept praising his efforts and reacted with enthusiasm to the students' work. This teacher not only felt proud of himself but also knew his teammates were proud of his ability to try something new that reaped positive student outcomes.

Teachers who have traditionally used textbooks exclusively have said they have adopted other instructional materials. Teachers who previously have had students work individually talk about having students working in small groups. Teachers who previously felt they needed to know the answers to everything reported that they have replied to students' queries by saying, "I don't know; let's find out together." Teachers who previously have only evaluated students via tests have assessed performance over time by reviewing work in portfolios.

It is important to stress that teachers' reflections on experimentation with new approaches are not always the glowing testimonials of total converts. It takes courage to try out radically different teaching styles, and teachers frequently speak of their struggles as well as their successes. We encourage this kind of frank assessment by asking teachers to consider what they would do the same or differently the next time they teach an I-Search Unit.

Seeing Students in New Ways

Teachers often talked about being surprised by how well students do in response to inquiry-based teaching. For example, one teacher talked about a student with learning disabilities who went to Town Hall to gather information on the history of the town's first housing development, conducted a survey of the residents while doing his paper route, and made a map of the development. His teachers commented on his persistence: "The more we tell him that he's doing a good job, the more [information] he comes back with!" They nicknamed him "King of the I-Search."

Teachers feel pride in "bringing out the best" in students, helping them achieve and make progress as learners and thinkers. Teachers in Massachusetts had a sense of shared pride when one eighth-grader wrote as part of his I-Search paper:

> Our class acted like a family by coming together in helping each other through the research. The class also acted like a tree, the limbs were the questions we researched, the trunk was our topic, and the soil and the nutrients were the teachers helping us grow in knowledge.

Harriet, the facilitator in the New York school, was particularly pleased when she overheard one of her students discussing which graphs to use to convey information about the number of deaf people in the United States. Todd was using a computer program that easily allowed him to move among bar graphs, line graphs, and pie graphs. Commenting aloud, Todd weighed the advantages and disadvantages of each type of graph in relation to the information he wanted to include in his report. As Todd looked at the line graph, he said:

> The point I want to get across is to show how many deaf people there are in the world, by thousands. The circle graph is not good; it's too crowded and bunched up. The bar graph isn't good either—it's not what I wanted; it's too bland. This is the one I like, the line graph. It helps you see my point and it's easy to read out. It shows the years and

numbers of people, and the increases and decreases of numbers of deaf people over time.

CAVEATS

Not every team grows as professionals by engaging in the interdisciplinary curriculum design process. Through reflection on our work with teams that fall along the successful–unsuccessful continuum, we have identified an emerging set of factors we believe can promote or hinder success.

The first factor is that there needs to be a *shared desire* among team members to engage in the change process, on both an individual and a team basis. We have seen teams headed for a speedy "divorce" when specific individuals on the team, either passively or aggressively, resisted change. When one principal heard two teachers on a team openly complaining in the teachers' room about being forced to participate in interdisciplinary curriculum design, he put up a sign in the main office reading, "Change is inevitable, growth is optional" (Fullan & Miles, 1992), as a way of articulating the school's philosophy.

Second, we have seen how important it is for teachers on the team to respect and *trust each other as professionals.* Some teams enter into the process with this mutual respect; for some, respect grows as individuals come to know one another; and, unfortunately, for others, the respect is not forthcoming. A lack of respect for one professional by another can be subtly transmitted to students. This can have a negative impact on the morale of the whole team, including students and teachers alike.

The third critical factor is the team's *shared view of the teaching/learning process.* When teachers openly disagree about the role of the teacher, what promotes the construction of knowledge, or how to assess student growth, divisiveness is evident. Even when teachers read the same professional articles, attend conferences, and discuss student portfolios, there is no guarantee that they will develop a shared mindset. A major problem that can arise is that each teacher wants to "prove" his or her method is the right one. Students can become pawns, pulled and tugged in different directions. Thus the most basic principle of interdisciplinary work is violated.

Finally, it is critical for a team to recognize that *curriculum design is a recursive process.* The process is not to be carried out once and then forgotten—there's too much energy required and too much at stake. It is the repetition of the process, accompanied by built-in reflection, that can make a difference. Teams that have willingly committed to repeating the process year after year have themselves recognized that they are engaged in an ongoing process, one that provides them with an important opportunity for professional growth.

SUMMARY

In this chapter, we have described a process of interdisciplinary curriculum design that middle schools teachers across many states are currently using. This process asks teachers to work together to construct knowledge, to anchor their work by focusing on how best to meet the needs of developing adolescents, to think repeatedly about complex issues, and to revise their thinking. The process gives them support and encourages reflection so that they can make sense of the teaching/learning experience. Many teachers who engage in this process feel it has helped them change in positive ways—to develop a set of skills and strategies to be used in future curriculum design, to work more effectively with team members, and to see students in new ways. However, what many teachers say they prize most about the process is that they see themselves as learners who have engaged in a meaningful learning experience. With first-hand experience of what it takes to construct knowledge within a social context, they have developed a clearer vision of the kind of learning and teaching they want for their students.

ACKNOWLEDGMENTS

My deepest appreciation goes to Catherine Cobb Morocco, Arlene Remz, and Shira Persky for their help in developing and testing Make It Happen! In addition, they contributed to the production of this chapter. A tremendous thank-you goes to Shelly Clark for her help in preparing this manuscript.

REFERENCES

Alexander, W. M., & George, P. S. (1993). *The exemplary middle school* (2nd ed.). New York: Holt, Rinehart & Winston.

Ames, N., & Miller, E. (1994). *Changing middle schools.* San Francisco: Jossey-Bass.

Beane, J. A. (1990). *A middle school curriculum: From rhetoric to reality.* Columbus, OH: National Middle School Association.

Beane, J. A. (1992). Turning the floor over: Reflections on a middle school curriculum. *Middle School Journal, 23*(3), 34–40.

Blumenfeld, P., Soloway, E., Marx, R., Krajcik, J., Guzdial, M., & Palincsar, A. M. (1991). Motivating project-based learning: Sustaining the doing, supporting the learning. *Educational Psychologist, 26,* 3–4.

Bransford, J. D., Sherwood, R. S., & Hasselbring, T. (1988). The video revolution and its effects on development: Some initial thoughts. In G. Foreman & P. Pufall (Eds.), *Constructivism in the computer age* (pp. 173–201). Hillsdale, NJ: Erlbaum.

Brown, J. S., Collins, A., & Duguid, P. (1989). Situated cognition and the culture of learning. *Educational Researcher, 18*, 32–42.

Bullough, R. (1989). Teacher education and teacher reflectivity. *Journal of Teacher Education, 40*(2), 15–21.

California State Department of Education. (1987). *Caught in the middle: Educational reform for young adolescents in California public schools.* Sacramento: Author.

Carnegie Council on Adolescent Development. (1989). *Turning points: Preparing American youth for the 21st century: The report of the Task Force on Education of Young Adolescents.* Washington, DC: Author.

Clift, R., Houston, W., & Pugach, M. (1990). *Encouraging reflective practice: An examination of issues and exemplars.* New York: Teachers College Press.

Cuban, L. (1992). What happens to reforms that last? The case of the junior high school. *American Educational Research Journal, 29*(2), 227–251.

Dewey, J. (1933). *How we think.* New York: Heath.

Englert, C. S., & Palincsar, A. S. (1991). Reconsidering instructional research in literacy from a sociocultural perspective. *Learning Disabilities Research and Practice, 6*, 225–229.

Eylon, B., & Linn, M. C. (1988). Learning and instruction: An examination of four research perspectives in science education. *Review of Educational Research, 58*(3), 251–301.

Fullan, M. B., & Miles, M. B. (1992). Getting reform right: What works and what doesn't. *Phi Delta Kappan, 73*(10), 745–752.

George, P. S., Stevenson, C., Thomason, J. K., & Beane, J. (1992). *The middle school and beyond.* Alexandria, VA: Association for Supervision and Curriculum Development.

Hill, J. P. (1980). *Understanding early adolescence: A framework.* Carrboro: University of North Carolina at Chapel Hill, Center for Early Adolescence.

Jacobs, H. H. (1989). *Interdisciplinary curriculum: Design and implementation.* Alexandria, VA: Association for Supervision and Curriculum Development.

Johnson, D. W., & Markle, G. C. (1986). Mainstreaming and cooperative learning strategies. *Exceptional Children, 52*, 553–561.

Kinnaman, D. (1990). Staff development: How to build your winning team. *Technology and Learning, 11*(2), 24–30.

Lester, N. B., & Onore, C. S. (1985). Immersion and distancing: The ins and outs of in-service education. *English Education, 17*(1), 7–13.

Linn, M. (1987). Establishing a research base for science education: Challenges, trends, recommendations. *Journal of Research in Science Teachings, 24*(5), 191–216.

Lipsitz, J. S. (1983). *Successful schools for young adolescents.* New Brunswick, NJ: Transaction Books.

Lounsbury, J. H. (1991). *As I see it.* Columbus, OH: National Middle School Association.

Macrorie, K. (1988). *The I-search paper.* Portsmouth, NH: Boynton-Cook.

Merenbloom, E. Y. (1988). *Developing effective middle schools through faculty participation.* Columbus, OH: National Middle School Association.

Morocco, C. C., Dalton, B., Tivnan, T., & Rawson, P. (1992, April). *Supported inquiry science: Teaching for conceptual change in the urban science classroom.* Paper presented at the annual meeting of the American Educational Research Association, San Francisco.

Perkins, D., & Blythe, T. (1994). Putting understanding up front. *Educational Leadership, 51*(5), 4–7.

Poplin, M. S. (1988). Holistic/constructivist principles: Implications for the field of learning disabilities. *Journal of Learning Disabilities, 21*, 401–416.

Resnick, L. B. (1983). Mathematics and science learning: A new conception. *Science, 220*(4), 447–478.

Schön, D. (1983). *The reflective practitioner.* New York: Basic Books.

Sizer, T. (1992). *Horace's school.* Boston: Houghton Mifflin.

Slavin, R. E. (1983). Where does cooperative learning increase student achievement? *Psychological Bulletin, 94*, 429–445.

Slavin, R. E. (1990). *Cooperative learning: Theory, research, and practice.* Englewood Cliffs, NJ: Prentice-Hall.

Smith, F. (1989). Overselling literacy. *Phi Delta Kappan, 70*(5), 360–364.

Tateyama-Sciezek, K. M. (1990). Cooperative learning: Does it improve the academic achievements of students with handicaps? *Exceptional Children, 56*(5), 426–437.

Vygotsky, L. S. (1978). *Mind in society: The development of higher psychological processes.* In M. Cole, J. V. Steiner, S. Schribner, & E. Souberman (Eds. & Trans.). Cambridge, MA: Harvard University Press.

Wiles, J., & Bondi, J. (1986). *Making middle schools work.* Alexandria, VA: Association for Supervision and Curriculum Development.

Zorfass, J., Morocco, C. C., Tivnan, T., Persky, S., & Remz, A. (1991). *Evaluation of the integration of technology for instructing handicapped children (middle school level).* Newton, MA: Education Development Center.

Zorfass, J., Morocco, C. C., Tivnan, T., Russell, S. J., & Zuman, J. (1989). *Evaluation of the integration of technology for instructing handicapped children (middle-school level).* Newton, MA: Education Development Center.

CHAPTER 10

The Diagnostic Teacher

MILDRED Z. SOLOMON AND CATHERINE COBB MOROCCO

This volume began as self-exploration, an effort by a group of colleagues from within the same organization who had worked for many years on separate, quite independent projects. We set out to write about our experiences working with teachers, principals, curriculum coordinators, and professional development staff with the expectation that through our own in-depth accounts we would gain further insight into the nature of our work.

We conceived of each chapter as a portrait of a particular staff development effort-in-process, with a particular emphasis on narrative descriptions of classroom activities. Through in-depth storytelling, story sharing, and reflection, we hoped to uncover common themes that would be useful to others who share our commitment to developing the very strongest kind of teaching and learning possible for our schools.

The most important and, in our view, helpful finding from this process of self-inquiry was that all of us, no matter the subject area or grade level within which we worked, seemed to be striving to cultivate a particular kind of stance in the teachers with whom we worked. This stance, which we have termed "diagnostic," became clear to us only at the end, after all the chapters were arrayed.

Webster's dictionary states that the word "diagnostic" comes from the Greek *diagnostikos*, meaning "being able to distinguish." After defining its more prominent medical usage, the dictionary then offers a second meaning that wonderfully captures the sense of the word as we are using it. In this second kind of usage, diagnosis means "critical scrutiny or its resulting judgment."

It is exactly a stance of critical scrutiny that we aim to promote through our use of the term "diagnostic teacher." It seems to us that the most powerful theme running throughout the chapters of this volume is that, in each case, the authors were attempting to create strategies and structures that would encourage teachers to look closely, to discern and distinguish through close attention to detail, and then to draw inferences and make judgments on the basis of those observations. Thus we use the term not just as a literary trope but to capture a specific vision of teaching. Moreover, in the course of reviewing the chapters in this volume, we discovered that the authors and their professional development colleagues had a vision of diagnostic teaching—though they did not call it that—which impelled, shaped, and motivated the staff development approach.

Detailed observation, analysis, judgment, experimentation on the basis of that judgment, renewed observation, and further reflection—this recursive process of detailed observation, action, and reflection seems to us central to and characteristic of each of the otherwise very diverse professional development projects described in this volume. Certainly, a critical stance is what Mark Driscoll (Chapter 4) was hoping teachers would develop through their creation of "authentic assessment tasks." Molly and Daniel Lynn Watt (Chapter 3) set forth a series of very specific questions and procedures for looking closely at student work. Judith Zorfass (Chapter 9) speaks of the criteria and guidelines teachers can use at each stage of the curriculum design process to scrutinize the clarity and relevance of the concepts they want to teach. Ada Beth Cutler and Faye Nisonoff Ruopp (Chapter 6) describe teachers in a slowed down, detailed engagement with mathematical problems. In James Hammerman's (Chapter 8) inquiry groups, teachers also examine detailed mathematical problems, exposing with frankness and candor their own thinking about those problems and the conceptual stumbling blocks they personally encounter. As a way of focusing on student thinking, Deborah Schifter, Susan Jo Russell, and Virginia Bastable (Chapter 2) ask teachers to write descriptions of classroom episodes, including detailed notes on students' mathematical discussions and samples of their written work. Carolee Matsumoto (Chapter 7) insists on the importance of uniting principals and teachers in close scrutiny of their joint science learning experiences. Maureen Keohane Riley and Catherine Cobb Morocco (Chapter 5) select instances of effective classroom teaching and student learning for in-depth analysis, so that teachers can "unpack" their successes and learn from them.

In all of these projects, teachers were encouraged to begin by looking outward, observing their students' skills, understandings, and misunderstandings. Teachers were asked to make decisions about which teaching practices or strategies to employ only after they had had the chance to assess student needs and subject-matter goals. Although this sequence—beginning first with student needs and teaching goals—seems straightforward, almost simplistic, it is in fact the opposite of what one usually sees in everyday practice.

Typically, staff development and teachers' curriculum planning focus on the *teacher's* behavior, as though it could be determined and evaluated independently of student needs. Too often the focus is on what the teacher will or will not, did or did not, do; rarely are teachers invited to begin by looking closely at what individual students understand or can do, or would find motivating and relevant. Diagnostic teachers, then, are ones whose gaze can focus clearly outside, as well as inside, themselves. Such teachers actively strive to assess students' understandings, misunderstandings, and skills in the light of their teaching goals, realizing that the choice of particular tasks and pedagogical strategies should follow from their goals and observations.

In this chapter, we describe in further detail what we mean by the diagnostic teacher, using examples from the preceding chapters to illustrate the concept. We argue that while some teachers strive for and do achieve critical scrutiny in their work, there is much to be gained by explicitly naming the concept and actively seeking to cultivate it more broadly. Otherwise, a diagnostic orientation to teaching and to teacher development will remain, as it too often is now—nameless, invisible, and, therefore, even where individual teachers do manage to achieve it, highly vulnerable. In Chapter 11, the final chapter of this volume, we go on to describe the roles that people charged with the responsibility for facilitating the professional development of teachers can play to support diagnostic teaching. The chapter includes suggestions for what schools and school systems might do to create a professional community capable of sustaining this kind of teaching and learning.

DIAGNOSIS OF WHAT?

It is one thing to claim that teaching ought to be a diagnostic enterprise, but what is the purpose of that diagnosis? What exactly do we hope that teachers will closely scrutinize? And why should they do so?

We believe that the diagnostic teacher is one who can observe closely and make judgments in three distinct but related domains: students' skills and understandings, subject-matter and disciplinary knowledge, and teaching practices and classroom pedagogy. These three domains are very similar to what the scientist David Hawkins called the triangle of "I, thou, it" by which he meant the essential relationships among teacher, student, and subject matter (Hawkins, 1969).

Although it is the key to achieving educational reform, most calls for reform have stressed the importance of a number of factors far removed from that central triangle, things such as tougher graduation standards, more standardized tests, more homework, and a longer school year. Much less has been written about what should happen within the triangle, and even less about how to influence what goes on within it, so we wholeheartedly agree with the emphasis Lightfoot calls for on these three domains and their interrelationship.

However, in this chapter we wish to emphasize a different order for the three domains and to call attention to their interrelationship. As noted above, we would put concerns about teachers and teaching practices at the end of the list, assuming that these should grow out of an assessment of both student needs and teaching goals, that is, the disciplinary knowledge one is hoping to encourage in students. We turn now to a discussion of the vital role that diagnosis can play in each of these three domains.

Diagnosis Focused on Student Thinking

Diagnosis focused on student thinking attempts to assess what individual students know, understand, and can do. Optimally, it should also seek to determine what individual students find funny, fascinating, surprising, or intriguing. However, recent research has documented how elusive the individual student can be in the teacher planning process. In the field of writing instruction, for example, Morocco, Riley, Gordon, and Howard (1996) found that teachers tended to focus their planning on a vague and general sense of the class as a whole. When teachers did think about individuals, their focus was mainly on students' emotional and social needs, not their conceptual thinking or academic skills. When pushed to articulate what they knew of student's cognitive understandings, the teachers often talked about students' skills and thought patterns as if they were enduring personal traits, beyond the reach of teacher influence.

In other words, students were seen as having this or that special talent or deficit. Very little attention was placed on coming to understand a student's *particular* thinking patterns, current understandings, or misconceptions. By emphasizing social and emotional issues or seemingly characterological descriptions of students, many teachers downplayed their own ability as teachers to influence student outcomes, missed the opportunity to discover more about student learning needs, and were therefore less able to choose appropriate teaching strategies.

Importantly, this emphasis on close analysis of students' academic strengths and needs is true of staff development efforts across the curriculum, not just in the area of writing instruction. As we look across the diverse projects described in this volume, we are struck by the emphasis that all the authors place on assessing the needs of *individual* students. Watt and Watt (Chapter 3) as well as Riley and Morocco (Chapter 5) are explicit about this, offering the wonderful term "focal" students.

Moreover, throughout our work reported here, there is an insistence on *coming to understand* students' understandings, not *judging* them. For a diagnostic teacher, assessment is part of a recursive cycle of observation, selection of teaching strategies, reflection, and readjustment of one's strategies. The focus is on diagnosis in the service of choosing more appropriate teaching strategies, not on testing for the purpose of rank-ordering student achievement.

Moreover, the need to begin with better observation of student thinking is not just a nice add-on to enhance one's teaching or something to do because of a general belief in individualized instruction. Teachers who are committed to diagnosing individual students' skills and understandings and *using* that diagnosis to inform their teaching practice are likely to have a fundamentally different view of teaching and learning. The diagnostic teacher, in the sense that we are advocating, is one who will be more focused on helping students grasp large concepts and construct their own knowledge in ways that are meaningful for them. Such a teacher will be less likely to see education as the transmission of isolated knowledge or discrete, decontextualized skills.

For example, in the writing research by Morocco and colleagues (1996) mentioned above, there were teachers who did think more about individual academic strengths and needs and were, therefore, able to construct learning activities that kept more students engaged and on-task. The researchers point out that a critical distinction between the teachers who focused more on individual students' academic strengths and those who did not was the beliefs or mindset that teachers had about the nature of teaching and learning:

> If teachers view reading and writing as a set of separate skills and assume that their students are equally deficient in those skills, then they will continue to drill on those skills without learning about other areas of their students' learning process. If, on the other hand, teachers view reading and writing as meaning-building processes, then they will need to know their students' individual language, reading, writing, and learning needs in order to gauge how best to scaffold that meaning-making. (Morocco et al., 1996, p. 172)

In other words, diagnosis of an individual student's particular ways of thinking or solving problems is a fundamental *necessity*, not an optional add-on, for teachers committed to a more holistic concept of teaching and learning. Such teachers see close-up analysis of student thinking as essential information if they are going to be able to help students grasp what Schifter, Russell, and Bastable (Chapter 2) have called "the big ideas."

Indeed, we see a compelling *reciprocal* relationship between assessing students' needs and disciplinary knowledge. Teachers whose disciplinary knowledge is limited have a less powerful lens for observing and assessing students' understandings and learning needs. One cannot assess something without having a sense of what one is striving for. Teachers who have a strong fundamental grasp of, say, mitosis, or who are themselves agile writers, or who have insight into how historians ask questions about the world—such teachers will be well equipped to help students understand cell reproduction, develop their own writing skills, or initiate a historical inquiry. When observing student work, teachers without a solid grasp of disciplinary knowledge will simply see less.

Bearing in mind the intertwined and reciprocal relationship between diagnosis of students' needs and disciplinary knowledge, we turn now to a more detailed discussion of the latter, examining how diagnostic teachers make use of disciplinary knowledge to create teaching practices capable of developing students' skills and understandings.

Diagnosis Focused on Disciplinary Knowledge: Assessing What's Worth Teaching

While all too often teaching focuses on transmitting a list of key concepts and principles or developing a set of decontextualized skills, diagnostic teachers are guided by an overarching assessment of what they think is *worth* teaching and why. The *purposes* to which concepts and skills are going to be put remain in sight and help to steer both assessment of students' current learning needs and selection of appropriate pedagogical strategies. Diagnostic teachers ask: What are the important concepts I want my students to grapple with and why do I want them to understand them? What problems do these concepts help people to solve? What are the methods and modes of inquiry in mathematics, science, history, social studies, and literature that I want my students to develop? Why? What sorts of questions will these disciplinary perspectives and methods help to illuminate? Why are they important? What "take-home" message should I encourage students to hold in memory when they conclude their work with me on this topic?

Defined in this way, the concept of the diagnostic teacher is similar to what Donald Schön, whose research focuses on the preparation and socialization of architects, physicians, and other kinds of professionals, has called the "reflective practitioner." According to Schön (1987), rather than simply carrying out algorithms, reflective practitioners apply their special knowledge and expertise flexibly and creatively not just to solve but also to identify new problems and opportunities.

For example, an algorithmic approach to mathematics teaching would simply teach students the procedures for addition and subtraction. As important as it is to enable students to learn their addition and subtraction facts, a skilled diagnostic teacher, a reflective practitioner, will see an opportunity to move beyond the doing of the arithmetic. A teacher who grasps that addition and subtraction are inverse mathematical operations will see that simply knowing one's number facts is not all that matters. In addition, such a teacher will want to help students develop meta-knowledge about mathematics as a system for describing the world. Such teachers will strive to demonstrate that mathematics is a system of symbols, operations, concepts, and conventions that is powerful because it enables us to model observed relationships between phenomena and to discover new relationships that we would not have been able to see without the help of that system.

Jill Lester, the teacher described in Chapter 2, has this orientation—a commitment to helping students grow not only in their capacity to perform arithmetic procedures but in their deep, and therefore more flexible, grasp of mathematical concepts and operations. Focused as she is on cultivating disciplinary knowledge and mathematical insight, Lester listens carefully, diagnostically, for what puzzles and intrigues her students about how mathematics works—finding opportunities for growth even, perhaps most especially, in their misunderstandings or bewilderment.

For example, as Schifter, Russell, and Bastable report in Chapter 2, Lester discovered a certain theme emerging year after year among her second-graders:

> The issue first arose the year she gave her class the following problem: *I have 24 pencils. I give 1 to each of 18 children in the class. How many am I left with?* Although all of her students came up with the answer, half arrived at it by taking away 18 from 4, while the other half added 6 onto 18 to get 24. But what struck Lester was the children's conviction that those who had "done it the other way" had solved the problem incorrectly. It seemed that because they understood the two operations as distinct and contrary actions, they were unable to concede that this problem could be solved using either one.
>
> When the issue again arose the following year, her new crop of second-graders had already had experience with problems that could be solved in different ways. Still, they were intrigued that the same problem might be solved by either adding or subtracting. (Chapter 3)

Wonderfully, it is the kids themselves who want to know why they could arrive at the same answer via different routes. Instead of providing an answer that would likely only short-circuit the children's own thinking, Lester offers a strategy for helping them grapple with their own question. As Schifter, and colleagues, report:

> Taking advantage of their curiosity, Lester assigned the children to work in pairs—one partner having solved the problem by addition, the other by subtraction—making up and then testing similar problems with missing addends. After 1 week most children were satisfied that if adding on worked, so would taking away, and vice versa. (Chapter 3)

Lester chooses instructional strategies that allow her students to confront addition and subtraction as the inverse operations they are. Moreover, she doesn't tell or describe. Instead, she listens. Then, having discovered her students' curiosity about an important mathematical concept, she orchestrates an activity that will speak for itself.

In *Rethinking Knowledge in School: The Recovery of Meaning in Disciplinary Understanding* (1995), Boix-Mansilla asserts that "knowledge in schools needs to be reconceptualized within a framework encompassing three interrelated aspects of knowledge," (p. 7) and she goes on to describe those three domains, as follows:

(1) *The substance of knowledge*: The powerful frameworks, systems of ideas or narratives in a domain or discipline that are most likely to illuminate a specific problem we would like to understand (e.g., the theory of evolution in biology, the ideological origins of the American Revolution) (Schwab, 1987);
(2) *The nature of knowledge*: The methods and procedures by which this knowledge is built and validated as reliable or warranted (e.g., systematic naturalistic observation, interpretation of written sources);
(3) *The purposes of knowledge*: The interests that motivate the construction of these bodies of knowledge and their uses to reinterpret and transform the world we live in (e.g., explaining, predicting, and controlling nature; developing national identity). (Boix-Mansilla, 1995, p. 7)

"Knowledge in history, science, carpentry, film-making, or architecture emerges," writes Boix-Mansilla, "from a dialectical relationship between the human concerns and needs in everyday life (purposes and interests) and the bodies of knowledge that are available to a society at a given moment in time (powerful narratives, frameworks, etc.)" [pp. 7–8]. She goes on to assert that schools can develop educational experiences for students that are both more rigorous in terms of disciplinary and subject-matter standards and more relevant to students' lives and interests if teachers focus on developing appreciation in their students and in themselves for all three kinds of disciplinary knowledge.

The Jill Lester example on inverse mathematical operations seems to us to meet Boix-Mansilla's definition of these kinds of disciplinary knowledge. Through the task that Lester invented, she engaged her students in the big idea that addition and subtraction are inverse operations; she placed the students in the role of mathematicians using mathematical tools to solve a given problem; and if she had chosen to, she could have gone on to help students see that addition and subtraction, in addition to being intriguing processes to study and understand, can help people solve everyday problems. In this one, simple example, we see the dynamic relationship among Boix-Mansilla's three types of disciplinary knowledge: a big substantive idea worthy of teaching, immersion in mathematical ways of thinking, and recognition of the intellectual and social purposes that impel the need for and invention of mathematics as a system of thought.

It is inconceivable that Jill Lester could have responded so flexibly and appropriately to her students' curiosity and confusion without her own in-depth disciplinary knowledge. Only teachers who have deep and flexible understanding of their disciplines can create instructional strategies capable of helping students make these kinds of connections. Disciplinary knowledge, in all three of the ways Boix-Mansilla describes, provides a lens for viewing student work—a template against which to evaluate student understanding. The sorts of questions teachers will ask, and their perceptions and discoveries about student understanding, are diminished if their own disciplinary knowledge is limited.

Certainly, many of the authors in this volume seem to be calling attention to the importance of teachers' disciplinary knowledge. Across the diversity of these projects, we see Education Development Center (EDC) staff creating opportunities for teachers to deepen their own subject-matter expertise and their mastery of discipline-specific skills and procedures. Riley and Morocco (Chapter 5) developed analogue writing tasks not only so that teachers could see how conversation can be used to prepare students for writing, that is, not only as a model of a pedagogical technique. They also developed analogue experiences so that they could engage teachers *as* writers. Cutler and Ruopp (Chapter 6), Schifter, Russell, and Bastable (Chapter 2), Driscoll (Chapter 4), Hammerman (Chapter 8), and the Watts (Chapter 3) all carefully chose mathematical problems that would stretch teachers' own mathematical understanding.

This was equally true in other disciplines as well. Matsumoto (Chapter 7) selected science problems that would engage teachers and principals in their own scientific thinking. And Zorfass (Chapter 9) pointed out a problem that can occur when teachers are unclear about the disciplinary knowledge they wish to impart, characterizing a lack of sufficient clarity as a problem of "fuzzy" concepts.

Furthermore, these authors all felt that their approaches to professional development were succeeding when there was evidence of changes not only in teacher's classroom behavior but also in their subject matter or disciplinary expertise. As Schifter, Russell, and Bastable put it:

> When challenged at their own levels of mathematics competence and confronted with mathematical concepts and problems they have not encountered before, they [teachers] both increase their mathematical knowledge and experience a depth of learning that for them is unprecedented. Such activities allow teachers, often for the first time, to encounter mathematics as an activity of construction rather than as a finished body of results to be accepted, accumulated, and reproduced. (Chapter 3)

Only teachers with a solid grounding in the large, generative concepts of a field of study and in the established methods of inquiry of an academic discipline can create instructional strategies capable of helping students make connections like the ones that Jill Lester was aiming for. There seems to be no shortcut, no substitute for disciplinary knowledge in all three of its aspects.

Diagnosis Focused on Pedagogy: Selecting Appropriate Curriculum Activities and Teaching Strategies

Although diverse in the specifics of its approach, each chapter in this volume describes how professional development staff and teachers worked together to select appropriate curriculum activities and teaching strategies. All the authors helped teachers select strategies and curriculum tasks that would help them assess students' understandings and skills, extend student thinking, and/or provide good points of entry for exploring the teaching goals they had in mind.

While selecting curriculum activities and teaching strategies was a component of every professional development approach described in this volume, Chapters 5 and 9 explicitly focus on the role that curriculum design and planning can play not only in selecting appropriate pedagogy but also in shifting teachers' mindsets about what teaching and learning can be.

In Chapter 9 Zorfass describes a professional development project, the I-Search Process, in which facilitators help interdisciplinary middle school teams develop a long-term investigation (approximately 6 to 8 weeks) on a socially relevant theme (such as ecology or justice) that intrigues early adolescents. Each student chooses a personally meaningful question to investigate, then gathers data individually and in small groups from a variety of sources, and finally develops a presentation or report that synthesizes what has been learned.

Zorfass and her colleagues developed a model of professional development to help teachers mount these I-Search Units. One of the important steps in the process is to encourage teachers to "test" the validity of the curriculum plan all along the way. For example, the staff developers encouraged the teachers to ask critical questions of the curriculum activities they were planning, such as: Will the activity introduce, define, or elaborate one or more of the overarching concepts we wish students to grasp? Does the activity elicit prior knowledge and invite students to build new knowledge? Is the activity linked closely enough to one or more desired student outcomes? How long will this activity take? What are costs and benefits of spending that amount of time on this activity?

In Chapter 5 Riley and Morocco describe "scaffolding" teachers' development toward a more holistic approach to writing instruction by engaging teachers in a curriculum planning process aimed at generating the production of personally relevant, meaningful writing in a variety of genres. Like Zorfass, Riley and Morocco encouraged their teachers to take a diagnostic stance toward the tasks they were setting for students. In particular, they encouraged teachers to build "thinking frameworks," lists of the kind of thinking and writing that different tasks would require of students. As architects and builders must do, these teachers were being asked to become conscious of the sorts of demands and choices different task constructions and different writing genres would allow.

Although Chapters 5 and 9 describe long-term curriculum development and planning processes, a desire to cultivate a diagnostic stance toward one's choice of teaching strategies runs throughout the chapters, regardless of how large scale the curriculum development effort is. Although the teachers in

Driscoll's CAM project were purposefully inventing far more self-contained, briefer tasks than were the teachers in the Zorfass or Riley and Morocco programs, it was equally essential for the CAM teachers to be able to describe what demands and choices their tasks would allow and to develop criteria for sorting more useful tasks from less useful ones. Thus, Mark Driscoll (Chapter 4) writes about "developing good taste," by which he means cultivating an explicit set of criteria to help recognize "worthwhile tasks" and refining tasks when it is discovered that they do not move students in the intended direction.

Finally, it is important to note that a diagnostic view of pedagogy involves scrutiny not only of the *tasks* or curriculum *problems* that teachers set for students but also of the instructional and classroom management *methods* that teachers decide to rely upon. For example, Riley and Morocco (Chapter 5) point out that in addition to helping teachers develop thinking frames to better name the kinds of thinking that a particular writing assignment will provoke, they also concerned themselves with helping teachers to think more reflectively and analytically about the virtues and limitations of one-on-one writing conferences in which a teacher talks individually with a student about his or her particular piece of writing.

In this case, the professional development strategy for developing critical awareness was to role-play writing conferences. Working in pairs, some teachers played the role of student and some, the role of teacher. Yet the "students" were unaware of the fact that those playing the teacher role were being asked to adopt one of two very different conference styles. While both sets of teachers were asked to be pleasant and friendly, one set was told to be directive, corrective, and full of recommendations for change. The other set was asked simply to show appreciation for the student's ideas and to ask open-ended questions that followed the student writer's lead, building more details into the story through conversational rapport between teacher and student. By interacting with the more authoritarian, less conversational "teacher," "students" developed first-hand experience of the limitations of that approach to conferencing, while interaction with the more conversational partner modeled the ways that teachers might cultivate that style of conferencing in their own practice.

Moving Flexibly Through the Three Diagnostic Domains

In our view, the diagnostic teacher is one who moves flexibly through the three diagnostic domains, constantly assessing students' needs, teaching goals, and pedagogy, reassessing each domain in light of what is learned in the other two. To switch the metaphor, the diagnostic teacher is one who knows how to use three different sets of lenses. At any given moment, one pair of lenses provides just the information that is needed, so that is the pair the teacher wears for that moment. Yet, the teacher knows that it will be important to see the world through the other two pairs of lenses as well, because they will illuminate different facets of reality. When the second and third pair are worn, what was in the background comes to the fore. Without the help of all three lenses, the full teaching landscape cannot come into view, and the complete array of information we need for powerful teaching will remain inaccessible.

In the activity we described above, Jill Lester, the teacher in Chapter 2, orchestrated an intellectual and emotional experience for her students, an "ah-ha" experience that tapped their curiosity and heightened their insight into mathematics as a system of thought. In doing so, she was operating as a diagnostician simultaneously across all three diagnostic domains.

From within the diagnostic domain of "disciplinary knowledge," she had to make an assessment about what mathematics was worth pursuing. From one year to the next, she had observed that her second-graders were having similar questions and uncertainties about the relationship between addition and subtraction. In observing their confusion and the fact that it was likely to recur from one group of second-graders to the next, this teacher recognized what Schifter and colleagues have called a "big idea." Jill Lester valued this major concept, seeing it as having greater importance than simply encouraging children to memorize addition and subtraction facts. She saw their interest and curiosity as an opportunity to help them develop insight about addition and subtraction being inverse operations. Importantly, her assessment of what to emphasize in her teaching grew out of careful, diagnostic listening and close-up engagement with the students' thinking, conjectures, confusion, and fascination.

Lester's diagnostic skills were also called into play when she had to choose problems to pose that would engage her students and lead them to the "ah-ha" experience she wanted them to have. According to Schifter, who worked closely with Lester, some addition/subtraction problems are more likely to invite an inverse operations discussion than are others. Wording can be critically important. Consider, for example, the following two problems:

(A) Miranda admires the Teddy Bear in the window on sale for $25. She has saved $13. How much more will she need if she wants to buy Teddy?

(B) Jason had 52 pieces of candy. At supper he ate 16 pieces. How many are left?

Problems with type A structure and wording are more likely to lead students to discussion of inverse operations than problems of the type B sort—a discovery that Lester and other teachers working with Schifter made as they sought to craft good problems for their students.

In addition to selecting appropriate problems, diagnostic teachers also have to consider the pedagogical techniques they will use to pose those problems. Jill Lester's selection—having pairs of students working simultaneously on the same problem, but solving the problem via alternative routes—was an inventive solution to what must have been yet another distinctive set of questions she was asking herself. This time, the questions focused not so much on students' thinking or on the particular problem to present to students, but on which strategy in particular would lead to the teaching goals she wanted to promote. In fact, question-asking, whether conscious and explicit or conducted as a nearly unconscious interior dialogue, seems to be a key feature of diagnostic teaching.

The Importance of Question-Asking and the Centrality of Community

The importance of questions in diagnostic teaching reverberates throughout this volume: Nearly all the EDC projects vigorously encouraged teachers to ask questions. Moreover, a detailed analysis of the professional development activities described in this book shows, in our view not accidentally, that the questions staff developers encouraged teachers to ask are questions that could help teachers operate within each of the three diagnostic domains. Such questions help teachers make judgments about what is worth teaching; assess students' understandings, misconceptions, and interests; and select appropriate problems and pedagogical techniques in the light of both students' interests, knowledge, and skills and one's own teaching goals. Figure 10.1 presents a sample of the sorts of questions EDC staff encouraged teachers to ask, organized by diagnostic domain.

If we could follow the thinking process of any one teacher, we would see it making shifts from what is important to teach, to what approach is going to work for most of my students, to what do I know about individual students that requires that I adapt my approach. The "executive" in each teacher is always asking, "What question is important now? Where do I need to focus?" In planning any specific lesson, the three domains of question and asking come together.

Moreover, throughout the projects described in this book, teachers were not only encouraged to ask these kinds of questions of themselves, but to do so openly and collectively. Question-asking was not a silent, private conversation with oneself, but an active and public dialogue with one's colleagues. The cultivation of a professional community within which people felt safe to openly and honestly ask questions, expose failures, and take risks appears to have been a common, indeed crucial, characteristic of the approaches described in this volume.

Figure 10.1. Important Questions

Assessing What's Worth Teaching and Why

- What issues, problems, concepts will grab my students' curiosity?
- What developmental issues are they dealing with that suggest topics that would be of interest to them?
- What are the important concepts in each disciplinary domain that I think my students should grapple with?
- Why are these concepts important?
- What problems do these concepts help people to solve or to investigate?
- Which disciplinary skills (i.e., what modes of inquiry in mathematics, science, history, social studies, or literature) do I want my students to develop? Why?
- What sorts of questions or problems will these disciplinary modes of inquiry illuminate?
- What "take-home" message should I encourage students to hold in memory when they conclude their work with me on this topic?

Assessing Students' Thinking and Skills

- Are there recurrent beliefs, conceptions, or misconceptions that my students hold about this subject?
- What is the meaning my students seem to be making of this subject? What do they see as its relevance or import?
- What specifically do individual students understand of this problem? How have the "focal" students I've followed approached the problem? What does each child's method of approach reveal about his or her understanding?
- What skills does each child bring to bear in solving the problems I pose? What additional skills would I like him or her to develop?
- Have the children I have observed approached the problems in new ways I might not have considered? How can I build on their approaches?

Assessing Appropriate Problems and Effective Pedagogy

- What problems should I pose to the students that will build on their curiosity and invite their entry into the conceptual domains I want to open for them?
- Did this particular problem do what I wanted it to do? If not, why not? What is it about its structure (or wording) that worked or didn't work?
- What would be the best way to pose this problem? How should I "engineer" the way in which they are going to encounter it? Should students work privately first and then compare answers? Should we begin with group brainstorm and then move to individual work? Are there any game-like strategies, rules, or special roles that would be helpful?

Teachers developed their knowledge about what students know, understand, and can do as they talked together about specific classroom lessons and the work of specific students. In that process, colleagues often helped one another to see beyond their initial, often limited, expectations for their own students.

Collegiality and the cultivation of professional communities were evident throughout these projects in many other ways as well. Teachers needed one another in order to build consensus about what constituted important subject-matter knowledge and to deepen their own understanding of the big ideas they were currently exploring or planning to explore with their students. Collegiality and professional exchange were also essential for building a richer and more relevant repertoire of classroom teaching practices. Throughout these projects, we see teachers observing in each others' classrooms, analyzing one another's classroom videotapes, and discussing multiple examples of how new ways of thinking about teaching and learning might be played out with students. In other words, professional communities become the means for continually linking new knowledge with daily practice.

For all these reasons, we believe that the cultivation of a professional community is essential to the very notion of teaching and learning we have been advocating—a claim that should come as no surprise. If one believes that knowledge is socially constructed, then it follows that active interaction with colleagues is as essential to adult learners' professional growth as collaborative enterprises are for students. If we are serious about teachers developing greater subject-matter expertise and deeper knowledge of their craft, then we have to create the social conditions that would make that learning possible. Diagnostic teaching requires that practitioners actively connect themselves both to a prior body of disciplinary knowledge and to one another as they share and construct new knowledge in their field.

In our view, the approaches described in this collection argue for a radical reconceptualization—both of teaching and of teacher development. Rather than seeing professional development as the transmission of knowledge and practices *from* staff developer *to* teacher, we need to invent a new model. Such a model ought to strive to articulate ways in which staff developers and teachers can join *with one another* to build a common professional community. In the next and final chapter of this volume, we describe some of the ways that staff committed to the professional development of teachers and teachers themselves could co-construct this kind of professional community. We recommend five action steps that would lead to a new model of staff development—one that would be more diagnostically oriented and more fully professional.

REFERENCES

Boix-Mansilla, V. (1995). *Rethinking Knowledge in school: The recovery of meaning in disciplinary understanding* [unpublished paper]. ATLAS Seminar, Harvard Project Zero, Cambridge, MA.

Hawkins, D. (1969, Spring) I, thou, it. *Mathematics Teaching*.
Morocco, C. C., Riley, M. K., Gordon, S. M., & Howard, C. L. (1996). The elusive individual in teachers' planning. In G. G. Brannigan (Ed.), *The enlightened educator: Research adventures in the school* (pp. 155–178). New York: McGraw-Hill.
Schön, D. (1987). *Educating the reflective practitioner.* San Francisco: Jossey-Bass.

CHAPTER 11

Revitalizing Professional Development

CATHERINE COBB MOROCCO AND MILDRED Z. SOLOMON

The assumption in these Education Development Center (EDC) projects, that professional development takes place within *communities* of practitioners, runs deep in many professions. Whether in law, medicine, architecture, or physics, a sense of connection to other contributing members is at the very core of what it means to be a professional. By definition, a profession is a group of individuals who have pursued specialized knowledge, defined by the group itself as important. Professionals are identified not only by their specialized learning but also by their socialization into membership organizations and their affiliation with colleagues who are the source of new knowledge and lifelong learning. Professionals usually define their own standards of excellence, mentor and monitor their peers to ensure high-level skills, establish licensing and credentialing procedures, and provide career ladders so that practitioners can be rewarded for progress in attaining ever higher levels of skill. Historically, professionalism has also implied a sense of mission and meaning in one's work that goes beyond the doing of mere tasks and sometimes, as in the case of law and medicine, a fiduciary relationship with a client or patient built on mutual trust and the personal virtue of the professional.

In the field of education, the concept of communities of competent professionals actively and interactively building on one another's knowledge of students, their disciplines, and pedagogy is a radical departure from most current conceptions of teaching and, consequently, of professional development. In the majority of schools today, "staff developers," often with minimal classroom teacher participation, plan and provide in-service "training." Most often, these trainings take the form of single workshops, or sometimes a course involving several sessions. The emphasis is on the staff developer presenting or transmitting pedagogical strategies that teachers will apply to their own particular students and classrooms. A "deficit" model frequently underlies this conception, with the assumption that teachers' missing skills have been identified.

In addition to arranging for workshops or courses, staff developers may move from classroom to classroom "ministering" to individual teachers by providing literature selections, identifying supplementary materials, or demonstrating strategies. While this role of individual coach or resource may be helpful to individual teachers, it does not connect teachers to one another in a common culture of inquiry. It therefore misses and, in our view, actually undermines the opportunity for teachers *themselves* to build and participate in a shared professional culture.

A number of studies and reports in addition to EDC's projects find that teachers are receptive to more collegial approaches (e.g., Corcoran, Walker, & White, 1988; Johnson, 1990; Little, 1990; McLaughlin & Talbot, 1993). Moreover, teacher collegiality appears to benefit student learning. Recent findings of major school-restructuring studies by the Center for the Organization of Schools support collegial professional development models by documenting the link between "teacher professional community" and student achievement. Louis, Marks, and Kruse (1996) find that when teachers work together, engage in professional conversation, and focus on student work, they develop a shared sense of responsibility for student learning. It is this variable, shared responsibility for student learning, that correlates with higher overall student achievement in the schools studied.

Moving teaching from solo practice to active membership in a professional community capable of reflection and active construction of its own knowledge and skills is essential if we are to prepare teachers and students adequately for the challenges of the next century. In this final chapter, we offer an alternative view of the role of "staff developer" as a collective role with broad and permeable participation. We recommend five actions that professionals in education can take in order to create a diagnostically oriented and more fully professional model of staff development.

RECONCEPTUALIZING THE ROLE OF STAFF DEVELOPER

Rather than seeing professional development as the transmission of knowledge and practices *from* staff developer *to* teacher, we need to invent a new model in which staff developers and teachers join *with one another* to build a common professional community. In fact, the projects described in these chapters imply a productive blurring of boundaries between teachers and those responsible for facilitating teachers' professional growth. Several of the programs were explicitly designed with the goal of bringing teachers over time into the staff development body. Zorfass describes "trainer of trainer" institutes that build a body of colleagues who can provide ongoing support to one another and ongoing connection to mentors—in this case, EDC staff—as they learn to facilitate a curriculum design process. This structure was designed, Zorfass tells us, to enable new facilitators to have time and role models for experimenting with, and ultimately internalizing, the many new roles they will need to play over the cycle of design, implementation, and evaluation that constitutes an I-Search Unit. In most cases, these trainers were originally participants in the program, demonstrating that professional development is a spiraling process of ongoing growth over time.

Similarly, the design of "Teaching to the Big Ideas," in Chapter 2, calls for teachers in year 4 to begin to "take on leadership roles to introduce these notions to colleagues in their own school systems" The Watts build a "co-learner" notion into their model, which requires that no one be exempted from a research role by virtue of being the group leader or facilitator. Rather than reflecting an expert–novice relationship, experienced teachers and staff developers (many of whom will be or will have been teachers) in a truly professional learning community should be seen as co-equals who bring varied kinds of expertise to a collaborative learning process.

The boundary between staff developers and teaching practitioners should be intentionally permeable; the idea is to distribute expertise over time, among all the professionals in the community. Chapter 7 is a special reminder that principals are critical practitioner in this model, that the boundaries between designated school leadership roles and the leadership roles that teachers acquire over time are also flexible.

Further, teachers' own growth from novice to experienced teacher should be a natural evolution with clearly marked steps. The movement to enable experienced teachers across all grade levels and major subject areas to receive certification as accomplished professionals by the National Board for Professional Teaching Standards (NBPTS). In most other professions, there are clear career ladders with steps that signal varying degrees of expertise. Physicians in training move from medical student, to intern, to junior and then senior residents before they become staff or private practice physicians. After their formal training is complete, accomplished physicians play multiple, and often simultaneous, roles as clinicians, academic mentors, and researchers.

Hammerman noted in his review of an earlier version of this chapter how much the common dichotomy of teacher and staff developer permeates our language, and documents his own difficulties in coming up with appropriate terms:

> I'm a little uncomfortable with the use of the term "staff developer" to describe my work. Somehow this feels like an agent—the "developer" acting on an object, the "staff," in a way that undermines my sense of the essentially collaborative nature of the activity. I tend to call myself a "teacher educator," but I know not everyone does. Sometimes I

> describe my work as "professional development" because then the adjective "professional" modifies the kind of "development" that's being done but doesn't set up a hierarchical relationship. Names are always tricky, and trying to get them right is difficult but important.

As the observant reader will note, throughout the rest of this chapter, we either place quotation marks around the term "staff developer" or replace it with a variety of terms, including "professional coach," "facilitator," and "professional development leaders." None of these phrases strike us as perfect, but, like Hammerman, we wish to strive for a way to talk about what ought to be a fluid and collaborative relationship among colleagues as they play mutually supportive roles.

The teachers involved in the projects described in this volume were active partners with the school system's professional development leaders and the EDC staff who worked with them. Indeed, the actions we recommend for building professional learning communities that cultivate diagnostic teaching do engage professionals in working together in a variety of ways. And although formally designated "staff developers" may introduce and facilitate these activities, the goal is to embed the capacity for structuring and guiding such activities into the professional school community as a whole.

CULTIVATING PROFESSIONAL LEARNING COMMUNITIES: FIVE RECOMMENDATIONS

We recommend five substantive actions that professional development leaders can take to construct models of workplace-based, lifelong learning, capable of promoting and sustaining the professional growth of teachers. We urge professional development staff in U.S. schools to:

1. Craft analogue experiences to engage teachers as learners in their own right.
2. Use assessment tools that reveal students' understanding and thinking.
3. Facilitate intimate professional conversations about teachers' beliefs and practices.
4. Use documentation strategies that encourage reflection-in-action and connect teachers with a wider professional community.
5. Advocate for a "blanket of support" from the school and district organization to enable teachers to learn together.

All the projects described in this volume undertook these actions in some form or another. Each action seems essential to the building of a professional community engaged in, or developing the capacity to engage in, diagnostic teaching. These actions were not seen as something to be done *to* teachers. Rather, each was a critical feature of how teachers, in their roles as classroom practitioners, and professional development staff, in their roles as facilitators, were interacting to co-construct a community of professional inquiry and mutual support.

Craft Analogue Experiences

Teachers cannot work with their students in more active, inquiry-based ways unless they themselves have experienced this kind of learning first-hand. Knowing this, most of the authors developed what Riley and Morocco (Chapter 5) specifically term "analogue experiences," tasks in which teachers do science or mathematics, conduct historical inquiries, or undertake writing assignments similar in purpose to those that they will ultimately be asking their students to do. These must be truly intellectually challenging experiences for teachers; in some cases, the stimulus material they use may be different from what they will give students, so that they will be fully challenged as adults. The purpose of these analogue experiences is twofold. First, analogue experiences help teachers understand what it feels like to be given an open-ended, exploratory assignment, how different from more didactic teaching such learning activities are, and how energizing they can be. Analogue experiences are important for helping teachers to understand a more active, inquiry-based approach and to come to know what it's like to engage in that sort of work from the learner's perspective.

Second, analogue experiences are essential for helping teachers build their own understanding of their discipline. As we looked closely at the kinds of experiences EDC staff and their school-based colleagues designed for teachers in these projects, it became apparent that they engaged teachers in building the three kinds of disciplinary knowledge discussed in the previous chapter: deeper personal understanding of the big ideas in a given subject area; a more profound understanding of the ways of observing, knowing, or validating truth that have developed, and are relied upon, in any given intellectual discipline; and more self-conscious reflection about the kinds of questions, needs, and societal problems that different disciplines are best equipped to address.

Professional development staff have a critical role to play in forming and supporting professional communities where teachers jointly construct these three levels of disciplinary knowledge. While few of the authors explicitly discuss what it takes to design such important adult learning tasks, we are aware of the many hours required to invent an analogue task such as the ones Driscoll and his colleagues did in mathematics (Chapter 4); to craft writing assignments that would help teachers discuss and internalize the different sorts of demands and opportunities posed by different literary genres, as Riley and Morocco did (Chapter 5); or to design the component of an I-Search Unit in Zorfass's program that would engage teachers themselves in joint inquiries that prepare them to design similar sorts of units for their students (Chapter 9). Such experiences must be fashioned out of an understanding of the teachers one is working with, the kinds of disciplinary knowledge to be highlighted, and a sense of what would be a fresh and compelling collaborative learning experience for the teachers. Generative, yet highly targeted, adult learning experiences don't just happen!

In Chapter 8, Hammerman gives us a glimpse of a professional coach thinking out loud about how to structure teacher inquiries that will move teachers themselves into deeper disciplinary knowledge. Hammerman's words make clear that he was intending to engage teachers in Boix-Mansilla's first two types of disciplinary knowledge (discussed in Chapter 10) and that he is thinking about how to promote this knowledge development within the teacher group:

> I brought to the group knowledge about both mathematics content—which mathematical ideas are important and potentially generative—and mathematics as a discipline—what it means to work "mathematically," to look for patterns, make conjectures, and try to find reasoned arguments that will prove or disprove these conjectures. I used this knowledge to make more or less subtle judgments in selecting the materials and problems I brought to the group. (Chapter 8)

Hammerman describes an activity he designed for teachers that moved them not only into deeper understanding of multiplication and mathematical ways of working but also into Boix-Mansilla's third type of disciplinary knowledge—recognition of the purposes to which disciplinary knowledge is put and metacognitive awareness that disciplines are emerging bodies of knowledge and methods of exploration that change over time. As part of an exploration of multiplication, he asked the group to examine a number of algorithms from different cultures throughout history, including Egyptian and "Russian peasant" multiplication, which both involved keeping track of successive doubling and halving and Lattice/Gelosia multiplication. Hammerman's report and the teachers' diaries offer evidence that this experience helped participants develop a deeper sense that mathematics is something that has been and can continually be invented to help solve everyday needs.

Use Assessment Tools That Reveal Students' Understanding and Thinking

As we noted in the previous chapter, the richest part of a teacher's repertoire usually is his or her instructional strategies, and teachers tend to lead with these strategies rather than with an appraisal of student understandings. Assessment tools can play a critical role—by redirecting teachers' focus away from a predetermined pedagogical strategy to an appreciation for what students understand, believe, can and cannot do or for what students may find confusing, interesting, or productively puzzling.

The chapters suggest that there is no reason to rely on a single way to reveal students' knowledge, skills, or interests. Depending on the content and purpose, a variety of tools, sometimes in combination, may be helpful. Driscoll (Chapter 4) suggests three broad categories of assessment and, indeed, they include most of the varied approaches we see across the chapters: ***asking questions of students*** (including talking with students about their work); ***observing students at work*** (observing videotapes of students working on problems or conversing about content; serving as observers in one another's classroom; transcribing conversations from their own classrooms); ***examining student products*** (students' journals, homework, problem notes, drafts, portfolios; classroom test results).

Because traditionally classroom assessments have been carried out to *judge* student mastery of content or skills, teachers can find it difficult to add to their repertoire assessments which require that they initially simply *describe* what is in the student's work. But neutral description—involving close-up looking—is the first, important step in this kind of assessment; as a result, some "scaffolding" of teachers' collaborative assessment of student work is usually necessary. Teachers in the Watts' action research groups are offered a highly formalized procedure to help them talk together constructively about student work. Structured conversations "are used to facilitate reflection, documentation, and description." Starting with a printout of a student's Logo drawing and procedure, the group brainstorms answers to a specific set of questions: "What knowledge is Kathy [the focal student] using?"; then "What potentially useful knowledge is Kathy not using?"; then "What teaching interventions would you take . . . Why?" When teachers are ready to make inferences, the Watts ask them to examine and critique those inferences carefully together.

The group may spend up to an hour describing a piece of student work and developing interpretations about what the student knows and does not know, "making a point of not overlooking the obvious or dismissing any knowledge as trivial" to create as complete a picture as possible of what the student understood. The group then suggests next steps the focal teacher might consider taking, and discussion focuses on the rationale for choosing a particular step and the methods one might use to undertake the recommended action.

Several other streams of work in professional development emphasize the importance of jointly examining student work to better understand or, as we have been putting it, "diagnose" individual students' thinking and skills (Allen, Blythe, & Powell, 1996). Seidel's (1991, 1996) collaborative assessment approach, developed at Harvard Project Zero, and David Allen's (1995) "Tuning Protocol," developed for the Coalition of Essential Schools, both use structured assessment protocols that require the teacher presenting a given student's work to initially simply listen to the other participants' comments about the work in order to fully take in others' observations and perspectives.

Joe McDonald, who has worked with the Coaliton of Essential Schools on developing new methods to look at student work, finds that discussions of the *qualities in* (rather than the *quality of*) a student's work benefit from multiple perspectives. A "diplomatic" protocol makes communication safe for expressing different viewpoints. In the process, participants "often find common ground and can move more surely toward creating the conditions in which teachers and students might do better throughout the system" (Cushman, 1996). These protocols fill an important role in "interrupting business as usual," since deep examination of student understanding *prior to* designing curriculum and instruction as well as ongoing *collaborative* investigations into student thinking are not, in most cases, the usual work of teachers.

The primary purpose of these assessment tools and procedures is to reveal students' ways of thinking, so that instructional purposes and teaching methods can be crafted to suit students' understandings and interests. These assessment protocols can also, in the process, change teachers' practices and their stances toward one another as professionals in important ways. Seeing the variety of ways students went about dividing fractions led teachers in Driscoll's CAM project to design curriculum and instructional strategies more specifically targeted to individual needs (Chapter 4). Shifter, Russell, and Bastable found that the mere act of transcribing student dialogue prompted teachers to listen to students more carefully, which in turn caused students to speak more thoughtfully (Chapter 2).

Facilitate Intimate Professional Conversations About Beliefs and Practices

One of the more subtle and complex roles that professional coaches play in these projects is facilitating what we have come to call "intimate conversations" among teachers. These are *conversations* because they are truly collaborative, often very informal, discussions with full give-and-take between the parties—a far cry from demonstrations of technique or didactic presentations. They are *intimate* conversations because they create a context in which teachers grow increasingly comfortable revealing their thinking, their uncertainties, their fears, and the limits of their own risk taking. In intimate conversations, skillful coaches are subtle conversational partners guiding, eliciting, supportively probing or playfully challenging, and as a result teachers become willing to share their failures as well as their successes.

Facilitating such conversations requires a high level of skill, knowledge, and flexibility, in part because the purpose of the talk changes over time. Most projects are long-term, iterative processes that extend for at least a year, in some cases several years, and the "agenda" of the group evolves. Several of the projects described in this volume had explicit developmental phases, with different kinds of conversations appropriate for each phase.

In the first year of Teaching to the Big Ideas project, described in Chapter 2, important conversations take place in developer–teacher dyads when coaches come to observe in participating teachers' classrooms. They ask questions—such as "What do you want your students to learn? How will you find out what they already know?"—that leaven the reflective process in these early intimate interactions. Conversations around videos of students' work or teacher transcriptions of student dialogue during the first year serve another purpose—to focus teachers' attention on what their students understand and what confuses them. The facilitators' questions are likely to catalyze teachers' observations and their reports of how this new kind of seeing is affecting their teaching.

Conversations are also intimate sites for supporting individual teachers in their own varied growth processes. Teachers are not all at the same level in their understanding and skills as diagnostic teachers. In Chapter 1, Nelson discusses recent work by Schifter and Simon [1992] describing four different stages that seem to characterize the developmental phases teachers go through as they change their instructional practice in mathematics. In stage 1, teachers' views of learning are not at all learner-centered, but then the teachers progress until, at stage 4, they focus on students' learning from a constructivist perspective and can design instruction based on students' perspectives.

In Cutler and Ruopp's portraits of individual teachers (Chapter 6), interview conversations provide a supportive and personalized context for teachers' reflections on their learning. Establishing rapport and safety are clearly important, given the honesty with which Jane admits, "I know I'm not great at it yet," and Lynn shares her triumphant, "Sometimes I can't believe how far I have come." In a conversation following an observation of her class, Lynn freely admits she was unable to present her students with a concrete model for multiplying integers. Yet she was not embarrassed by her "failure," because in order to provide a broader and deeper understanding of mathematics for her students, she recognized she had to take the risk of going outside her comfort zone with her own content knowledge.

There is no established script for professional coaches to rely upon in facilitating intimate conversations about teaching and learning. Hammerman captures the intensity of one coach's interior dialogue about how best to facilitate teachers' inquiry in the changing conversational landscape and to provide teachers the tools for carrying out their own reflection. He asks, "How explicit do I need to be about my 'moves'—the reasoned choices I make as group facilitator—to create a culture of mathematical investigation in a group if I hope that it will become institutionalized and maintained in the long term?" (Chapter 8).

While seasoned coaches probably have varied "moves" for catalyzing professional conversation, we observe some basic moves common to facilitators across all these projects. Some relate to establishing a safe environment for teachers to reveal their understandings and beliefs; more than one author mentions the importance of creating a nonjudgmental tone in response to teachers' as well as students' contributions. Other moves relate to deepening teachers' thinking by posing questions that encourage teachers to make connections between their own learning, in analogue experiences, and their students' learning (Morocco & Phillipsen, 1997).

Indeed, as we claimed in the previous chapter, questions play a central role in fermenting respectful exchange and critique of ideas. While good facilitators clearly have deep content knowledge and are themselves expert practitioners, truly experienced facilitators tend to hold back from telling the answers. Because they are coaching teachers to listen to students' ideas, skillful facilitators model how to listen and build on teachers' ideas and observations. They do not withhold their expertise and sometimes do simply state a principle, make a direct observation, or share their wisdom in some other way. However, most often a skillful facilitator's emphasis will be on selecting just the right *question*—the one that would be most helpful in moving a teacher or the group in the direction that the facilitator thinks is beneficial at that particular moment in their time together. Rather than telling or judging, skilled coaches let their expertise shine through their questions.

Use Documentation Strategies

One of the most intriguing roles for professional coaches in these chapters is that of guiding the documentation of the ongoing work of the professional community. The assumption of the programs in this volume is that the collaborative work of the group and the particular ways that participants implement new ways of teaching in their classrooms are grist for all members' learning and therefore need to be recorded and revisited in various ways.

Some of the chapters explicitly describe the documentation strategies and ways in which group "data" were used to move individuals forward. In fact the chapters themselves—with rich stories, detailed examples, think-alouds, and verbatim participant comments—are evidence of the extensive amount and array of documentation that took place. Projects that were funded as research projects had specific resources, activities, and staff devoted to gathering data around specific research questions. Riley and Morocco and project staff (Chapter 5) engaged in ongoing tape-recording of meetings, teacher interviews, classroom observation, charting of conversations in meetings, and collections of teacher lessons—some of which became material for group analysis and some of which remained "data" for later analysis by researchers.

Yet even those projects that were not funded as research efforts created "cultures of documentation." The Watts identify documentation as central to the kind of researcher accountability that is an essential part of action research. Teachers examine their practice by systematically gathering data, reflecting on it, "in order to make teaching decisions grounded in evidence rather than in hunches" (Chapter 3). According to the Watts, sharing the results of this data analysis and formulating consistent teaching decisions are not only an effective tool for professional development but also "a moral imperative for the action researcher and an integral part of the research." This pervasive process of documentation is not an accident but rather reflects a fundamental, shared view of teaching and learning as a constructive process. Documentation of the sort done in these projects serves to "slow down" the work, capturing it in a form that allows it to be examined, reflected upon, and shared.

In fact, we detect four different purposes for documentation with each project, reflecting one, or some combination, of these purposes:

1. Scaffold (i.e., provide temporary and flexible support for) the immediate, ongoing collaborative learning process in the group.
2. Enable participants to track their own personal growth over time.
3. Provide case material for analysis and reflection by others outside the group.
4. Contribute to the published professional literature.

As we discuss throughout the remainder of this section, each purpose requires a different role for professional coaches and implies a different audience for the data that are being recorded.

The first two kinds of documentation serve the learning needs of group members themselves; the audience for the third is practitioners in other contexts; and the audience for the fourth is a broader range of professionals concerned with teacher development and school change—teachers, professional development staff, administrators, educational researchers, and policymakers. Hollingsworth (1994) has observed a similar distinction between what she calls internal and external audiences for the work of inquiry groups, noting that documentation helps group members with the "reflective development of [their] own knowledge" and yet can also provide the group a way to "make public and fuse what [they are] learning with the larger world of education research" (p. 9). Our examples in the brief discussion of the four documentation examples below demonstrate that, in many cases, the same data can be helpful for both internal and external audiences.

Internal Audiences: Scaffold the Immediate Collaborative Learning Process. While many of the authors imply that they chart discussions during meetings, build individual and group "portfolios" of student work, record teacher reflections, or transcribe classroom dialogue, Zorfass (Chapter 9) explicitly traces the role of documentation in each stage of work. As teachers engage in interdisciplinary curriculum design, an I-Search facilitator records (always highly visibly, on large chart paper) the student characteristics that teachers visualize in the first meeting to remind the group that "they are embarking on a student-centered approach to teaching and learning." In a follow-up discussion of a small-group simulation activity designed to stimulate teachers' reflection on collaborative learning, she writes their concerns on chart paper as they voice them in order to be able "to return to these issues for further discussion at appropriate times." Charting lists of ideas from brainstorming and presenting possible themes for interdisciplinary units allow group members to categorize and draw connections among ideas. The ongoing "group writing" makes ideas visible for reflection and elaboration and is an integral part of the close scaffolding this project provides for its teachers.

Documentation helps professional coaches create opportunities for teachers to become more aware of the beliefs that shape their daily decisions. Teachers' writing, the student work they choose to bring, and their commentaries on that work reveal teachers' thinking and understanding in the same way that students' work reveals their understanding. In a recent paper on how teachers develop their own mathematics, Schifter (1998) describes how coaches use notes from classroom observations and one-on-one consultations not only to inform upcoming seminars and classroom activities, but also to evaluate ways in which the seminars were affecting classroom practice.

Internal Audiences: Participants Track Their Own Growth Over Time. Documentation that scaffolds idea-building in these professional groups also makes "data" available to teachers for reflection on their own growth and change. While Zorfass (Chapter 9) emphasizes the role of *facilitator as documenter*, Schifter, Russell, and Bastable (Chapter 2) highlight the role of *participants as documentors* of their own evolving thinking and practice, building toward a future stage when teachers will focus their questions on their own professional development. The question teachers pose to themselves—"What is it that I have learned about learning and teaching mathematics that is important for me to communicate to other teachers?"—is a step toward writing their own "autobiographies of change."

Goswami (1996) and colleagues in the Rural Sites Network, which creates "small professional learning communities" in the Breadloaf Summer Writing Program, found that documenting practitioners' ongoing follow-up conversations about their work on the Internet had a powerful impact on teachers. Project staff transcribed the conversations and periodically all the teachers read sections and discussed the themes and concerns they heard themselves working through. Previewing transcripts and facilitating conversations about them proved an important role for the staff developer who took on that job in the project.

External Audiences: Providing Case Material for Others' Analysis and Reflection. Written documents not only consolidate teachers' own growth but also build their capacity to support and lead others. For example, the change autobiographies that teachers wrote in the Teaching to the Big Ideas project led naturally to preparing papers designed to communicate their learning to other teachers beyond their project group. Developing an interpretive framework for understanding one's own growth and polishing that interpretation into a publishable document builds participants' identification with the role of writer and leader, and can provide models and images of practice for other teachers.

Case materials can take a variety of forms, for example, tracking the development of an idea among students over several months or describing the growth of particular students. Watt and Watt describe two cases of teachers following individual, challenging "focal" students over time in the context of a supportive, rigorous action research collaborative. These teachers integrated students' work and their own reflections into narratives that illustrated how other practitioners, in other research collaboratives, could study "one student's work in rich detail [and how that could in turn lead] teachers to revise teaching practices for all their students (Chapter 3).

These kinds of teacher writings and project cases should convey vivid images of how teachers and students work together, and include numerous examples of students' thinking or detailed descriptions of one lesson. Others in the educational research community (Clandinin, Davies, Hogan, & Kennard, 1993; Davenport & Sassi, 1995; Hollingsworth, 1994) have also observed that teachers' constructing and sharing stories of their own development as practitioners are and should be valued, core activities in professional development.

External Audiences: Contributing to the Published Professional Literature. Because cases embody principles and theoretical concepts in highly memorable, contextualized story form and because they provide models for emulation and reflection, we believe that they should play a central role in the development of teachers. Certainly, case-based learning has had a long and respected place in the development of other professional groups. Case analysis is the central pedagogical tool used to initiate and socialize professionals-in-training in medicine, business, and law.

Cases are one form of publishable material made possible by close documentation of the ongoing work of professional learning communities and are a natural outgrowth of the work described here. Professional development staff, including principals, can play a very helpful role by grouping cases, providing a theoretical context for their use, or providing tips for facilitating case-based discussions. A professional coach can also take on the important role of developmental editor, working with teachers to write their cases for a more general audience. This editorial role is one that a number of EDC staff took on in order to bring rich project documentation to a wider professional audience (see Miller & Kantrov, 1998a, 1998b). Schifter's (1996a, 1996b) book series on teaching mathematics evolved from carefully documented teacher experiences and writings about exploring more constructivist ways of teaching mathematics. Watt and Watt (1993) published cases of teacher investigations of Logo learning that are now being read by participants in a national network of action research collaboratives, Zorfass's forthcoming book on the I-Search model integrates case material on student and teacher growth.

While documentation around these four purposes does require time and effort, as demonstrated in the EDC projects, it can also be efficient when teachers' rich case examples that had been helpful for structuring their groups' learning then "travel" to another group in the form of a book or article. Moreover, putting one's ideas forward for public scrutiny and debate is at the very heart of what it means to be a professional. If we are serious about the "professional" in "professional development," then we should encourage teachers to reflect on their work and publish their insights.

Advocate for a "Blanket of Support"

All the projects described in this volume were designed, organized, and carried out by groups of EDC staff together with colleagues in collaborating school districts, individual schools, universities, and, in the case of Cutler and Ruopp (Chapter 6), community industries. In no case was a lone individual designing or implementing an intervention. Indeed, each project offered what Driscoll in Chapter 4 calls a "blanket of support." He uses this term to refer to a constellation of human resources and logistical supports for innovation that included "time for planning; regular team meetings; district encouragement, and the direct support and involvement of the mathematics supervisors" as well as support for the other key elements of a program, which can also include attendance at national conferences and participation in information exchanges and professional communication through an electronic network.

Driscoll's use of the word "blanket" strikes us as particularly apt. It connotes the need for *comprehensive* support, so that teachers across grade levels and content areas can be included in the restructuring. "Blanket" conveys an image of safety and protection for the personal risk taking that is involved. It also implies the safeguarding of time and establishment of new work norms, so that teachers can engage in new kinds of adult learning and classroom practice. The incipient professional communities described in these chapters were able to get a toehold because someone, or some group of individuals, created time for teachers to meet and work with other teachers and professional development staff.

In short, these chapters have outlined interventions that are promising and successful because they have allowed for far more supports and new forms of collaboration than one can find in the usual school system. Without extra support, professional development activities of the kind outlined in this volume simply cannot work. As Darling-Hammond and McLaughlin (1995) point out, it is foolish to expect new teaching approaches to grow out of conventional structures. If our nation is serious about revitalizing professional development, then we have to be willing to reinvent the school day, change students' and teachers' schedules, restructure teachers' roles and responsibilities, and encourage a wholly different set of workplace norms.

What would the school day have to look like to enable teachers to work in these ways? What kind of a workplace for teachers (and for students) would our schools have to become, and how could we move them in that direction? What sorts of logistical supports would teachers and students need to work in these ways every day, as a matter of routine practice? Although we cannot attempt a definitive or exhaustive response to these questions, we offer some tentative responses that we hope will serve as a starting point for further discussion.

ENVISIONING A NEW WORKPLACE AND A NEW KIND OF SCHOOL DAY

In her study *Teachers at Work* (1990), Susan Moore Johnson describes the need for more informal, flexible schools and the reason they are so elusive:

> Bureaucratic forms in education are resilient because they keep costs down and permit schools to cope with large numbers of students in a seemingly orderly way. They do not, however, meet the needs of teachers and students who are engaged in the business of teaching and learning rather than management and accounting. If schools were structured from the inside out, rather than the outside in, if they derived their form from the needs of teachers and students rather than the priorities of administrators and business, they would be smaller, more flexible, and varied organizations. (p. 107)

A more flexible, less bureaucratic school would allow for at least two important kinds of restructuring: changes in how time is structured and changes in teachers' roles and workplace norms.

Time

Lack of time has been the Achilles heel of most efforts to reform classroom practice and professionalize teaching. Indeed, the problem is so significant that the National Education Commission, which titled its 1994 report on school reform *Prisoners of Time*, warned readers to be wary of the false premise that schools can be transformed for students without giving teachers the time they need to "retool themselves and reorganize their work" (p. 3).

As the 1996 report of the National Commission on Teaching and America's Future insists and our own experience validates, teachers need time to make "professional development an ongoing part of [their] daily work through joint planning, study groups, peer coaching and action research" (p. 21). The National Staff Development Council (NSDC) board has determined that adequate time for staff learning and collaborative work should be 20% of an educator's week. NSCD considers any of the following to be productive learning opportunities: observing in others' classrooms, planning lessons with colleagues, attending seminars, participating in a study group, mentoring a new teacher, developing curricula, doing school improvement planning, conducting action research, and examining new technological resources to supplement lesson planning (Sparks & Hirsh, 1997).

Furthermore, the need for teacher time cannot be separated from students' needs for time. The average 50-minute class period in most schools limits students' intensive engagement in learning. It makes the kinds of science inquiry, mathematical thinking, and interdisciplinary research and writing discussed in the preceding chapters nearly impossible. Moreover, the push for "coverage" places counterproductive pressures on teachers and students alike. A curriculum that requires teachers to move at breakneck speed over too many facts and concepts undermines their ability to engage in diagnostic teaching.

In quiet efforts by many schools, there is now a localized movement across the country to create time for teachers to work and plan together. These local approaches reflect a number of general strategies with unlimited possibilities for variation, depending on the purpose for collaboration and the structures and activities that serve that purpose. One approach is to alter the daily school schedule to provide the extra time that teaches need for joint planning and peer coaching, while allowing for a curriculum that focuses in depth on big ideas. Many middle schools have restructured around block scheduling, with interdisciplinary teams of teachers in charge of a common group of students. When those students are involved in special activities, such as art and physical education, teachers are free to meet.

Another approach is to "bank time" by beginning school early or releasing it a few minutes late each day to accumulate enough minutes for a schoolwide early release or late start format once a week (Sparks & Hirsh, 1997). The approach allows all staff, specialists, and art and physical education teachers to be involved in joint planning or curriculum design. Another approach involves a long-range program of community volunteers. Principals who are creating these programs tell us how time-consuming it is to start up such a program and yet how rich the rewards can be—not only in freeing teachers to work jointly but also in bringing new talent into the school and creating new school–community relationships. Other models involve creative use of teaching assistants; in one site a team of five assistants releases five teachers the first hour of school and another five teachers the last hour, so that two teacher groups meet every day (Murphy, 1995).

One of the new roles of professional development leaders is to contribute to school- and district-level discussions about strategies for creating time for collaboration. Another is to ensure that parents and community members understand, all along the way, how students benefit when teachers have time to learn and work together. Teachers need to tell their students and parents what they do in study groups, planning meetings, and curriculum design sessions, and to show students and parents the tangible results.

New Teaching Roles, Workplace Norms, and School Structures

International comparisons can be helpful in demonstrating the benefits of a new approach to the school day and a new vision of the teaching profession. Parents and community decision makers should know that most U.S. teachers have only 3 to 5 hours each week for planning and almost no regular time to consult together or reflect on their practice with their peers. This is in sharp contrast to teachers in many European and Asian countries, where teachers spend between 15 and 20 hours per week working jointly on refining lessons, coaching one another, and learning new instructional methods (Darling-Hammond, 1996; National Commission on Teaching and America's Future, 1996). In Japan and China, for example, teachers only teach 3 to 4 hours per day and have the remainder of the day for professional preparation and interaction with their colleagues (National Governors Association, 1995).

Other countries are able to afford these investments in teachers' knowledge and time because they hire fewer nonteaching staff and more teachers assume a broader range of decision-making responsibilities. In the United States, the number of teachers has declined to only 53% of public school staff, while the number of nonteaching specialists and other staff has increased (National Center for Education Statistics, 1993, as reported in Darling-Hammond, 1996). And of that 53%, only about three-quarters take primary responsibility for classrooms of children, with the remainder working in pull-out settings or performing nonteaching duties (Darling-Hammond, 1996).

Clearly, better pre-service education and licensing requirements will bring better-prepared teachers to our schools, but the schools themselves must be organized in ways that encourage and reward good teaching and that enhance the professional identities of the teachers who come to work there. Where teachers are allowed greater decision-making authority, they are more likely to see curriculum reforms accompany transformations in teaching roles (as reported in Darling-Hammond, 1996). Moreover, teachers from "restructured schools with more rigorous graduation standards, performance-based assessment practices, emphasis on in-depth understanding rather than superficial content coverage, accelerated learning approaches, connections between classroom practices and home experiences of students, and teacher involvement in decisions about school spending" are also "more likely to report that their schools provide structured time for teachers to work together on professional matters" [Darling-Hammond, 1996, p. 9].

Professional development staff, including teachers, curriculum coordinators, and principals, can play a crucial role in developing appropriate workplace structures that are capable of nurturing the kinds of professional learning communities described throughout this book. Professional development staff can enhance policy making and restructuring within their own districts by building a knowledge base of the strengths and limitations of various combinations of support strategies and by negotiating for the kinds of changes they think will be effective in supporting teachers' development and professional identity.

Professional development staff can, for example, encourage the creation of salary structures to reward professional learning and press hard for the establishment of a line item in the school budget to pay for teachers' travel to conferences or to provide incentive awards for teachers who publish accounts of their teaching practices in professional journals. If the professional development staff see their role as being an advocate for institutional change as well as a coach, they could also contribute to redesigning the school's daily schedule to preserve more nonteaching time, negotiate for significant amounts of common planning time for teachers, help teachers arrange observation time in one another's classes, or create partnerships with institutions of higher education capable of granting credit for a flexible array of professional development experiences. In deciding to take on this kind of institutional role, professional development staff would not only be changing the working conditions and workplace norms for teachers, but would also be reinventing their own roles within the system. They would be committing themselves to looking diagnostically at the needs of the entire teaching community.

CONCLUSION

Although ample lip service is paid to the notion that teachers are professionals, in fact teachers live isolated lives with little emphasis on their own learning. They operate mostly in self-contained classrooms without even the simplest rudiments of a professional life, such as a telephone, personal computer, or convenient access to professional journals and conferences. Colleagueship is episodic—for example, when teachers team up to develop a joint curriculum unit; but the time to cultivate an atmosphere of collegiality and the opportunities for colleagues to consult with one another in a meaningful way that is focused in detail on student learning and understanding is rare in most teachers' experience.

Historically, teachers were seen as the mechanism for transmitting knowledge and socialization to students in a school system built on an industrial model of inputs and outputs and a theory of learning more static and atomistic than our current conceptions. The children entered the schoolroom door, the teacher conveyed information, and the students left. But teachers who are simply conduits are not likely to be lifelong learners, problem solvers, or active contributors to a field of inquiry. Just as children are rendered too passive in this traditional model of schooling, so too are teachers.

If we are committed to a profession in which teachers jointly "diagnose" what level and kinds of understanding their students bring, what within their discipline is important to teach, and what strategies are appropriate for developing greater subject-matter expertise and deeper disciplinary knowledge, then we have to create the social conditions that make that learning possible. In the view of professional development implied by the stories in this volume, the primary condition for change seems to be that teachers must be encouraged to define themselves as part of a professional community of inquiry in which there is direct and collective engagement with challenging ideas and opportunities to critique, build on to, and refine each member's thinking.

Clearly, there are and must be many routes for professionalizing the craft of teaching, including more rigorous pre-service education, more emphasis on subject-matter expertise and disciplinary knowledge, standards for licensure and accreditation, more clearly delineated career pathways for experienced teachers, and more appropriate levels of financial compensation. However, regardless of how successful we are in these domains, ultimately teachers must do their work in schools. The school environments we build must be capable of attracting highly qualified, self-motivated teachers and must offer them the opportunity to join a vibrant professional community. Professional development staff, teachers, principals, curriculum coordinators, school committee members, and other community leaders, committed to building such professional communities within their own school systems, can play a vital role in the national effort to revitalize the teaching profession. The portraits presented by the contributing authors to this volume present promising ways to meet that challenge.

REFERENCES

Allen, D. (1995). *The tuning protocol: A process for reflection.* Providence, RI: Brown University.

Allen, D., Blythe, T., & Powell, B. S. (1996). *A guide to looking collaboratively at student work.* Cambridge, MA: Harvard Project Zero.

Boix-Mansilla, V. (1995). *Rethinking knowledge in school: The recovery of meaning in disciplinary understanding.* [Unpublished paper] ATLAS Seminar, Harvard Project Zero, Cambridge, MA.

Clandinin, D., Davies, A., Hogan, P., & Kennard, B. (1993). *Learning to teach, Teaching to learn.* New York: Teachers College Press.

Corcoran, T. B., Walker, L. J., & White, J. L. (1988). *Working in urban schools.* Washington, DC: Institute for Educational Leadership.

Cushman, K. (1996). Looking collaboratively at student work: An essential toolkit. *Horace.* The Coalition of Essential Schools, Vol. 13, No. 2, November.

Darling-Hammond, L. (1996). The quiet revolution: Rethinking teacher development. *Education Leadership, 53*(6), 4–10.

Darling-Hammond, L., & McLaughlin, M. (1995). Policies that support professional development in an era of reform. *Phi Delta Kappan, 76*(8), 597–604.

Davenport, L. R., & Sassi, A. (1995). Transforming mathematics teaching in grades K–8: How narrative structures in resource materials help support teacher change. In B. S. Nelson (Ed.), *Inquiry and the development of teaching* (pp. 27–36). Newton, MA: Education Development Center.

Goswami, D. (1996, March). The internet as a site for teacher conversations about writing. Paper presented at EDC, Newton, MA.

Hollingsworth, S. (1994). *Teacher research and urban literacy education: Lessons and conversations in a feminist key.* New York: Columbia University Press.

Johnson, S. M. (1990). *Teachers at work: Achieving success in our schools.* New York: Basic Books.

Krechevsky, M., & Morocco, C. C. (1996). *When ATLAS goes to school: Three tensions around professional development from a school reform collaboration.* Manuscript submitted for publication.

Little, J. W. (1990). The persistence of privacy: Autonomy and initiative in teachers' professional relations. *Teachers College Record, 91*, 509–536.

Louis, K. S., Marks, H. M., & Kruse, S. (1996). Teachers' professional communities in restructuring schools. *American Educational Research Journal, 33*(4), 757–800.

McLaughlin, M. W., & Talbot, J. (1993). *Contexts that matter for teaching and learning: Strategic opportunities for meeting the nation's goals.* Stanford, CA: Center for Research on the Context of Secondary Teaching, Stanford University.

Miller, B., & Kantrov, I. (1998a). *Casebook on school reform.* Portsmouth, NH: Heinemann.
Miller, B., & Kantrov, I. (1998b). *Facilitating cases in education.* Portsmouth, NH: Heinemann.
Morocco, C. C., & Philipsen, L. (1997, March). *Listening to study groups in restructuring schools.* Paper presented at the annual meeting of the American Educational Research Association, Chicago.
Murphy, C. (1995). Whole-faculty study groups: Doing the seemingly undoable. *Journal of Staff Development, 16*(3), 37–44.
National Commission on Teaching and America's Future. (1996). *What matters most: Teaching for America's future.* New York: Author.
National Education Commission on Time and Learning. (1994). *Prisoners of time.* Washington, DC: U.S. Government Printing Office.
National Governor's Association. (1995). *Transforming professional development for teachers: A guide for state policymakers.*
Schifter, D. (Ed.). (1996a). *What's happening in math class? Vol. 1: Envisioning new practices through teacher narratives.* New York: Teachers College Press.
Schifter, D. (Ed.). (1996b). *What's happening in math class? Vol. 2: Reconstructing professional identities.* New York: Teachers College Press.
Schifter, D. (1998). Learning mathematics for teaching: From the teachers' seminar to the classroom. *Journal for Mathematics Teacher Education, 1*(1), 55–87.
Schifter, D., & Simon, M. A. (1992). Assessing teachers' development of a constructivist view of mathematics learning. *Teaching and Teacher Education, 8*(2), 187–197.
Seidel, S. (1991). *Collaborative assessment conferences for the consideration of project work.* Cambridge, MA: Harvard Project Zero.
Seidel, S. (1996). *Learning from looking.* Cambridge, MA: Harvard Project Zero.
Sparks, D., & Hirsh, S. (1997). *A new vision for staff development.* Alexandria, VA: Association for Supervision and Curriculum Development, and Oxford, OH: National Staff Development Council.
Watt, M., & Watt, D. (1993). Action research, teacher research: The case of the Logo Action Research Collaborative. *Educational Action Research Journal, 1*(1), 35–63.

Afterword

When we speak of professional development, we most often focus on the roles that people play: teacher, principal, staff developer, school board member. Many readers of this volume live in these roles; each involves strong notions of competence already achieved and expertise ready to be put into play.

My hope is that *The Diagnostic Teacher* breaks the mold of these notions and helps us as practitioners and researchers to start from different premises: That we are all learners; that none of us is fully prepared for our work as educators, caregivers, and guides to our children; that the future most certainly hasn't been invented yet; and that change will be a constant in our lives. If we accept these premises, then access to new knowledge and know-how is essential for all of us. "Learning" is therefore the key word. It is the distinguishing characteristic for defining the diagnostic teacher. It assumes by definition that knowledge about students and about how to encourage better teaching is provisional.

As an organization with a long history, we have had firsthand experience with the provisional nature of such knowledge. For a brief period during its earliest years as an organization, Education Development Center (EDC) made several attempts to develop curricula influenced by the misguided goal of being "teacher-proof." Yet, the chapters in this volume show how far we have come from that ill-conceived, indeed foolhardy, notion. All of the language used to tell these stories refutes such a stance. Even in the early days, we quickly moved to innovative "parallel curriculum" for teachers on the content and pedagogy of new materials. Then came, over time, in-depth workshop experiences, enriching teachers' disciplinary knowledge. Presently, as this volume demonstrates, teachers are engaged as co-constructors with EDC staff in developing instructional materials, and as researchers and developers in their own communities of practice with EDC staff as guides and critical friends. This book, then, very much represents a journey, taken over several decades. It reflects the current conceptions of EDC staff, as the organization turns 40.

It is generally acknowledged today that teachers need to break out of the isolation of the classroom and join together in such communities of practice. EDC's work, whether with adults or with youth, has been strongly influenced by this and other theories of social learning. Many of the chapters in this volume state explicitly that knowledge is socially constructed, and is gained through active, hands-on experiences and opportunities to reflect with one's colleagues. The emerging language and literature around "communities of practice" has therefore been of special importance to our work in teacher development. These learning communities are, quite simply, groups of people united by common enterprise, and as Solomon and Morocco point out in their two concluding chapters, the vigor of these communities is at the heart of their professionalism.

This afterword would be incomplete without including the thinking of David Hawkins, one of EDC's earliest and most distinguished teacher educators. Exactly 30 years ago, Dr. Hawkins presented to the world of mathematics teachers his thoughts on what he termed "the triangle" of I-Thou-It: student, teacher, and the stuff of learning that must be in a relationship together if the classroom is to be a rich world of learning. He wrote and spoke eloquently about the essential connection of the human duet—the "I" and the "Thou"—with the "It"—the curriculum and its tangible experiences. His formulation was the precursor to the work of Sarah Lightfoot and others, including staff of EDC.

What is even more astonishing and delightful is that 30 years ago, David Hawkins also wrote about the "diagnostic teacher." While we believed throughout the development of this volume that we had created this powerful descriptor for ourselves, what I uncovered in his work was the deep-running tradition of EDC's theory into practice that launched our ensuing decades of commitment to the development of teaching as a profession. This brought us back, through intuitive and analytic means, to the same language as David Hawkins used himself so long ago.

I leave the reader with a few quotations from David Hawkins' article, "I-Thou-It," published in EDC's *ESS* (*Elementary Science Study*) *Reader* in the late 1960s.

> The function of the teacher . . . is to respond diagnostically and helpfully to a child's behavior. . . . I'm speaking as one very much in favour of richness and diversity in the environment, and of teaching which allows a group of children to diversify their activities and which—far more than we usually think proper—keeps them out of their hair. What seems very clear to me—and I think this is a descriptive, factual statement, not praising or blaming—is that if you operate a school, as we in America almost entirely do, in such a style that the children are rather passively sitting in neat rows and columns and manipulating you into believing that they're being attentive because they're not making any trouble, then you won't get very much information about them. Not getting much information about them, you won't be a very good diagnostician of what they need. Not being a good diagnostician, you will be a poor teacher. . . . It doesn't

say that you *will* but that you *can* get more significant diagnostic information about children, and can refine your behavior as a teacher far beyond the point of what's possible when every child is being made to perform in a rather uniform pattern. . . .

Of course, you certainly aren't going to succeed all the time with every child in this diagnostic and planning process. There are going to be several misses for every hit, but you just say, "Well, let's keep on missing and the more we miss the more we'll hit." The importance of this in the "I-Thou" relationship between the teacher and the child is that the child learns something about the adult which we can describe with words like "confidence", "trust" and "respect".

It seems to me that many of us, whether our background was in science or not, have learned something about ourselves from working with children in this way that we've begun to explore. We've begun to see the things of the physical and biological world through children's eyes rather more than we were able to before, and have discovered and enjoyed a lot that is there that we were not aware of before. We don't any longer feel satisfied with the kind of adult grasp that we had of the very subject matter that we've been teaching; we find it more problematic, more full of surprises, and less and less a matter of the textbook order.

One of the nicest stories of this kind that I know comes from a young physicist friend who was very learned. He had just got his Ph.D. and of course he understood everything. (The Ph.D. has been called "the certificate of omniscience".) My wife was asking him to explain something to her about two coupled pendulums. He said, 'Well now you can see that there's a conservation of. . . . "Well, there's really a conservation of angle here." She looked at him. 'Well, you see, in the transfer of energy from one pendulum to the other there is . . ." and so on and so on. And she said, "No, I don't mean that. I want you to notice this and tell me what's happening." Finally, he looked at the pendulums and he saw what she was asking. He looked at *it*, and he looked at *her*, and he grinned and said, 'Well, I know the right words but I don't understand it either." This confession, wrung from a potential teacher, I've always valued very much. It proves that we're all in *it* together.

As indeed we are!

Janet Whitla
President
Education Development Center, Inc.
Newton, Massachusetts

About the Contributors

Virginia Bastable is the director of the SummerMath for Teachers Program at Mount Holyoke College. During the course of a 20-year career as a secondary school mathematics teacher, she earned a master's in mathematics and an Ed.D. in mathematics education. Since 1986, Dr. Bastable has been working in the field of teacher education, designing and conducting summer institutes and academic-year courses in both mathematics and mathematics education for teachers of grades K–12. She is currently working in collaboration with EDC and TERC to create a professional development curriculum designed to allow teachers to engage with the mathematical ideas of the elementary curriculum and to examine the way students develop those ideas.

Ada Beth Cutler is a professor in the department of curriculum and teaching at Montclair State University and director of the New Jersey Network for Educational Renewal, a school–university partnership of Montclair State and 17 school districts. Prior to joining the faculty at Montclair State, Dr. Cutler spent 6 years doing qualitative research on teacher education, school reform, teacher staff development, and educational policy at Education Matters, Inc., and the Consortium for Policy Research in Education. Earlier in her career she was an elementary school teacher and then principal of a K–8 school. She holds the Ed.D. from Harvard University.

Mark Driscoll is a project director at EDC for such projects as Assessment Communities of Teachers, which implements professional development programs focusing on student assessment, and Leadership for Urban Mathematics Reform, aimed at helping urban teachers become reform leaders. Dr. Driscoll received his Ph.D. in mathematics (differential geometry) from Washington University in St. Louis and has an extensive background in mathematics and mathematics education, ranging from research in mathematics to curriculum development and teacher training. He has been co-chair of the NCTM's Task Force on Reaching All Students with Mathematics, a member of NCTM's Educational Materials Committee, and a member of the writing team for NCTM's Assessment Standards for School Mathematics. His publications include "Professionals in a Changing Profession," which was co-authored with Brian Lord for the 1990 NCTM Yearbook, and *Teaching Mathematics: Strategies That Work*, which Dr. Driscoll co-edited for Heinemann Educational Books.

James K. Hammerman is a senior research associate at the Center for Development of Teaching at EDC and a doctoral candidate in learning and teaching at the Harvard Graduate School of Education, where he is a Pforzheimer and Harvard Graduate National Fellow. He is primarily interested in collaborative models for teacher professional development that draw their strength from joint inquiry into mathematical and pedagogical issues grounded in specific examples of teaching practice. Jim taught elementary and middle school for several years in what can most aptly be described as an "urban one-room school." He has developed mathematics and geography curricula for elementary, middle, and secondary levels, and has worked extensively as a teacher educator through SummerMath for Teachers and EDC.

Carolee S. Matsumoto received her Ed.D. in teaching, curriculum, and learning environments from the Harvard Graduate School of Education. The focus of her current work at EDC is in the development of systemic learning communities, leadership development, and equity. Currently, she is the director of Systemic Learning Organizations at EDC and the principal investigator of the Region 1, New England, Comprehensive Technical Assistance Center funded by the U.S. Department of Education. This follows her work as co-director of the National Science Foundation Technical Assistance Project for the Statewide Systemic Initiatives (SSIs) in 25 states focusing on education reform, science, and technology in schools, districts, and states across the United States, Brazil, and Japan. Prior to coming to EDC, Dr. Matsumoto was the assistant superintendent for curriculum and instruction for the Concord and Concord-Carlisle (Massachusetts) public schools.

Catherine Cobb Morocco's work weaves together professional development, school reform, and literacy development. She has served as principal investigator of several classroom-based research projects on writing development, integrating technology into the curricula, and teachers' planning for academically diverse classrooms. Currently she is conducting research and consulting with school districts on the role of teacher inquiry groups in bringing about culture of professional inquiry in restructuring schools. She is the author of *Writers at Work* (SRA, Inc.) and numerous articles and book chapters on writing instruction, technology integration, and professional development. She holds an Ed.D. in language and literature from the Harvard Graduate School of Education.

Barbara Scott Nelson is senior scientist and director of the Center for the Development of Teaching at EDC. She holds the B.A. degree in philosophy from Mt. Holyoke College, an M.A.T. from Johns Hopkins, and an Ed.D. from Harvard University. She has long been interested in the relationship between teachers' ideas about learning, teaching, and subject matter, and the particular social and intellectual contexts in which their teaching is embedded. The Mathematics for Tomorrow project, which she directs, looks at the systemic implications of a mathematics teacher-enhancement program based on a constructivist view of teachers' intellectual development. Currently, she is working with school- and district-level administrators on the implications of mathematics education reform for the intellectual culture of schools and for their own work.

Maureen Keohane Riley has wide experience turning theory into practice working with pre-service and in-service teachers as associate professor of psychology and education at Lesley College in Cambridge, Massachusetts. Her specialization is in the field of cognition. She brings her appreciation of cognitive diversity to her expertise in the areas of assessment and curriculum design for inclusive classrooms. She has been director of EDC projects such as Teacher as Composer, a four-year study on Thinking in Science, and the Inclusion Outcomes Project. Presently, as director of academic services for students with learning disabilities at Lesley College, she is developing a program that establishes instructional policies and practices at the post-secondary level that honor the regulations of the Americans with Disabilities Act.

Faye Nisonoff Ruopp is principal investigator of the EDC staff development project Reaching Every Teacher, a local systemic change initiative funded by the National Science Foundation, where she is working with 200 teachers of mathematics in the district of Waltham, Massachusetts. This project also uses an industry volunteer model, developed by Ms. Ruopp, to release teachers from their classes during the school day. Previously at EDC she directed Teachers, Time and Transformations, designed to examine the content of algebra across the curriculum for teachers in grades 4–12. Ms. Ruopp also directed the project Improving the Math Performance of Low-Achieving Middle School Students from 1990 to 1992. From 1972 to 1993, Ms. Ruopp taught mathematics at Lincoln–Sudbury Regional High School in Massachusetts. In 1986 she was named a Lucretia Crocker Fellow by the Massachusetts Department of Education and provided technical assistance to school districts on the use of cooperative learning to promote minority achievement.

Susan Jo Russell is a principal scientist at TERC, a nonprofit organization that works to improve mathematics and science education. She has an M.S. in early childhood education from Bank Street College and an Ed.D. in mathematics education from Boston University. After 10 years of classroom teaching and staff development in elementary schools, Dr. Russell became involved in research and development. At TERC, she currently directs the project Investigations in Number, Data, and Space, which is developing a complete mathematics curriculum for grades K–5 and support materials for teachers engaged in changing their mathematics teaching. She is co-author of *Beyond Arithmetic: Changing Mathematics in the Elementary Classroom.* Her work focuses on the development of children's mathematical ideas and on understanding how practicing teachers can learn more about mathematics and about children's mathematical thinking.

Deborah Schifter has worked with SummerMath, a nationally acclaimed mathematics education program at Mount Holyoke College, since the program's inception in 1982, becoming the director of SummerMath for Teachers in 1988. She has also worked as an applied mathematician and has taught elementary-, secondary-, and college-level mathematics. She has a B.A. in liberal arts from Saint John's College, Annapolis, an M.S. in applied mathematics from the University of Maryland, and an M.S. and Ph.D. in psychology from the University of Massachusetts. In March 1993, Dr. Schifter moved to EDC, where she directs a major teacher development and research project. She co-authored, with Catherine Twomey Fosnot, *Reconstructing Mathematics Education: Stories of Teachers Meeting the Challenge of Reform*, and edited a two-volume anthology of teachers' writing, *What's Happening in Math Class?*

Mildred Z. Solomon, Ed.D., editor for this volume, is the director of the Center for Applied Ethics and Professional Practice at EDC. A senior staff person at EDC for more than 20 years, Dr. Solomon has developed curricula and professional development programs on subjects ranging from middle school American history to modern medical ethics. In the 1980s, she served as project director for a comprehensive school health education program and was responsible for the design and implementation of its large teacher education component. Fifteen years later, the program is currently in use in approximately 20,000 classrooms nationwide.

Dr. Solomon consults broadly, both in the United States and abroad, on the design of educational programs to promote the development of practicing professionals and professionals-in-training, including teachers, physicians, nurses, social workers, and counselors. She has taught middle and high school language arts in a rural Massachusetts school system, and designed and carried out training programs for classroom teachers in the United Kingdom on the use of drama to encourage more hands-on participatory approaches to teaching. She holds a B.A. degree from Smith College and an Ed.D. from

Harvard University, where she specialized in educational research and adult learning.

Daniel Lynn Watt is a senior research and development associate at EDC. He has worked extensively as a teacher, teacher educator, curriculum developer, and researcher in mathematics and in science and technology education. He serves as a consultant to Mathematical Inquiry Through Video (Cambridge, Massachusetts) and Building Bridges, a science and mathematics professional development project focused on teaching modeling as a thinking strategy in the elementary grades (University of Wisconsin, Madison). In addition, he has taught at the upper elementary, secondary, college, and graduate school levels, most recently as assistant professor of mathematics and science education at Keene State College. In addition to the books he has co-authored with Molly Lynn Watt (see below), he is author of the widely used book series *Learning with Logo* (McGraw-Hill, 1983, 1984, 1985). His recent publications include "Mapping the Classroom Using a CAD Program: Geometry as Applied Mathematics" (in *Designing Learning Environments*, Richard Lehrer and Daniel Chazan, eds., Erlbaum, in press).

Molly Lynn Watt, a senior associate at EDC since 1985, has been actively engaged in the professional development of teachers for more than 30 years. Co-founder of the Brookline, Massachusetts, Teacher Center in 1973, she has published more than fifty articles, chapters, curricula, and books. Her K–6 curriculum and teacher's guides, *Welcome to Logo!,* written to accompany a D.C. Heath mathematics text, were chosen as exemplary new materials in 1987 by *Teaching and Computer Magazine.* She is currently editing a book, in press with Teachers College Press, for educational leaders and staff developers, relating action research to mathematics and science education reform. She is co-director of the Danforth Foundation–sponsored project Develop Leaders for Action Research and project director for PainLink, the Mayday Fund's joint project with EDC to provide technical assistance to 50 health care institutions mobilizing for better pain management. She was also the principal investigator for an NSF-funded project linking action research to the national reform initiatives in mathematics and science education.

As collaborators, **Daniel Lynn Watt** and **Molly Lynn Watt** have worked together on a number of publications and EDC projects. They co-directed Developing Leadership in Action Research, a 2-year leadership development program for leaders of school-based action research groups, and the Logo Action Research Collaborative. They co-authored "Teacher Research, Action Research: The Case of the Logo Action Research Collaborative" (*Educational Action Research Journal*), *Logo Learning: Strategies for Assessing Content and Process* (International Society for Technology in Education, 1992), and *Teach-*

ing with Logo: Building Blocks for Learning (Addison-Wesley, 1986). They also co-edited the NECC Monograph *New Paradigms in Classroom Research on Logo Learning*, published in 1993 by ISTE, which shares a range of practical methodologies using practitioner research to improve Logo teaching practice and solve implementation issues.

Judith M. Zorfass is associate director for the Center for Family, School, and Community at EDC. She manages multiple projects that focus on research, professional development, technical assistance, and product development and dissemination. She concentrates her work on middle school curricula and instruction, technology use, special education, and teacher development. Dr. Zorfass is a frequent presenter at national conferences on such topics as middle school reform, interdisciplinary curricula, language development, and special education, and she writes often for journals on these topics. She has an Ed.D. from Harvard University, where she specialized in reading and language development.

Index